Project PLANNING
AND IMPLEMENTATION

JIM KEOGH

Avraham Shtub • Jonathan F. Bard • Shlomo Globerson

UNIVERSITY OF PHOENIX
COLLEGE OF INFORMATION SYSTEMS AND TECHNOLOGY

Pearson
Custom
Publishing

CONTENTS

Congratulations...

You have just purchased access to a valuable website that will open many doors for you! The University of Phoenix has chosen to enhance and expand your course's material with a dynamic website that contains an abundance of rich and valuable online resources specifically designed to help you achieve success!

This website provides you with material selected and added to powerful online tools that have been seamlessly integrated with this textbook, resulting in a dynamic, course-enhancing learning system. These exciting tools include:

> Online Study Guide
> Online glossary
> Links to selected, high-quality websites
> And more!

You can begin to access these tremendous resources immediately!

www.pearsoncustom.com/uop: The opening screen of the University of Phoenix website includes book covers of all the Pearson Custom Publishing books in the BSBIS and BSIT programs. Click on the book cover representing your course. This will launch the online study guide for the course in which you are currently enrolled **and** the glossary of key terms for all the University of Phoenix BSBIS and BSIT courses.

CD-ROM: The accompanying CD-ROM includes key terms underlined within the online book that are linked to the World Wide Web. Use the enclosed CD-ROM to launch websites selected to reinforce your learning experience.

TAKE THE FIRST STEP ON THE ROAD TO SUCCESS TODAY!

Pearson
Custom
Publishing

PROJECT MANAGEMENT AND THE ORGANIZATION

We tend to take for granted the complex systems that keep our lives running smoothly. Nearly everything in our life is influenced by technology—some that we see and some that works quietly behind the scenes.

Take, for example, a system used by some utilities to handle customer inquiries. The customer calls the utility. A recorded voice answers and presents a menu. Making the correct selection connects the caller to a customer service representative who greets the customer by name and is able to answer questions about the customer's account almost instantaneously.

Within a split second after the caller makes the selection, the system uses caller ID to identify the customer's telephone number. The system searches the company's database for the telephone number and the account information associated with that number. The call and the account information are routed to the next available customer service representative.

Someone in the organization came up with this idea for improving customer service by routing calls automatically and making account information available immediately so the representative can attend to the customer's needs. Someone else in the organization had to take this idea and bring it to reality. This person is called the project manager.

A project manager has the most challenging responsibility in any organization. He or she must design, build, and implement someone else's idea—an idea that is intangible and nearly invisible.

Imagine yourself as the project manager who is given the assignment to make the customer relations system a reality. All you are given is the idea from a manager who probably knows little about computers or what it takes to build a computer system. To further complicate matters, you know little about the operations of the customer relations department.

So it is your job to develop a complete understanding of the organization's needs, and then translate those requirements into a computer system. The system must be delivered within an agreed-upon timeframe, within budget, and it must work flawlessly the day the system is turned on. How you accomplish the objective is entirely your responsibility.

Typically, management is impatient and feels the system should have been completed yesterday or at least within the current budget year. Your staff of technicians may not adhere to your schedule, making it impossible for you to meet the deadline. If you rush your staff, the quality of the system is in jeopardy. Furthermore, management holds you to the original deadline regardless of the situation. Your job is to delicately balance all the demands placed upon you and deliver a perfect system.

In all such situations, taking an idea from concept to reality requires three major components. These are people, the management of those people, and a project plan. We will explore each of these components in this section.

THE PEOPLE COMPONENT

■ THE PROJECT MANAGER'S ROLE

The success and failure of the project is in the hands of the project manager. He or she must be an advisor, a planner, a manager, an effective communicator, a politician—as well as knowledgeable about the business and about technology.

The project manager is looked upon as the expert in technology, the person who can advise management on whether a business operation can be economically computerized. For example, the manager who devised the idea of automating the customer relations department likely has little or no concept of whether or not this is achievable. Two questions which must be answered in this type of situation are:

- Is technology available to develop the system?
- Will the cost of developing the system outweigh the benefits to the organization?

These are issues that the project manager must explore and resolve before beginning to develop the system. The project manager must answer another series of questions once it has been determined that the system is feasible to develop, including the following:

- What tasks must be completed to build, test and implement the system?
- What is the order of these tasks?
- Which tasks must be performed before other tasks?
- Which tasks can be worked on simultaneously?
- Who will perform these tasks?
- Where will these tasks be performed?
- What computer hardware and software is required to build the system?
- What computer hardware and software is required to run the system?
- How will the new system be introduced to the organization?
- How will employees be trained to use the new system?

Once these questions are addressed, the project manager will develop a plan for creating the system. Next, the project manager must hire a staff of technicians and acquire office space to house the staff and the equipment needed to build the system, and manage everyone so the system is developed on time and within budget and works perfectly. To accomplish this, the project manager must:

- Plan to handle unanticipated delays such as missed deadlines and staff illnesses.
- Provide management with ongoing status reports.
- Enlist management's help to overcome obstacles within the organization and have changes in the original plan approved.
- Make sure each team member is completing tasks accurately and on time.
- Handle new deadlines and changes imposed by management.

Reading through these lists of questions and responsibilities, you are probably wondering if anyone possesses all the skills necessary to undertake the job of a project manager.

Although there are numerous jobs that must be performed to deliver a system, the project manager does not need to perform all those jobs him- or herself. Instead, the project manager must know what questions must be answered, what tasks must be performed, when they must be performed, and who should perform them.

For example, although the project manager needs to know that there must be a cost benefit analysis performed on a proposed system before any funds are dedicated to its development, the organization's accounting department can be called upon to perform this analysis. Likewise, the project manager must know that the system requires data storage; however, a database analyst will develop specifications for the database.

The project manager must:

- Like making things that are useful to others.
- Like taking a general idea and addressing all the complex issues involved with making that idea become reality.
- Like constantly learning about business and technology.
- Like building something that works perfectly.
- Like dealing with all kinds of people.
- Like working on the details of a project.

In addition, there are six skills the project manager must bring to the project. These are:

- The ability to select the right staff to create the system. Each member of the staff must be a team player and have the interpersonal skills and the technical knowledge to assure the objectives of the project are met.
- The ability to delegate responsibilities to the appropriate staff member.
- The ability to motivate staff members and ensure they remain focused on their tasks.
- The ability to understand the technology used for the system and how to use that understanding to keep the project on course.
- The ability to communicate effectively to the staff and to management in terms they can fully understand—that is, to be able to speak technically with the staff and non-technically with management.
- The political acumen necessary to manage the project through the maze of office politics.

■ MANAGEMENT'S ROLE

An organization is created for a specific purpose by its founding members. This purpose is called a *charter* and it becomes the objective for the existence of the organization. For example, two or more people form an organization to deliver utility services to customers and return a profit to stockholders. These people typically become the initial stockholders of the organization.

Stockholders elect a *board of directors* whose role is to establish short- and long-term goals that will enable the organization to fulfill its charter.

A *short-term goal* is an objective that can be achieved within a three- to five-year period, such as "to increase the customer base by 25%." A *long-term goal* is an objective for a period longer than five years, such as upgrading the technological infrastructure of the organization.

The board of directors hires a *chief executive officer* (CEO) to carry out the short- and long-term goals. Sometimes the CEO is called the *president* of the organization and/or the chief operating officer (COO). The titles fluctuate depending on the size and political structure of the organization.

The CEO assembles a management team of experts in specific areas who collectively establish the strategic plan for reaching the organization's goals. In many firms, the management team is called *senior management*, and each member oversees an operational division of the organization.

The senior management team is usually composed of the following:

- The *chief information officer* (CIO), who is responsible for technology.
- The *chief financial officer* (CFO), who is responsible for the organization's finances.
- The *chief administrative officer* (CAO), who is in charge of administrative activities (i.e., personnel).
- The *marketing director*, who identifies and fulfills customers' needs.

These are a few of the common titles you'll find in an organization. However, many organizations have expanded or different senior management positions, depending on their charter and the complexity of the organization.

The senior management team handles *strategic planning* and creates a broad approach to achieving the organization's charter. In addition, each senior manager develops a middle management team. Each member of the *middle management team* is responsible for managing an aspect of the senior manager's area. In addition, this team must devise a *tactical plan*, which is a roadmap for achieving a segment of the strategic plan.

For example, the CIO may have a middle manager responsible for applications development, for network operations, for hardware operations, and for vendor relations. These are a few responsibilities found in some organizations; however, each organization will have its own set of functions.

The lowest management level is called the *first-line management team,* which is responsible for operational planning and day-to-day operations. An *operational plan* carries out an aspect of the strategic plan. For example, while a tactical plan might declare that the organization must upgrade its network to fiber optics, the operational plan determines when to upgrade with the minimum impact on the operation of the organization.

■ MANAGEMENT AND THE PROJECT

A major component of an organization's strategic plan is a computer system. Since technology gives most organizations the competitive edge in the market place, managers at all levels within an organization typically have influence in many computer systems. The degree of influence depends on the level of management.

The project manager must plan to involve the appropriate levels of management in the development of a system. There are two ways in which managers can become an integral and productive part of the development team: as members of the executive committee or of the project steering committee.

The *executive committee* for the project consists of senior managers who are responsible for approving the project and determining whether or not the completed project met its objective. The executive committee is likely to receive general monthly reports on the status of the project.

Any number of executives can be on the committee and usually one member of the committee is considered the project's sponsor. A *project's sponsor* is the manager who proposes the system as a solution to an aspect of the strategic plan. Once approved by senior management, the sponsor oversees the development and implementation of the system and handles major obstacles that stand in the way of the completion of the project.

The *steering committee* is comprised of appropriate middle and first-line managers who function as advisors to the project manager. They provide the project manager with business direction and resolve conflicts among various stakeholders in the project. The steering committee is involved in a more detailed level of the project than the executive committee. It will meet weekly to review the current status of the project and approve and readjust priorities necessary to keep the development moving along.

A *stakeholder* is any person in the organization who has a vested interest in the success of the project. This person can be a senior manager, middle manager, first-line manager, or any employee who will be affected by the system and can influence the system's success or failure.

For example, a shift supervisor in the customer relations department might find the account information screen difficult to read. Since his comments can greatly influence the perception of the system by people he manages, he is a stakeholder in the project.

■ JOINT APPLICATION DESIGN (JAD)

It is imperative that all those who will be affected by the project are also brought into the design phase of the project because they know details of the business operations and requirements.

One method to accomplish this objective is to hold a series of meetings with these users, called *Joint Application Design (JAD)* meetings.

The project manager or the appropriate member of the project management team must meet with key users regularly to gather and verify information necessary to develop the project. Each JAD meeting must focus on a particular issue confronting the project team, such as determining the contents and flow of the customer account screen. Only users who can provide constructive input to the issue should attend the meeting. That is, every user in attendance must have a vested interest in the topic.

JAD meetings act as focus groups whereby participants provide quality input to the project development. Members of the project management team have an opportunity to present users with components of the project such as the data model, processing of data, and the flow of the system.

Participants are made aware by the project manager that what they are seeing is work in progress and that at times they are seeing a "straw man" of an idea. A *"straw man"* is a method used by project managers to open discussions about an issue. Based on preliminary information, the project manager puts forth a way of addressing an issue, and then encourages participants to modify the proposal. The proposal is a way to help participants focus on an issue.

For example, a project manager could ask participants to describe what they want to see in an account screen. While the question is pertinent to the project development, it is open-ended and can lead participants to wander in unproductive directions. An alternative is for the project manager to design a preliminary account screen, then ask participants to remove unnecessary items and add items that are missing.

A project manager can expect to hold a series of JAD meetings on the same issue. Each meeting produces results, which are incorporated into the project and then reviewed and revised if necessary at the next JAD meeting.

The number of attendees at a JAD meeting can vary from a single person to a small group. The actual number will depend on the nature of the issue. In the case of an account screen, the group of users who will access account information should attend the meeting, whereas only the first-line manager need attend a meeting that reviews the flow of incoming customer calls.

JAD meetings have a downside. Employees at times feel meetings are too time-consuming and don't see a benefit in attending the meetings. Attendees tend to come to the meeting unprepared regardless of the preliminary information sent by the project manager before the meeting.

Another potential drawback is the person selected to moderate the meeting, called the facilitator. It is the facilitator's responsibility to make sure all the attendees have an opportunity to ask questions and present their views. A poor facilitator may lose control and allow one participant to dominate the meeting.

■ THE PROJECT MANAGER AND MANAGEMENT

A project involves many persons in the organization, from senior management to the worker who uses the system or the results of the system daily. These employees must be involved with the development of the project from the onset so their needs and wants can be considered in the design.

Usually, only the project manager is aware that input from employees is essential to the success of the project. This is probably the first experience for most in the organization to be directly involved in a project's development. Therefore, it is the responsibility of the project manager to give all affected employees a role in the development of the project. If he or she fails to do this, then key information remains unknown until the completed project is introduced to the organization.

For example, imagine that a just-in-time inventory system delivers a week's supply of parts to a manufacturing plant. This system involves coordination of the organization's computer systems with those of vendors. In addition, staffing and warehouse construction and other non-computer systems are components of a just-in-time inventory system.

The project manager and the organization's management assume that demand for the product can be predicted with a degree of accuracy a week in advance. This is a reasonable assumption. However, a few weeks after the system is introduced a sales representative asks how the system handles unpredictable heavy demand, since for several weeks during every year major clients are known to require 125% of a manufacturing-week's worth of products. These orders are not known seven days in advance, but still must be filled. The current manufacturing method has met this demand because there was always more than a week's supply of parts on hand and the plant was placed on overtime to produce the products.

The bottom line is that the new just-in-time inventory system cannot perform as well as the existing system, and because of this the organization will lose business and possibly major clients. You can imagine the embarrassment of both the project manager and the project's sponsor. After years of planning and development, the "new" technology can't perform as well as the "old" system.

This dilemma could have been avoided if the project manager had consulted with all the stakeholders in the system during its development. Instead, the project manager accepted the approval of the marketing director, assuming he knew everything there was to know about the marketing and sales operations.

■ THE PROJECT MANAGER'S RESPONSIBILITIES

The project manager's job is to deliver the project on time, within budget, and in perfect working order the first day the project is implemented. This is a broad responsibility that begs questions, such as when is the deadline for the project? How much will the project cost to develop and implement? How will we know if the project is working perfectly?

Try to answer these questions and you'll discover that they are not easily answered. Yet it is your responsibility as project manager to find the answers before the development of the project begins. If you fail to answer these questions, then you allow each manager to devise his or her own answer, which will be used to determine whether your project is successful. This means that if your organization has 30 managers, then there will be 30 definitions of success—none of which might reflect the actual success of the project.

A project manager must take control over every aspect of the project from its inception, and must remain in control until the project is fully implemented. Your job is to manage everyone who is involved in the project, including senior management, the executive committee, the steering committee, stakeholders, and the project team who directly report to you.

Each one has a specific role in the project's development. You must define their role, then make sure they fulfill it. This is not an easy task since most of the participants do not report to you, so you will have to use your influence and political talents to assure that you receive the information you need to complete your assignment.

Here is a checklist that summarizes the steps you must address:

- Develop a consistent definition of the project. Specifically, what is the project to achieve? Be as specific as possible. A broad definition allows for various managers to devise their own interpretations. This could lead to false expectations that can result in the failure of the project.

- Identify the scope of the project. What are the constraints imposed on the project by management? What are the realities of the situation? Is there a business reason for an imposed deadline on the project? Does the organization have financial constraints that prohibit the project from meeting management's expectations? Are there technological limitations?

- Identify and develop a rapport with the project sponsor. This is the person who determines whether or not the project is allowed to continue through to implementation. Keep in mind that the project can be stopped at any time if the project sponsor feels doubt that you can deliver the project.

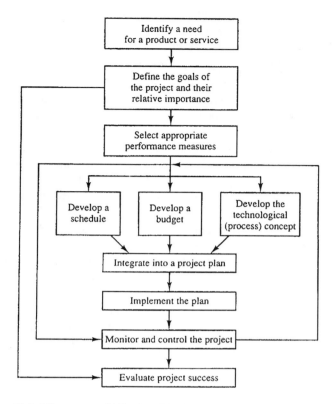

FIGURE 1-1   *Major Processes in Project Management*

- Identify and develop a rapport with stakeholders. These are the people who will be working either directly or indirectly with the project once it is implemented. They are also the people who know the detailed operations of the organization, information you need to build the project.

- Identify the benefits of the project. How will the organization be better off once the project is completed? The answer to this question provides a concrete purpose for everyone to work towards the same goal.

- Determine what tasks must be performed to complete the project. Even the smallest task must be identified—otherwise cost and time estimates will be inaccurate and a critical component of the project could be overlooked, leading to the failure of the project.

- Develop and maintain a schedule of tasks. Determine when something must be done, by whom, and the dependencies of each task. A *dependency* is a task that must be performed before other tasks can be started.

- Identify milestones. A *milestone* is the completion of a key portion of the development process, such as the user acceptance test. The *user acceptance test* is the time in the development of the project when the users test the system and agree that it meets the original specifications.

- Identify deliverables. A *deliverable* is a piece of the project such as a report, a computer screen, or the foundation of a building that is an indication of progress.

■ RISK AND UNCERTAINTY

A key role of every project manager is to manage risks and uncertainty. Risk is present in most projects, especially those that use cutting-edge technology where there is little experience using the technology in business. It is prudent to assume that what can go wrong will go wrong. Principal sources of uncertainty include random variations in component and subsystem performance, inaccurate or inadequate data, and the inability to forecast satisfactorily due to lack of prior experience. Specifically, there may be:

1. *Uncertainty in scheduling.* Changes in the environment that are impossible to forecast accurately at the outset of a project are likely to have a critical impact on the length of certain activities. For example, subcontractor performance or the time it takes to obtain a long-term loan are bound to influence the length of various subtasks.

2. *Uncertainty in cost.* Limited information on the duration of activities makes it difficult to predict the amount of resources needed to complete them on schedule. This translates directly into an uncertainty in cost. In addition, the expected hourly rate of resources and the cost of materials used to carry out project tasks may also vary widely.

3. *Technological uncertainty.* Technological uncertainty may affect the schedule, the cost, and the ultimate success of the project. The integration of familiar technologies into one system or product may cause technological uncertainty as well. The same applies to the development of software and its integration with hardware.

4. *Organization and political uncertainty.* New regulations might affect the market for a project, while the turnover of personnel and changes in the policies of one or more of the participating organizations may disrupt the flow of work.

■ THE PROJECT TEAM

A project is similar to a football game where the project manager is the coach and members of the project team are the players who win or lose the game. The comparison between a project and a football game is probably the best way to fully understand the role of the project team.

The project manager plots a game-winning strategy, then determines the talent required to carry out his or her plan. The type of project determines the kinds of positions that must be fulfilled; for example, a systems project requires different players than a construction project, a distinction that is similar to the difference between a football game and a baseball game.

Each position on the team requires a certain skill set. For example, the customer relations project discussed throughout this section requires a project team member to design the account database. However, the proficiency level can vary among players who have the same skills. For example, a database designer who might be a whiz at getting the most efficiency from a Sybase database may be less than a super star if the database is built using an Oracle system.

It is the job of the project manager to assess the breadth and depth of skills required to play a position on the project team. Then he or she must find the talent to fill the position. And, just as in sports, there are constraints that limit the choice of talented players.

First of all, does such a person exist? The job description for the position might describe a person with an unusual set of skills and there are few players who can meet the requirements. If there is such a person, then how is the project manager going to find him or her? And if the person is found and interested in pursuing the position, will the project manager be able to convince him or her to join the team? Then there is the ultimate limitation—price. Are there sufficient funds in the project budget to compensate the prospective player?

These are many of the same constraints facing a coach of a football team. Talented players demand high compensation. When their price is higher than the amount budgeted for the position, the coach must lower his sights and redefine the job description.

However, before the project manager can start looking for talented players, he or she must determine the skills necessary to complete the project. The project manger should use the zero-based staffing rule to staff the project. *Zero-based staffing* is similar to zero-based budgeting. Each project starts without any staff except for the project manager—every project requires a project manager.

Every position on the project team must be justified based on tasks that need to be performed. In the customer relations project, it can easily be assumed that a database designer is required. However, the decision to create such a position must occur after the project manager determines there is a need for a database.

The project's task list initiates the generation of positions on the project team. Each task requires one or more team members to complete the task. In addition, the project schedule determines the number of positions on the project team.

Let's say five stakeholders must be interviewed for a day to gather details about the existing system. Typically a business analyst handles this kind of job. One business analyst is required if the project schedule allows five days to complete the task. However, five business analysts must be hired if one day is dedicated for the interviews. But if there isn't room in the budget for five business analysts, then the project manager must revise the project plan to coincide with funds available to complete the task.

Staffing a project is a balancing act among constraints that are beyond the control of the project manager. By using tasks and the project schedule as a basis for staffing, the project manager is able to identify players necessary to complete the project.

Once a balance is struck between the requirements of the project and a visible pool of candidates, the project manager must choose players for the project team. This is likely to be one of the most critical decisions that will determine whether the project team wins the game. The game is doomed even before the launch of the project if the project team doesn't gel with personalities, attitude, and technical skills.

A good player must have the desire to work within a team rather than for individual glory. Knowing this principle, a major international Wall Street firm has a policy of requiring candidates to work through several rounds of interviews. Each round requires the interviewer to determine whether the prospective employee has met a requirement of the position.

The question the interviewer has to answer in the first round is whether or not the candidate's personality fits with the organization's culture and with that of the team. The firm doesn't want an ego to get in the way of progress. Each team member is expected to help the others regardless of job assignment. If the candidate doesn't meet the first criterion, he or she is rejected regardless of experience or expertise.

The second round consists of technical interviews where the expertise of staff challenges the candidate's skills. Typically, technicians from various disciplines within the company probe the candidate's depth of knowledge of technology and business as it relates to the project.

No one grades the candidate. Instead, each interviewer subjectively determines the candidate's level of knowledge in each area. The results are submitted to the project manager who determines the proper blend of skills he or she wants on the team.

The remaining rounds of interviews center on whether or not the personality of the candidate clashes with that of the project manager, project sponsor and other managers involved in the project.

THE PEOPLE SKILLS COMPONENT

■ MANAGING EXPECTATIONS

When is a project successful? This is one of the hardest questions to answer for both project manager and others involved in the project. Each person has his or her own definition of success based upon whatever criteria the person deems important.

Think about it. Your success as a project manager is being judged subjectively by the executive committee, steering committee, stakeholders, and your boss. You are bound not to meet someone's definition of success.

Our perception of success is based on our expectations of a result. If a project meets our expectations, then we tend to say the project is successful. Let's say a customer service representative's expectation is to have accurate account information displayed on the screen when a customer call is received. As long as the project meets this expectation, then the customer service representative feels the project is successful.

A Typical Project Team for a Systems Project

Programmer/Analyst
A programmer/analyst defines and analyzes aspects of the project using CASE tools. A *CASE tool* is used to collect information about a project and to automatically produce specifications and project reports. A programmer/analyst then interprets the specifications into a program.

Systems Analyst
A systems analyst interacts with the business unit and the business analyst to translate the business needs into specifications from which a programmer/analyst can create a component of the application. The systems analyst also creates prototypes of screens, reports and other aspects of the project.

Database Analyst/Administrator
A database analyst/administrator is responsible for the installation and maintenance of the database management system, which stores and retrieves data for the system. In addition, a database analyst/administrator designs and tunes the database used by the system. *Designing a database* involves organizing the data required by the system. *Tuning the database* involves taking advantage of all the features of the database management system to obtain the most efficient operation of the database.

Technical Analyst
A technical analyst is responsible for various hardware and software components of the system such as networking, communication, and assuring that components of the system work together. Many technical analysts have in-depth knowledge of a particular technology used in the project, e.g., data communication.

Business Analyst
A business analyst interacts with the business units to define the business requirements of the project. The business requirements are then submitted to the systems analyst, who translates the requirements into the specifications needed for the programmer/analyst to write the application.

Data Analyst
A data analyst extracts the data requirements from the business requirement. The data requirements are submitted to the database analyst/administrator who creates the database for the application.

Likewise, the project sponsor expects the project to increase customer satisfaction. If customer complaints rise, especially when customers are forced to respond to a telephone menu, then the project sponsor feels the project failed.

The project manager has the responsibility to manage the expectations of everyone who is involved with the project so that the project will meet all the expectations. One of the major reasons why projects don't meet expectations is because the expectations are not realistic. For example, there are many factors other than the customer relations system that cause customers to be dissatisfied with an organization. The project manager must point out these factors before the project is launched.

Managing expectations is an ongoing responsibility. Throughout the project, the project manager and the project team must monitor expectations and use reality checks to bring the expectations closer to the true benefits of the project.

The fact that people tend to rely more on their instincts than the word of another poses a dilemma for project managers. Since many managers have little experience with the development of a project, their instincts, uninformed by experience, can cloud their expectations and their judgment of the project's success or failure. It is like a skunk caught on the highway with an 18-wheeler bearing down. The skunk realizes this is a life-threatening situation and instinctively raises its tail.

A project manager must overcome the influence of a manager's instincts by being persuasive. The manager must be convinced that his or her initial impression may not be correct. There are several techniques you can use to persuade a manager. First, gain the manager's trust by being honest, and provide a rational basis for your arguments.

You must be an effective communicator and use terms the manager can easily understand. Let's say the manager expects to have telephone, video, and computer data transferred anywhere in the organization within a fraction of a second. However, you realize the communication infrastructure is unable to meet this expectation because there is insufficient bandwidth.

Bandwidth is a technical concept that is difficult to appreciate unless you are a technician. However, you can easily make an analogy to a highway to illustrate the problem. The organization's communications infrastructure is a four-lane highway. This needs to be increased to a 16-lane highway to meet the manager's expectations.

Another technique to manage expectation is to deliver on a promise. You can pose a rational argument why the manager's expectation isn't reality. However, a little doubt will always remain until you are proven true. Therefore, you must establish achievable goals at the beginning of the project. Those goals must be shared with the manager—and the goals must be achieved.

◼ AVOID THE PITFALLS OF DEALING WITH MANAGERS

The start of every project is predictable. The project sponsor and others involved in the project are confident the project will succeed. Special care is taken to approach the project systematically in an effort to avoid errors of previous projects.

This is called the *honeymoon period* when the project manager, the project sponsor, the steering committee, and the project team form a partnership and define their roles in the project. However, the honeymoon is short lived and soon adversarial relationships develop.

The lack of trust is the basis for the partnership to become unwound. A project manager makes many small and major commitments to management. Fidelity becomes a concern once a commitment is not met. Fail to live up to a commitment, and trust is lost, which is very difficult to regain.

Not every commitment can be met due to factors beyond your control and honest errors in judgment. Managers are supportive only if you are truthful. Support immediately drops once managers discover they are being deceived.

Your role is to deliver bad news to management. You must avoid panic and present the problem objectively. Don't minimize or embellish the situation. Be prepared to explain what you think caused the situation to occur—even if you or a member of the project team made an error.

Explore options to resolve the issue with the manager, and then collectively arrive at a course of action to rectify the situation and prevent it from reoccurring.

◼ BUILDING A RAPPORT WITH MANAGERS

A project manager plays various roles in the project, including coaching the project team, advising management, and making sure a variety of personalities are pleased with the progress of the project. Another key role is to develop a solid rapport with the project sponsor and steering committee members, for these are the people who determine the success or failure of the project.

People tend to become familiar with each other by finding something in common besides working on the project. It is important for the project manager to locate things unrelated to the project that will bring him or her closer to the manager—for example, sports, books, films, family, and education.

Once the relationship is built on common ground, the project manager must be sure not to violate unwritten guidelines of business ethics. For example, appropriate formality and informality can be used depending on the rapport developed between you and the manager. Use comfortable mannerisms and speak in everyday language at all times.

You must be prepared to sell the project sponsor and others involved with the project on various proposals, such as changing the project specifications or hiring another member for the project team.

Trust and respect go a long way to making the sale. However, you must be sure the customer—in this case the manager—doesn't feel rushed into adopting the proposal. Otherwise, the customer may feel you are "putting one over" on him or her. You can avoid this problem by understanding the steps involved in acceptance of a proposal.

Let's use the analogy of selling a car to illustrate this process. First, the customer needs to be aware the car exists. This is called the *awareness step*. Car manufacturers and dealerships tend to accomplish this by showing the benefits of the car in advertisements. The object is to get the customer's attention.

If successful, the customer explores the car further by visiting the show room and asking general questions such as fuel mileage and cost. This is called the *exploration step*. These questions are designed to qualify the car and determine whether the car meets the customer's needs.

If this step is also successful, the customer begins to see the merits of the car and enters the *examination step*. It is here where the customer investigates the details of the car such as the color, CD player, options, and availability.

If the examination step is successful, then the customer is willing to enter the test step. The *test step* is where the customer tries the car, looking for any reason not to make the purchase. If the test step goes well, then a sale is made. This is referred to as the *adoption step*.

Steps of Adoption

1. Awareness
2. Exploration
3. Examination
4. Test
5. Adoption

◼ HANDLING AN ANGRY MANAGER OR TEAM MEMBER

When a project doesn't proceed as planned, people involved with the project become frustrated, which typically manifests as anger directed at the person responsible for the project—you, the project manager.

You are placed in a difficult situation. There is likely a sensible reason why the project isn't meeting expectations. However, rarely will any reasoning avoid the angry response. Instead, the anger is vented towards you, who are likely helpless to provide immediate satisfaction.

There are steps that can be taken to manage the anger and leave the other person with a positive feeling for the project. You must remain in control at all times and not take the anger personally. The anger is directed at the situation and not you.

Stay calm and let the person know you are sincerely interested in his or her concerns and disappointments. Give the user time to vent the anger, after which he or she will be in a better frame of mind to address the situation rationally.

The objective is to have the person talk about the problem, during which time you can acknowledge facts and defuse myths. Any misperceptions must be resolved. Ask questions that isolate the issues that disturbed the person.

You must remain detached from the situation; otherwise, your emotions will impede your role of being an advisor and manager. This technique is similar to that used by emergency room physicians. No matter the condition of the patient, the physician's job is to identify facts, isolate the problem, explain the reality of the situation to the patient and have the patient agree to a treatment.

An agreed-upon course of action cannot be considered until the person's anger has dissipated. Until then, you must be a good listener and fact-finder. Anger over a project can lead to the break in rapport and damage the bond built between the project manager and others on the project team. You cannot let this happen.

Once the other person is calm, you must rebuild the rapport by showing that both of you are on the same team, working towards the same objective. You must recognize a problem exists and lead the other person towards a solution.

Let's say the project sponsor noticed that critical data are missing from a prototype data entry screen. He anticipates this will cause a month's delay in the project. After the project sponsor has vented his anger, you must provide a reality check and identify the missing data and the effort it will take to revise the screen.

People tend to lose track of the significance of a problem. Small problems take on major proportions in the absence of an understanding of the facts. You must help the person define the magnitude of the problem. Is it really a big problem or a small problem that seems big?

Start by agreeing to what is correct about the situation. This shows that progress has been made. Move on to what is incorrect about the situation, which shows issues that need to be addressed. Next focus attention to a solution. Agree upon how and when the issue will be resolved. It is critical that the solution will work and will be delivered on time. Avoid under- or over-estimating effort required to fix the problem.

■ THE FEAR FACTOR

A project manager must be aware of apprehensions of managers who are involved in the project. We tend to assume everyone is beginning the project with a "gung-ho" attitude. However, managers are likely to approach the project timidly because a project can be a minefield that can kill a successful career.

Behind the manager's game-face is fear. It is important to recognize this fact and plan to ease any fears. The initial fear is of you. The success or failure of the project—and possibly the manager's career—is in your hands. Will you deliver the project on time and within budget?

There is also the fear of the unknown. No one, including you, knows if the project will be successful. This fear is increased when the fate of the project is out of the manager's hands, as is the case for the project sponsor. For him or her, the experience is like being a passenger on an airliner. The pilot is responsible for getting you to your destination. You and the pilot cannot guarantee that you'll get there—even though the probability is high. You try to recognize problems in flight based on previous bad experiences, but you're never sure if they are serious problems. And you're not sure that the pilot is telling you the truth when he says everything is OK.

Then there is the fear that the project sponsor may lose his or her job. Is the project urgent enough to take such a risk? The sponsor is authorizing expenditure of funds for a project that might fail; he or she is risking making bad decisions and losing face with colleagues and senior management.

It is your job to identify these and other fears and try to minimize their effects on the project.

■ THE ART OF INTERVIEWING

A substantial amount of project management time is typically spent interviewing executive committee members, the steering committee, project sponsor, and other stakeholders. Interviews can elicit important information needed to complete the project. It is your job and the job of anyone else who conducts interviews to design meetings for the productive exchange of information.

Meetings are usually conducted in one of three ways: very *structured,* such as a town hall meeting with a formal agenda and rules of order to follow; *semi-structured,* where there is a known topic and an objective for the meeting; or *ad hoc,* where no planning or control is implemented.

Experienced project managers avoid *ad hoc* meetings, at least to the degree that they depend on the meeting to identify key information for the project. Likewise, a town hall meeting approach rarely is conducive to a free flow of ideas. Most meetings regarding a project are semi-structured. The meeting is called for a particular purpose, such as determining the flow of a process. The meeting also has a clear objective; that is, at the end of the meeting specific information necessary to complete an element of the project is known.

You must carefully plan every meeting to assure it provides for an open exchange of ideas and yet still benefits the project. Below are techniques used by experienced project managers to ensure that project meetings are productive.

First, set an objective each time you meet with someone regarding the project. You should not require a formal agenda, but you must establish the topic before the meeting and share this information with all attendees so they too can prepare to discuss the topic. Limit the meeting to no more than two topics. Meetings are only productive for an hour so you probably won't be able to explore more than two topics.

In addition, only invite to the meeting people who can contribute to the topic. Don't allow anyone to "sit-in" for someone else. For example, a common practice is for a key manager to send a staff member as his or her representative to the meeting. Unfortunately, that staff member is rarely in a position to make decisions or answer questions on behalf of the manager. The meeting is likely to be unproductive.

Begin the meeting or interview by easing into the conversation rather than starting abruptly like a baseball game. It is your meeting, and you set the tone. Make sure everyone is at ease. Your job is to ask questions and keep the meeting focused on the topic. Ask questions respectfully and never sound as if you are interrogating anyone. Let others in the meeting do most of the talking as long as they remain on the topic. Listen carefully, take notes and never dominate the conversation. Give each person time to present his or her thoughts.

Don't be afraid to encourage someone to elaborate on a thought. Likewise, ask test questions to be certain others in the meeting feel the meeting is staying on track. For example, you may ask someone, "How do you feel about what we've discussed? Is there an important issue that you feel we haven't discussed?" If the answer is yes and off the topic of the meeting, then schedule another meeting to explore the issue, and make sure you determine who must make the final decision on the issue.

For example, attendees might be staff employees who have important information and opinions on the topic, but who are not authorized to decide on a course of action. You need to know who are the decision-makers and what information is required for them to make the decision. Then provide the information and have them make the decision.

Maintain eye contact when someone is responding to your question. Looking away implies disinterest or that what is being said is not important to you. Keep the conversation moving and don't allow anyone to get bogged down in unnecessary details. For example, a conversation discussing a data entry screen should not wander into opinions on a PC monitor or the computer running the screen.

Make sure you clarify each point made by someone. Feedback is the best method to assure you have a firm understanding of what is being said and a way of letting the person know that you are listening. Always try to see the point from the other person's perspective. This helps you to understand their emotions and commitment to the project.

Avoid speaking about politics, religion, or other controversial topics, or allowing negative remarks to be made about anyone during the meeting. These are sensitive areas for most of us and usually have little or nothing to do with a project. They also may cause a difference of opinion that hampers progress.

Always end a meeting on a positive note by having everyone agree on something—even if it is a small item, such as having the notes of the meeting sent to everyone.

Above all, you must maintain your integrity during the meeting—and during the project. Each of us has set our own standards that should not be compromised for the sake of a project. There are two important questions that should be asked before you take any action: Would I want someone to do this to me? Would I be proud to see my actions on the nightly news? If you answer no to either of these questions, then don't do it.

■ DYNAMICS OF A MEETING

A project manager must be a good facilitator. A facilitator understands the dynamics of people working as a group, and uses this knowledge to assure that the interaction during a meeting results in a consensus.

Let's say you called a meeting to discuss a specification change that will delay the completion date by three months. The appropriate people are invited to attend. Each brings to the meeting expertise, motivation, personality, personal objectives, and opinions. You must manage the meeting so these characteristics don't prevent the group from agreeing to a solution.

Project managers are able to achieve a consensus by using guidelines taken from the study of *group dynamics*. There are three roles that must be managed at every meeting to assure that the group makes a rational decision. These roles are called the *task roles*, the *maintenance roles,* and the *individual-centered roles*. Anyone in the group can take on one or more of these roles during the meeting.

TASK ROLES   *Task roles* are those required for the group to make a decision. There are five task roles: initiating, opinion giving/seeking, clarifying, summarizing, and reality testing.

The *initiating role* sets the objective of the meeting and a procedure for reaching the objective, which is inviting appropriate employees to the meeting to determine a course of action. Typically, the project manager fulfills this role, although it is not uncommon for the project sponsor to do the same.

The *opinion giving/seeking role* is demonstrated by someone who expresses his or her feelings on the issue or asks a question. Every attendee can find himself or herself in this role.

The *clarifying role* is fulfilled by someone who explores an issue mentioned during the meeting. The person restates the idea, asks for or offers a definition of terms used to describe the issue, and offers various interpretations of the issue.

The *summarizing role* is taken by someone who assembles the ideas on the table into a course of action. This is an attempt to reach a consensus. Several attempts might be made before there is agreement within the group.

The *reality-testing role* is one where the proposed consensus is critically analyzed. One or more members of the group ask whether or not the proposal is achievable. If the answer is yes, then the group has dealt with the issue; otherwise, the issue is revisited by someone taking on one of the other task roles.

MAINTENANCE ROLES   *Maintenance roles* are those that are performed to continue the decision-making process. Many influences can cause the meeting to go off track and impede movement toward a consensus. Maintenance roles bring the meeting back on track. There are five maintenance roles: harmonizing, gate-keeping, consensus testing, encouraging, and compromising.

The *harmonizing role* reduces tensions and attempts to reconcile disagreements among meeting participants. The person who takes on this role seeks to have differences resolved to the point where they are no longer interfering with the progress of the meeting.

The *gate-keeping role* maintains open communication channels. If the meeting becomes silent, the gatekeeper speaks in order to keep the discussion lively.

The *consensus-testing role* determines whether the group is prepared to reach a decision. The person filling this role might send up a trial proposal and see if there is any agreement. If not, the meeting continues.

The *encouraging role* fosters an environment conducive to exploring an issue. It is this role that seeks to have everyone voice his or her opinion and ideas. For example, some attendees tend to sit silently listening without contributing to the meeting. The person taking on the encouraging role must bring those people into the conversation.

The *compromising role* offers a solution that can be supported by everyone at the meeting. This role is critical whenever conflicts stand in the way of a consensus.

INDIVIDUAL-CENTERED ROLES   *Individual-centered roles* reflect personal traits that hinder a decision. Each of us at some point assumes most of the individual-centered roles during the meeting. You have the responsibility to recognize these roles as they manifest, and then to try to diminish their effect on the group, even to the point of taking a 10-minute recess. There are five individual-centered roles: aggression, blocking, dominating, out-of-field behavior, and special interest pleading.

The *aggression role* is taken when someone attacks a participant, the group, or the project without providing constructive criticism. Aggression, if out of hand, destroys the decision process and defeats the purpose of the meeting.

The *blocking role* is one in which an unreasonable effort is made to thwart the group's progress. Attendees can and should have a lively discussion that elicits opposing opinions; however, this must not prevent the group from reaching a decision.

The *dominating role* is seen when a person tries to manipulate members of the group by asserting either real or implied authority.

The *out-of-field behavior role* is one in which a person is not relating to the discussion. The person is physically attending the meeting, but is mentally somewhere else.

The *special-interest-pleading role* attempts to use the group as a tool to achieve an individual's objective rather than to address the issue related to the project.

Staying Alive

Here is a checklist for keeping a project on track.

1. Keep the project team focused on the mission.
2. Identify managers who make final decisions related to the project.
3. Make sure all plans are approved before work begins.
4. Make sure all changes to the plan are approved before work begins.
5. Manage the expectations of everyone involved with the project.
6. Avoid in-fighting within management groups.
7. Avoid surprising management and the project team.
8. Keep the project proceeding as planned.
9. Don't overemphasize any aspect of the project.
10. Don't allow a personality conflict to overshadow a valuable opinion.
11. Don't allow favoritism to influence objectivity.
12. Don't make judgments based upon preconceived notions.

THE PROJECT COMPONENT

■ THE PROJECT

There are many kinds of projects. Some involve building computer systems that automate an activity within an organization. Others involve constructing an office building or devising a better way to manage an aspect of a business. Regardless of the objective of the project, every project has similarities.

A *project* is the organization of tasks that must be completed to achieve a particular objective. A *task* is a job that must be performed in a logical sequence. For example, the task of laying a cinder block foundation cannot begin until the excavation is completed. Likewise, framing the structure must wait until the cinder block foundation is in place.

One or more resources are required to perform a task. Intuitively, we think of workers as resources since they perform tasks. However, materials and equipment are also considered resources. Therefore a *resource* is person or thing necessary to complete a task.

For example, masonry workers alone cannot complete the cinder block foundation. Cinder blocks, cement, masonry tools, trucks to deliver the cinder blocks and cement to the site, and equipment to unload the cinder blocks from the truck are all resources required to build the foundation.

Looking at this example, you'll recognize that many tasks are composed of smaller tasks called subtasks. A *subtask* is a task that must be completed before the higher task is completed.

For example, someone must determine the type and number of cinder blocks that are required for the foundation. Those cinder blocks must be ordered and delivered to the site.

Another resource must verify that the proper type and quantity of cinder blocks were received. The cinder blocks must be off-loaded from the truck, and the foreman must determine where each cinder block is to be laid to form the foundation. The correct type and quantity of cement must be determined; the order for the cement must be placed. The cement must be delivered at a precise time, and masons must cement each cinder block into the proper place on the foundation.

This example illustrates the detail of subtasks that are involved in a single task of a project. If just one of those subtasks is overlooked, the project can come to a standstill, its completion may be delayed, and the cost may be increased. Let's say that, due to this type of oversight, the cement is delivered a day late. The project manager must still pay the masons although they are standing around waiting for the cement to arrive—and then pay them to do the work the next day.

Projects are deceivingly simple to anyone who has never managed a project. Senior management often understates the complexity of the project by giving the project manager a general objective, such as, "Automate the inventory process." It seems an achievable objective since other organizations in the industry might have such a system in place, especially when you consider the advances in technology.

However, what once appeared simple becomes a complex maze of options and tasks when you scratch the surface and try to assemble the pieces of the puzzle. The key to development of the project is the project plan.

LAWS OF PROJECT MANAGEMENT

1. No major project is ever installed on time, within budget, or with the same staff that started it. Yours will not be the first.

2. Projects progress quickly until they become 90% complete, then they remain at 90% complete forever.

3. One advantage of fuzzy project objectives is that they let you avoid the embarrassment of estimating the corresponding costs.

4. When things are going well, something will go wrong.
   - When things just cannot get any worse, they will.
   - When things appear to be going better, you have overlooked something.

5. If project content is allowed to change freely, the rate of change will exceed the rate of progress.

6. No system is ever completely debugged. Attempts to debug a system inevitably introduce new bugs that are even harder to find.

7. A carelessly planned project will take three times longer to complete than expected; a carefully planned project will take only twice as long.

8. Project teams detest progress reporting because it vividly manifests their lack of progress.

■ THE PROJECT PLAN

It is the job of the project manager to create and manage the project plan throughout the life of the project. A *project plan* is a detailed roadmap of what has to be done, who is going to do it, and when it must be started and completed. In addition, the project plan must determine how to monitor the progress of the project with deliverables and milestones. And, to be complete, the project plan must identify the estimated cost of building the project.

A project plan consists of a list of tasks and subtasks that are necessary to complete the project. Dependencies are then drawn for each task and specific resources are assigned to each task. Based on the resources, the project manager estimates how long it will take to complete the task. This is called the task's *duration*.

Information is tracked by using a project management tool. Microsoft Project is a commonly used tool to manage projects, although there are other products available in the marketplace. Other software packages offer similar features.

Microsoft Project generates reports, charts, and schedules automatically based on a minimum amount of information about the project. These include a Gantt chart, PERT chart, the critical path, a resource sheet, a resource graph, a calendar of events, and customized reports.

The project management tool enables the project manager to concentrate on identifying details of the project and managing the project. The administrative duties of reproducing schedules and calculating dates are left to the project management tool.

A Gantt chart (Figure 1-2) displays basic task information such as name of the task, resources assigned to it, and its duration. The duration of each task is displayed as a bar along a grid of dates. Dependencies among tasks are depicted visually with bars that connect the dependent tasks. Many project managers use the Gantt chart to enter initial information about their projects into Microsoft Project. As changes are made to tasks, such as a longer or shorter duration, Microsoft Project automatically adjusts the Gantt chart to depict the changes. A *PERT chart* (Figure 1-3) displays tasks and dependencies as a network diagram in which each box on the diagram (called a *node*) represents a task. A line that connects nodes represents a dependency between two tasks. The PERT chart graphically shows tasks not yet started, those in progress, and those completed.

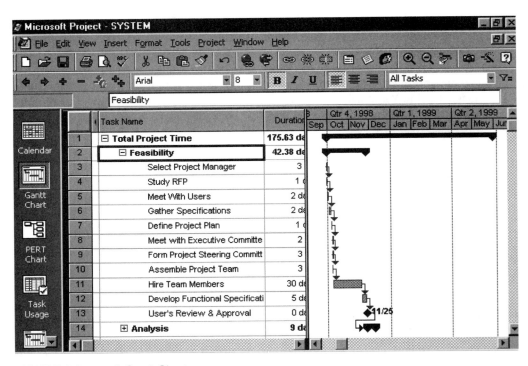

FIGURE 1-2   *A Gantt Chart*

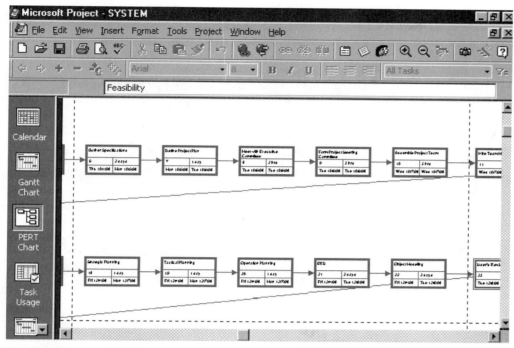

FIGURE 1-3   *A PERT Chart*

The *critical path* (Figure 1-4) represents the tasks that must be completed on schedule if the project is not to be delayed. Microsoft Project uses the dependency and duration of tasks to determine which tasks are on the critical path. Delays in completing tasks not on the critical path may not affect the end date of the project.

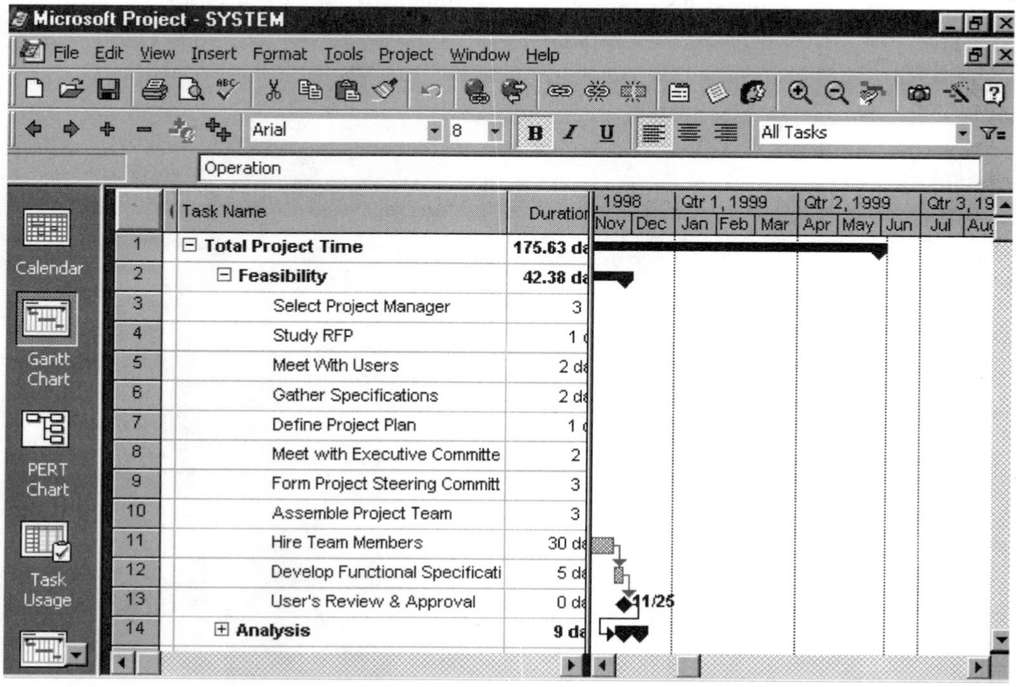

		Task Name	Duration	1998 Nov Dec	Qtr 1, 1999 Jan Feb Mar	Qtr 2, 1999 Apr May Jun	Qtr 3, 19 Jul Aug
1		⊟ Total Project Time	175.63 da				
2		⊟ Feasibility	42.38 da				
3		Select Project Manager	3				
4		Study RFP	1				
5		Meet With Users	2 da				
6		Gather Specifications	2 da				
7		Define Project Plan	1				
8		Meet with Executive Committe	2				
9		Form Project Steering Committ	3				
10		Assemble Project Team	3				
11		Hire Team Members	30 da				
12		Develop Functional Specificati	5 da				
13		User's Review & Approval	0 da	11/25			
14		⊞ Analysis	9 da				

FIGURE 1-4   *The Critical Path*

The *resource sheet* (Figure 1-5) is used to enter details of resources that are assigned to the project. Once the resource is entered, it can be assigned to tasks. Microsoft Project then generates a schedule for each resource that consists of a list of tasks, starting date and deadline, and duration.

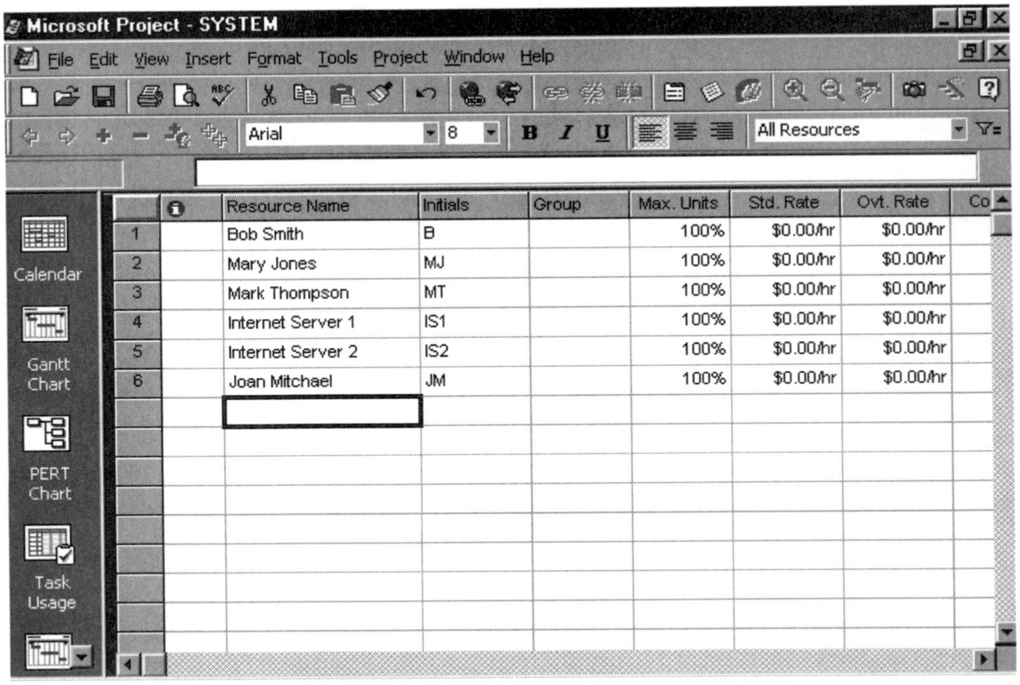

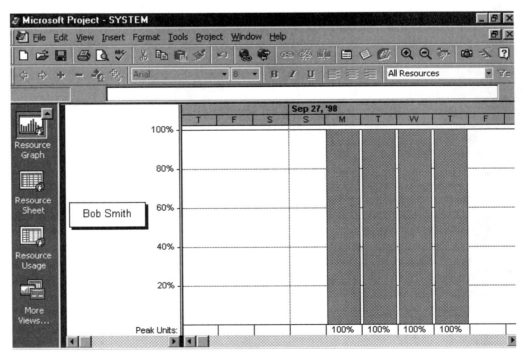

FIGURE 1-5   *The Resource Sheet*

The *resource graph* (Figure 1-6) depicts the allocation of a resource to the project. For example, while a resource can spend 100% of the time working on tasks for each day of the

FIGURE 1-6   *The Resource Graph*

workweek, the project manager may mistakenly assign the resource to more tasks than can be accomplished in a day. If this occurs, the resource graph shows that the resource is over-allocated, and that the project manager needs to reallocate resources.

The *calendar* (Figure 1-7) of events shows tasks on a calendar.

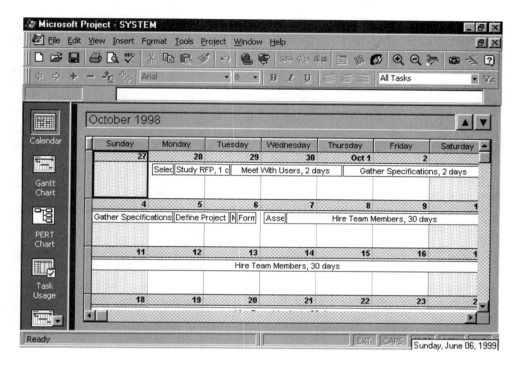

FIGURE 1-7   *The Calendar*

THE START OF THE PROJECT PLAN

All projects begin the same way. The project sponsor gives a project manager an objective; the project manager's job is to deliver the completed project. For example, if someone asks you to build a skyscraper and expects you to do so on time and within budget, most of us would panic, wondering where to begin. However, an experienced project manager simply says, "Will do," and then goes about creating a project plan.

The project manager is confident about fulfilling the objective because he or she knows that there are guidelines that help to develop a sound approach to completing the project. There are three kinds of guidelines project managers follow: the project life cycle, a design philosophy, and a project management methodology.

The *project life cycle* outlines phases of the project. Each phase describes the orders and the kinds of activities that must be undertaken. After each phase is completed, the project manager and the project sponsor review the status of the project and decide whether or not to move the project into the next phase.

A *design philosophy* is a philosophical method by which the project manager and the project team approach the project. A *project management methodology* is a step-by-step way of addressing every aspect of a project.

These guidelines provide the project manager with the framework within which to develop a detailed plan based on a general objective identified by the project sponsor.

THE PROJECT LIFE CYCLE

Every project, regardless of its objective, goes through standard phases called the *project life cycle.* The life cycle of a project is generally the same as that of human beings; we are born, grow up and get married, have and raise children; then we die.

A project too is born as the sponsor's idea and is developed by the project manager and his or her team. The project is implemented and at some point in the future, the implemented project is replaced by a new project.

The actual life cycle phases can vary depending on the nature of the project, just like our life cycle might differ from others if we don't marry or don't have children. A variation of the life cycle is called the *life cycle model.*

However, all projects can be divided into four phases. These are conception, definition, acquisition and operational.

The *conception phase* is where managers arrive at the objective of the project. That is, they identify a need, such as to improve the flow of a business operation; and then develop a general statement of how the need can be fulfilled.

The *definition phase* is when the details of the projects are explored. For example, the conception phase might state that a new warehouse is necessary to meet customer demand. The definition phase states the size, location, and other facets required to make the warehouse become a reality.

The *acquisition phase* is where the project is actually built. In the case of our warehouse, this is the period in the project where a site is purchased and the building is constructed.

The *operational phase* occurs when the project is implemented and becomes a working part of the organization.

A systems variation of the project life cycle covers the same ground, but uses different phases. The initial phase consists of a *definitive statement of the objective.* It is at this phase that the project manager determines whether a system can fulfill the objective of the organization.

Next is the *systems study phase.* This is where the existing systems are analyzed and various alternative solutions are evaluated. Once a viable systems solution is agreed upon, the project enters the design phase. The *design phase* is where the general concept of the objective is translated into logical and physical design specifications.

The *programming phase* follows, in which the design specifications are translated into a working computer system. The system then undergoes a test phase called the *system test.* This is the period when every aspect of the system is thoroughly tested before the system is turned over to the business unit.

When the project manager is satisfied that the system performs as expected, the project is moved into the next phase, called the *acceptance phase.* This is where the business unit tests the system to determine if the system meets its requirements. If it does so, then the system is considered accepted by the business unit and ready to be implemented.

The *migration phase* is where the accepted system is moved into production, thereby replacing the existing system. During this stage of the project, data from the old system is converted to the new system, software is installed on the appropriate servers, and other steps necessary to replace the existing system are completed.

The next step is the *operational phase.* This is where the old system is turned off and the new system becomes fully operational. The final step is the *maintenance phase* when the system is supported during normal operations.

■ DESIGN PHILOSOPHY

The design philosophy of a project determines how the project manager and the project team handle issues such as quality and organization of assignments, and how they react to specification changes during the development of the project.

Quality is of uppermost concern for every project manager. Every aspect of the project must be completed correctly and on time. Although this statement might seem obvious, it is difficult to fulfill, especially when you consider the complexity of a typical project and the number of people involved in the development of the project.

Take, for example, the customer relations system described earlier in this section. Within this project there are executive committee members, the project sponsor, steering committee members, stakeholders, the project manager, business analysts, system analysts, database designers, network engineers, communications engineers, database programmers, application programmers, and communications programmers. Each of these people has a role in the development of the system.

Furthermore, there are thousands of lines of programming code necessary to make the system operate properly. Each line of code must be written within a deadline, then tested to make sure it works with all the other lines of code that are designed by other analysts and written by other programmers.

Imagine that every facet of the project must be identified and specified in detail, and then assigned to the proper team member for development and testing. Even in ideal conditions an aspect of the project will be overlooked.

The *design philosophy* adopted by the project manager helps to strengthen this weakness in every project plan. Total quality management is a design philosophy that should be adopted for every project since it clearly assigns responsibility for the quality aspect of the project. *Total quality management* holds each member of the project team responsible for the quality of the entire project. Building the system is a team effort and if a part of the system fails to work, then the entire system is deemed not to work and the entire team is held accountable. This is much like a football team where it doesn't matter how well you play your position if the team loses the game.

An objective of total quality management is to instill in team members the knowledge that protecting their individual "turf" won't protect them from repercussions if the project fails.

Let's return to the customer relations system to see how a total quality manager can impact a project. This system requires that accounts are stored in a database and a program is written to query the database for account information. Typically, a database designer develops the database scheme and a programmer writes the query to access the data. Let's say there is a serious delay in retrieving the data. Customer service representatives are not receiving account information in a timely fashion.

It is common for the database designer to fault the query written by the programmer and the programmer to fault the database design. This is a catch-22 situation for the project manager since he or she is usually an expert neither in programming nor in database design. This kind of conflict is a common cause of unnecessary and unanticipated delays in the project that continue until someone resolves the conflict.

Under the total quality management philosophy, it doesn't matter who is to blame for the problem. It is up to the database designer and the programmer to analyze and resolve the problem without having to argue who is at fault and be prodded by the project manager to take action.

Another design philosophy is to *design bugs out of the system.* A *bug* is an error in logic that causes the system to do something unexpected. Every system will have bugs. However, it is up to the project team to eliminate all bugs before the system is released to the user for acceptance.

A common method of detecting bugs is not to allow programmers and other systems developers to test their own pieces of the system. Developers tend to make honest mistakes by assuming the system will perform with a particular response, and therefore fail to perform a thorough test. To overcome this problem, system testing is assigned to a quality assurance group whose staff tests every aspect of the system following a prescribed test plan. Bugs detected by the quality assurance group are reported back to the project manager and programmer.

The *top-down design approach* is another philosophy that helps the project manager approach a complex project. The top-down design approach requires the project manager to plan the project at the highest level, and then to divide the project into small functional modules, each of which is assigned to the project team.

Let's return to the customer relations system. The top level might consist of the customer service representative's workstation, data storage and retrieval, and telephone communications operations.

Each of these areas can be divided into smaller modules based on functionality. For example, telephone communications operations can be divided into the following: receiving incoming calls, determining the nature of the call (i.e., menu selection), request for data, determining which customer service representative is available, and routing the call to the customer service representative.

The top-down design enables the project to be divided into logical discrete units that focus the team on a functional aspect of the system.

The *Waterfall Model* is another useful design philosophy that should be incorporated into every project. The Waterfall Model states that the project team must be aware that each phase of the project will be touched more than once during the project.

Take, for example, a screen used by the customer relations representatives to view account data. A screen designer and programmer might have spent months developing the screen and consider the screen completed. However, the customer relations department staff may find aspects of the screen unacceptable. Therefore, the screen must be returned to the designer and programmer for redevelopment.

It is your responsibility to recognize that components of the system may require additional work after the work seems to be finished. Likewise, you must instill this reality in all the members of the project management team so they don't become frustrated when a completed component is returned for rework.

■ Project Methodology

A *project methodology* is a proven method used to complete a project on time and within a budget. It provides a clear roadmap, an ordered list of all the tasks that are necessary to complete the project. A *methodology* provides a checklist from which the project manager develops his own project plan.

You should employ a project methodology for all large, complex projects; otherwise, you risk overlooking a critical component of the project. However, projects fewer than three months in duration will not greatly benefit from the use of a project management methodology. Those projects are less complex and can be developed with less formality without risking their success.

It may seem that adopting a project management methodology solves many problems in the management of a project, but this isn't always true. A project management methodology requires you to follow formal procedures. *Procedures* offer structure to a project, but also impede flexibility, especially when unexpected problems arise.

Furthermore, procedures require you to follow steps that may not be relevant to the project, which tends to lengthen the project needlessly. In addition, a project management methodology can become a crutch rather than a tool. A project manager and the project team can rely too much on the methodology and assume that it will resolve all the issues involved with developing a project.

For example, a project management methodology will not make a poor project manager into a good project manager. It will not build the system. It will not assure that quality technicians join the project team. It will not come up with clever ways to solve problems.

Two of the more common project management methodologies are Rapid Application Development (RAD) and the Iterative Project Development Methodology (IPDM). Both methods bring the users closer to the project development by having the user work together with the project management team in creating the specifications for the system.

Through the use of prototypes, users are able to lend their expertise to the development process and test-drive the application long before the system is delivered. (A *prototype* is a working part of the system.) In this way, users gain a sense of participation and ownership of the project and will often do everything in their power to assure the success of the project.

However, there is a drawback to both methodologies. First, prototyping does not produce documented specifications for the system. The project team and users tend to develop the system "on the fly," using the development tool without considering formal specifications.

Also, both methods rely on a development tool. There are many to choose from. However, the wrong selection might require the project team to redevelop the prototype using a more desirable tool.

For example, the project team might use Microsoft Visual Basic to develop prototypes. However, the system might require a more robust tool such as PowerBuild to build the final system.

■ RAPID APPLICATION DEVELOPMENT (RAD)

The *Rapid Application Development methodology* centers on the use of prototypes of applications and processes to develop a system. For example, development of a working account screen for the customer relations system is a component that can be presented to the user as a prototype. That is, customer information is displayed in the same manner as it would be if the system were fully implemented.

Prototypes have the look and feel of the final system, and can be used by the project manager to demonstrate the system to the users and to receive user feedback. Users can interact with the system and define enhancements long before the system reaches the acceptance phase of the project. Once the user agrees to the prototype, that prototype becomes a fixed part of the system.

Project teams use software tools that help to flush out specifications for RAD projects. For example, using a RAD software tool, an architect could show a homeowner his plans for a new house. The homeowner would be able to simulate the experience of taking a walk through the house and determine if the plans meet his or her needs.

If they don't, the plans could be modified on line with the results immediately displayed on the computer. Once there is an agreement, the same software can generate detailed specifications for the project, including a list of building supplies.

■ THE ITERATIVE PROJECT DEVELOPMENT METHODOLOGY (IPDM)

The *Iterative Project Development Methodology (IPDM)* enhances RAD. It too uses prototypes to develop components of the system. However, IPDM expects components to be revised after the project manager and the users reach an agreement.

IPDM assumes that the project remains dynamic throughout the project life cycle. Specifications for components change based on changes in other components and the organization's needs. Those changes can be incorporated throughout the system if they are necessary for the current version of the system, or they can be held over for a later version.

Project managers who use IPDM find that the application delivers a short time period at a reduced cost with a high degree of user acceptance of the final system. In addition, IPDM lends itself to the project being divided into several smaller projects. Each piece can be independently implemented.

Let's return to the customer relations system. The call routing component can be implemented without the data retrieval and account display components. Likewise, the data retrieval and account display components can be implemented without the call routing component. This assumes that customer service representatives can recall account information from the account display component.

Remember Apollo I—Don't Take Short Cuts

Workers used short cuts to meet the unrealistic schedule to launch the Apollo 1 spacecraft. Instead of testing, workers assumed some systems would work properly.

Three astronauts died when their capsule caught fire during a preflight drill on the launch pad. No one stopped to realize that they inadvertently created a highly explosive bomb—the capsule itself!

They overlooked basic high school chemistry that would have prevented the accident. Oxygen ignited by a spark from an exposed electrical connection caused an explosion and fire in the spacecraft.

Keep in Mind . . .

. . . Plan to throw away your project because all projects are eventually replaced.

. . . The system doesn't change once you deliver it to the customer. No system is perfect.

. . . Fixing a problem with the system has a 50% chance of introducing new problems.

SUMMARY

Project management is the task of taking someone else's idea and making the idea become reality within a time schedule and cost. Accomplishing this objective requires the project manager who manages the project to balance various demands made by key people in the organizations.

These people fall into several groups called the executive committee, steering committee, project sponsor, stakeholders, and the project team. The project manager and members of the project team must interview all those involved in the project to determine their needs and expectations. A business analyst or systems analyst translates needs and expectations into specifications for the project.

The project manager must divide the project into functional components, each of which can be a phase of the project. A phase of a project can be developed and delivered without affecting the other phases. A phase is almost a project unto itself.

Each functional component must be divided into tasks which, when accomplished, complete the functional component. A task can be further divided into subtasks with each subtask being assigned a duration. Duration is the length of time required to complete the subtasks. The duration of all the subtasks of a particular task is the duration of the task. Likewise, the duration of all the tasks is the duration of the functional component.

A project methodology and project life cycle are used to provide guidance to the project manager and the project management team when developing the task list.

Once tasks and subtasks are identified, the project manager determines the skill sets required to complete the tasks and subtasks. Skill sets are translated into job descriptions, which are used by the personnel department of the organization to locate candidates.

The staff who fill those positions are called resources and become members of the project team. A resource is anything required to complete a task or subtask. This includes material objects such as computers, buildings, and office space, in addition to the staff. The project manager must assign resources to each task and subtask.

Furthermore, each task and subtask must be performed in a precise order. That is, some tasks may not start until a previous task is completed due to the flow of the project. Therefore, it is the job of the project manager to identify relationships among tasks. This is called dependency.

A project management tool such as Microsoft Project is used to devise and administer a project schedule. A project schedule consists of various documents and charts that help the project manager manage the project. The project schedule consists of a Gantt chart, resource schedule, critical path method and other tools.

A critical factor in project management is the skill required to manage everyone involved in the project. The project manager must be able to manage the expectations of stakeholders and the project team so their expectations are realistic and will be met when the project is delivered.

WORK BREAKDOWN STRUCTURE AND SCHEDULING

A project begins when a manager within the organization devises a way to meet an aspect of the organization's strategic plan. This idea is based on the manager's perception of the problem, his or her experience, and his or her idea of a solution, usually based on intuition rather than solid research.

This concept is likely presented to senior management and to various colleagues for input and criticism. Adjustments are made to the idea to reflect practical and political considerations. If there is enough support the manager takes on the role of project sponsor and begins the processes of making the idea come to fruition.

The initial step is for the project sponsor to formulate his or her idea into a request for proposal (RFP). Some organizations may draw up a project charter, an internal business case, a statement of work (SOW), or a feasibility study for this same purpose.

A *request for proposal* is a brief document that states a problem and a concept of how to solve the problem. The RFP might also include known limitations such as time, resources, and costs. The content of the RFP is based on the project sponsor's views and research.

The RFP becomes the focal point of discussions about the project with a likely project manager who will take this idea and make it come to reality. Candidates include outside consultants, staff project managers, and prospective project managers who might join the organization.

The RFP is the jumping-off point for the project manager to learn everything possible about the organization, the strategic plan, the problem, and the proposed solution. It is the project manager's job to develop the project on time, within cost, and in flawless working condition. To achieve this objective, the project manager must analyze the RFP to identify which aspects of the request are achievable and which aren't.

For example, the RFP might require the system to predict sales based on the weather forecast. Does the proposal mean to predict for a day, a week, a month or a season? Does the organization have historical sales data recorded by date and is this available electronically?

These are just a few questions that must be answered before the project manager knows whether this request is achievable. Let's say the organization has historical sales data stored electronically and the U.S. Weather Bureau can supply weather conditions for those dates. A statistician can be hired to develop a forecast model for the organization. Will the model accurately project sales based on weather? This question cannot be answered until the statistician completes his or her job; however, a process exists to explore this possibility. Therefore, this aspect of the project might be feasible.

Once the project manager identifies achievable aspects of the project and the project sponsor agrees, the project is divided into functional components. A *functional component* is a piece of the project that can be considered independently, fully developed and implemented apart from other components.

For example, a product tracking system in a supermarket has several functional components, two of which are a point-of-sale component and a product-ordering component. A point-of-sale component tracks the products sold. Each product is scanned into the system, and the price, tax, and other information is automatically recorded on the cash register and in the accounting system. A product-ordering component is the part of the system used to re-order products for inventory. Both functional components are part of the same project, but can be developed and implemented independently. You can consider each a subproject within the project.

The project manager must then divide each functional component of the project into sub-functional components and into tasks. A *sub-functional component* is a division of the functional component such as the data-gathering piece of the product-ordering component. This is the sub-component that gathers information needed to re-order products for inventory.

Tasks are the steps that must be completed to develop the sub-functional component. Tasks are divided into subtasks, sometimes called activities. A *subtask* or *activity* is a detailed step required to complete the task. For example, the data-gathering sub-functional component requires a data entry screen from which vendors' names and addresses are collected. Developing the data entry screen is a task. A subtask is to determine how stakeholders expect the data entry screen to work.

The project manager assigns duration and resources to each subtask and establishes the dependency among sub-functional components, tasks, and subtasks. This information becomes the basis for the project schedule. In this section, you'll explore the techniques used to develop the project schedule.

REQUEST FOR PROPOSAL (RFP)

A request for proposal is a document that takes on various forms depending upon the nature of the project and the formality of the organization (see next page). An informal RFP can be as simple as a memo that states in general terms the objective of the project and how the project sponsor foresees the system functioning when completed.

A formal RFP is divided into sections, each stating in relatively detailed terms an aspect of the project. For example, an RFP has a section that states the *objective* of the project and how it meets the business needs. Another section presents *background information* to justify the project. The RFP also has a section that describes *constraints* within which the project must be developed and implemented.

The project manager must look at the RFP as preliminary information to be analyzed, validated, and expanded. The RFP should not be considered fully credible regardless of its completeness or the staff who authored it.

Typically, RFPs are prepared for high-level review and adoption and contain insufficient information from which to develop a formal project plan. It is the responsibility of the project manager to embellish the RFP and fill in the missing pieces required to develop the project plan.

There are many questions that need to be answered before an organization underwrites any project. How much is the project going to cost? How long will it take to develop? What impact will the completed project have on head-count, facilities, and infrastructure?

These questions are not easy to answer without detailed analyses and the development of a proposed project plan. This means the project manager must find the information necessary to answer these and other questions and then provide those answers.

Developing a preliminary project plan is a process flawed by inevitable problems, since the project manager must make assumptions and estimates that may not be on target. For example, although a decision may be made about which technology to use in a project, more advanced technology might later become available and be included in the final project plan.

Request for Proposal

A four-store supermarket chain requires the creation of a point-of-sale inventory system. The manager of the chain envisions a system that will adjust inventory records as each item is entered into cash registers in stores.

Furthermore, the manager seeks to have the system track the location of products from the time the merchandise is received from the vendor to the time it is purchased by the customer. Therefore, the manager expects the system to electronically record merchandise as it is received at the firm's central warehouse, when it is stored at a location within the warehouse, when it is shipped, when it is received by the store, and when it is placed on the shelf.

Managers at all levels should be able to log into the system and track the current level of inventory and the location of inventory from any location: from their office, the warehouse, and the store.

The system is expected to recommend re-order quantities based upon historical sales, external factors such as weather, and special events such as sales and holidays. Furthermore, the system should provide executives with merchandise analyses.

These analyses should detect sales trends with and without relationships to other events, including the following:

- Tie-ins with other products (e.g., loss leaders).
- Special promotions (e.g., movies, ad campaigns).
- Price changes (e.g., price elasticity where a lower price generates more sales).
- Sales vs. shelf space for products.
- Sales vs. store location of products.

Management has reviewed vendors who supply such systems and has decided the store should create its own system.

Considering these pitfalls, the project manager still must deliver a preliminary project plan with the clear understanding that the plan is contingent upon the accuracy of the underlying assumptions.

COMPONENTS OF THE PROJECT PLAN

A project plan contains several components, many of which are dependent on the style of the organization and that of the project sponsor. Some organizations require a project plan to follow along strict guidelines, while in other organizations the form is left to an agreement between the project sponsor and the project manager.

Typically, a *project plan* consists of an executive summary and supporting exhibits. An *executive summary* is a document that highlights key points of the project and refers to exhibits for details. An *exhibit* consists of supportive documentation such as a project schedule, Gantt chart, and a financial spreadsheet that presents the detailed rationale for one or more statements made in the executive summary.

Let's say your project is divided into three phases and each phase will take six months to complete, cost $250,000, and require a staff of five technicians. The executive summary states these facts, and then refers to specific exhibits that provide details. These should include the tasks and duration for the six months, details of how you arrived at the $250,000 cost, and the specific type of technicians you require, as well as whether or not they are temporary or permanent staff, and what their assignments will be.

The executive summary addresses all the key issues regarding a project. After reading it, the project manager will have a high-level understanding of the project and a foundation from which to pose questions and review selected components of the document to learn details. Furthermore, the executive summary can be turned over to the support staff to review and verify the details in the exhibits. For example, it is common for the accounting department to review the cost details you provide in the executive summary.

Here are factors that should be covered in every executive summary:

- A statement of the business case. The *business case* is the justification for the project. It restates the problem and the solution proposed in the request for proposal. The business case also presents the rationale for the approach used to solve the problem.

- The *analysis of the request for proposal* and subsequent factors relating to the project. It is here where the project manager clearly states factors that are achievable and those that are not achievable along with a brief rationale for coming to this conclusion.

- The solution proposed by the project manager. The *solution statement* informs the project sponsor of how the project manager intends to solve the problem. This might be a restatement of the business case or a modification that reflects only the achievable aspects of the project. The solution statement goes into greater detail than the solution mentioned in the business case. Typically, the solution in the business case is that of the project sponsor while the solution statement is that of the project manager.

- A statement of assumptions is also necessary. A *statement of assumptions* lists the premises used as the basis for the project manager's proposed solution. That is, the project manager's solution will work as long as the assumptions remain true. If not, then there is doubt whether this solution can be achieved.

- A statement of limitations is required. A *statement of limitations* acknowledges the constraints within which the project manager must deliver the project. For example, the project sponsor might set a budget limit or a head count limit. *Head count* is the number of employees.

- A brief *history of the project* is necessary to properly set the stage for reading the executive summary. The brief history should include the events that brought the project to its current state, including previously failed attempts, the reasons for the failure, and steps the project manager intends to take to avoid those same mistakes in the future.

- A *high-level organization of the project* divides the project into functional components and identifies components as phases of the project. Also included in this section of the executive summary is the rationale to support this organization.

- A delivery date for the project and for each phase of the project must be given.

- Staffing requirements for the project and for each phase should be provided, identifying the number of permanent and part-time members on the project team. Furthermore, you must determine the number of staff members required for each phase and the number required once the project is implemented. Let's say that five permanent employees and three part-time consultants are necessary to complete phase 1. However, only two permanent employees are required for maintenance of the phase once it becomes operational.

- A *statement of major acquisitions* such as facilities, infrastructure, and hardware must be identified for the entire project and for each phase.

- A *summary of the cost* of the project and for each phase must be provided. It is sufficient to list totals and then refer to exhibits for the cost breakdown. The cost must include both one-time charges and ongoing charges. For example, the project team is a one-time charge because the charge stops once the project ends. However, additions to the operations staff to maintain the system are an ongoing charge.

- A statement of return on investment must be included. *Return on investment* is the financial gain or loss an organization has realized as a result of investing capital in the project. Assume the organization has $100 to invest. It could place the money in the bank at 5% interest and realize a return of investment of $5.00 at the end of the year, or it could take the same $100 and invest it in your project. Typically, a project will save the organization money or bring in new revenue. If the project saved the organization $50, then that is the same as the organization earning $50 on its investment. Likewise, if the project increases revenue flow by $50, then the project returns more than 5% and is a better investment. The next section discusses the cost of a project.

- A cash flow analysis must also be shown. *Cash flow analysis* describes when funds are required to pay bills during the development of the project. A monthly, quarterly, or annual summary can be included in the executive summary depending on the length of the project. A detailed cash flow analysis can be supplied as an exhibit.

STARTING YOUR PROJECT PLAN

All projects begin the same way. There is an idea that needs to be examined in detail to identify the tasks and resources necessary to complete the project. Although this appears to be a simple statement, you'll find that bringing an idea to fruition is a complex operation.

Your job is to formulate a project plan that lays out step-by-step procedures for bringing the idea to reality. The initial procedure is to determine which aspects of the project are achievable and which are not achievable.

The project sponsor must agree to exclude from the project those ideas that cannot be achieved before you proceed further with the project. It is highly probable that you will reach such an agreement if you present your rationale for the exclusion.

■ FUNCTIONAL COMPONENTS

Next you need to divide the project into functional components. A functional component is an aspect of the project that provides functionality to the organization and could, but might not necessarily be, developed and implemented without other functional components.

Let's say that you are upgrading the systems of a four-store supermarket chain. The request for proposal states that the new system must track products from the time they arrive in the warehouse through distribution to stores and when products are sold. Furthermore, the system should recommend when to re-order products and the quantity of products to re-order.

Without an extremely detailed analysis, you can intuitively divide the systems into four functional components. These are: an inventory receiving system that records when products are received in the warehouse, a product distribution system that allows stores to order products from the warehouse, a product stocking system that manages the restocking of store shelves, and a point-of-sale system that records products sold to customers.

Collectively, these functional components track products from point-of-entry into the warehouse through to products sold at the cash register. However, each component could be developed and implemented independently of the others.

A functional component can be considered a phase of the project as well as a subproject. That is, a functional component will have tasks, subtasks, resources, and expenses, all detailed in a project plan.

At any point in the development of the entire project, the project sponsor can decide to postpone or eliminate any phase; yet the organization receives the benefit from those phases that are completed and fully implemented.

Depending on the nature of the project, functional components can further be subdivided into *sub-functional components.* For example, the point-of-sale component might include a data collection subcomponent that allows the clerk to enter products into the cash register.

Likewise, there may be a presentation component that displays information about the transaction to the clerk and the customer. In addition, there might be a processing component containing product bar codes that are used to look up product information and pricing.

■ MILESTONES AND DELIVERABLES

The next step in the process is to identify milestones and deliverables. A milestone is the completion of a key portion of the development process. A phase of the project is a likely choice for being a milestone. Within a functional component, a completion of a sub-functional component can be considered a milestone.

A deliverable is a piece of the project such as a report, a computer screen, or the foundation of a building that is an indication of progress. Showing the finished product display screen is an ideal deliverable.

All milestones and deliverables must be identified in the proposed project plan so the project sponsor and other stakeholders have a framework within which they can determine whether the project is on course.

■ TASKS AND SUBTASKS

For each sub-functional component, you must identify all the tasks and subtasks (also known as activities) that are necessary to complete the sub-functional component. You must ask yourself what must occur to build the component; place all the tasks and subtasks on a list. It is important that the task list is complete, since otherwise a key element might be overlooked that could delay the project.

After you determine tasks and subtasks you must decide the dependencies. Ask yourself which tasks or subtasks must be completed before another task or subtask can be started. Identify tasks that can be performed concurrently.

For example, identifying the data for the inventory-receiving component must be performed before a technician can design the database for the component. However, design of the data entry screen used to enter products into the database as they are delivered to the warehouse can be worked on at the same time the database is designed. Each task can be developed independently once the data is identified for the component.

■ DURATION AND RESOURCES

Next you must determine how long each subtask will take to complete—that is, its duration. Later in this section you'll be shown techniques for setting the duration. Your estimate of duration plays a critical role in the project plan, for it is the basis for forecasting the time to develop the tasks, sub-functional components, functional components, and the duration of the project as a whole.

You must also analyze each subtask to determine the resources that are required to complete the task. Your choice of resources will influence the duration for some subtasks. Resources are discussed in detail in the next section.

WORK BREAKDOWN STRUCTURE

The blueprint for the execution of a project is a plan that defines the objectives, deliverables, and specifications for each task to be accomplished. In addition, a schedule, a budget, the required resources, and most important, an indication of individual responsibility must be provided. Tasks may be characterized by their length, work content, level of technology, and cost. Some tasks are complex and expensive, spanning months or years, whereas others are short and present little technical difficulty. It is often convenient to break the longer tasks down into subtasks of shorter duration. Once this is done, it is possible to arrange all tasks and subtasks in a network resembling a directed tree with a single root node. The resultant figure, known as the project work breakdown structure (WBS), is an important aid in planning and managing the project. The construction of an actual WBS is situation dependent. However, some guidelines relating to the design of military systems are presented in MIL-STD-881A, where the WBS is defined as follows: "A work breakdown structure is a product-oriented family tree composed of hardware, services and data which result from project engineering efforts during the development and production of a defense material item, and, which completely defines the project/program. A VMS displays and defines the product(s) to be developed or produced and relates the elements of work to be accomplished to each other and to the end product."

The WBS is a schematic presentation of the disaggregation-integration process by which the project manager plans to execute the project. This process, once again, is the heart of project management. The work content of a project has to be divided into tasks that can be assigned and performed by one of the participating organizational units. If such tasks cannot be defined, the project plan is not feasible. The definition of a task at the lowest level of the WBS should include the following elements.

1. *Objectives.* A statement is made of what is to be achieved by performing this task. The objectives may include tangible accomplishments such as the successful production of a part or a successful integration of a system. Nontangible objectives are also possible, such as learning a new computer language.

2. *Deliverables.* Some deliverables may be part of the hardware and software used in the project, like a pump in the hydraulic system of a new airplane. Other deliverables might include a report that documents the findings of an economic analysis, or a recommendation made after evaluating a number of scenarios with a computer model.

3. *Schedule.* For each task at least two milestones should be specified: its planned start time and its planned finish time. The elapsed time between these two dates is not necessarily the estimated duration of the task since some leeway may be built into the plan.

4. *Budget.* A time-phased budget should be prepared for each task. In so doing, projected outlays should be synchronized with the planned schedule and estimated cost of the respective task.

5. *Performance measures.* The successful completion of a task has to be judged by predefined performance measures. These measures are used during project execution to compare actual and planned performance in order to establish project control. A total quality management approach to project management integrates cost, schedule, and quality into a common performance measure called the earned value.

6. *Responsibility.* The organizational unit responsible for on-budget and on-schedule performance of each task has to be defined. This is done by associating a lower-level element in the WBS (a task) with an organizational unit in the project organizational breakdown structure (OBS). The entity that consists of a task to be performed by an organizational unit for a given schedule and budget is called a *work package.*

IDENTIFYING TASKS

A task is a paradox of project management. Identifying tasks of a project appears a rather simple job—list every job that must be performed to complete the project. Yet this is an exhaustive process that is bound to leave out some tasks.

Let's illustrate this point. A task in every project is to interview a stakeholder to determine his or her expectations. What are the subtasks that are necessary to complete this task?

A typical response to that question is to have the business analyst visit the stakeholder. No additional subtasks seem to be necessary. That's not true, although the business analyst does interview the stakeholder. Here are other subtasks to consider.

- Create a job description for the business analyst.
- Recruit candidates for the business analyst's position.
- Offer the position to a candidate.
- Negotiate employment terms with the candidate.
- Acquire office space for the business analyst.
- Acquire equipment needed for the business analyst to perform his or her job, such as a desk, telephone, computer, printer, and network connections.
- Provide the business analyst with a list of stakeholders.
- Determine the questions to be answered by the stakeholder.
- Arrange an interview date with the stakeholder.

Let's stop. You'll notice that many subtasks must be performed before the business analyst interviews the stakeholder. Some of these subtasks you probably assumed would have taken place prior to the interview. However, you cannot make any assumptions about tasks when you are planning the project.

When the task to interview a stakeholder to determine his or her expectations is raised, the assumption is commonly made that the business analyst is already on staff. Remember that the business analyst is a resource necessary to complete this task. Before making such an assumption, the project manager must be sure the subtasks necessary to hire the business analyst are addressed by the project plan.

Hiring the business analyst does not need to be a subtask of the task to interview a stakeholder to determine his or her expectations. The hiring task can occur earlier in the project plan.

The importance of identifying all the tasks and subtasks in the project plan becomes obvious when you consider the duration of tasks. Intuitively, you can estimate that an interview with a stakeholder should take an hour. However, while the interview itself may take an hour, it might take a week to arrange a date when both the stakeholder and the business analyst are available. Likewise, two days might be required for the business analyst to prepare for the meeting. You can easily see that the hour duration for this task is underestimated. Instead of an hour, it will really take seven workdays to complete.

This type of overlooking of tasks and subtasks is one reason a project manger may fail to deliver a project on time, within cost, and in perfect working condition. A case in point involved a major international investment banking firm. Managers of each business unit were given authority to do what they pleased so long as the business unit returned the projected profit.

Business unit managers hired revenue producers who demanded new systems. Costs for computer systems were treated as corporate overhead and not directly charged back to the business unit. Revenue producers turned to the information systems department and said, "I want . . . " and never considered the impact their requests would have on the firm. There was no formal plan.

Corporate overhead rose dramatically. Hundreds of technical and administrative personnel were hired and 10 recruiters were brought on board to handle recruiting. Floors had to be rented in nearby office buildings and temporary office space located to house the new employees while the permanent space was configured with walls, phones, and other essentials. This rapid growth stretched the capabilities of the existing telephone system and the firm's computer networking infrastructure, which also had to be upgraded quickly.

No one in the firm realized the ramifications of allowing revenue producers to do whatever they pleased to bring in money for the firm. It took a little over a year before the financial impact reached the bottom line. The firm had drastic cutbacks and layoffs, then instituted formal project management and cost controls.

■ HOW TO IDENTIFY TASKS

Identifying the tasks of a project is a challenge and there aren't any templates that will guarantee that you've identified them all. Your first objective is to divide the project into many small objectives. You start this by dividing a project into functional components, and then further dividing functional components into sub-functional components.

As described in the Functional Components section earlier in this book, a point-of-sale component could be divided into the following:

- A data collection component that allows the clerk to enter products into the cash register.
- The presentation component that displays information about the transaction to the clerk and the customer.
- A processing component containing product bar codes that are used to look up product information and pricing.

Focus on each sub-functional component. Ask yourself what tasks must be performed to develop the sub-functional component. Brainstorm and write down every task that comes to mind. Your list of tasks should be long.

Here are some tasks for the presentation component.

- Determine the data to display to the customer.
- Determine the data to display to the clerk.
- Determine the layout of the screen used to display data to the customer.
- Determine the layout of the screen used to display data to the clerk.
- Determine the functional requirements for the display screen for the customer.
- Determine the functional requirements for the display screen for the clerk.

Examine each task on the list and determine what other tasks are required to complete the task. For example, what other tasks are required to determine which data to display to the customer? Here are some likely possibilities:

- Determine the expectations of the store manager.
- Determine the expectations of the accounting manager.
- Determine the expectations of customers.

These tasks define the information the store manager, accounting manager, and customers would like to see on the customer display.

The process of identifying tasks continues by examining these tasks to determine other tasks that are necessary to reach these objectives. For example, the store manager must be interviewed to determine his or her expectations.

As you reduce the project further and further into tasks, subtasks, and sub-subtasks, you soon realize the true challenge of developing a project plan. Just when you think that you've reached the lowest level task, another list of subtasks can be developed.

■ GUIDELINES FOR IDENTIFYING TASKS

By now you realize the importance of considering all tasks in your project plan. If you overlook a few, then there could be a serious flaw in the plan that affects your ability to deliver the project. Yet there must be a balance between identifying finer tasks in the project and completing the project plan itself on time.

One of the first rules of developing a project plan is not to make the plan your project. That is, a project manager can spend an excessive amount of time on the plan, leaving little time for managing the project.

You can strike a balance by leaving some finer tasks to be identified by the resource that is assigned the task. For example, your project plan could stop at the task of determining the expectations of the store manager. There are subtasks that must be performed to complete this task, such as arranging the interview and preparing questions. These subtasks are best left to the resource to identify and do not need to be included in the project plan. However, you need to be aware that these subtasks must be performed and therefore consider them in estimating the duration of the task.

Likewise, the project plan might stop at the task of determining the expectations of stakeholders regarding a particular sub-functional component. The detailed subtasks required to achieve this objective are left to the resources that are assigned to the task.

The question you must answer is whether these tasks are too low-level or not low-level enough. The answer will depend on the importance the task has on the project.

Let's consider the task of determining the expectations of stakeholders regarding a particular sub-functional component. Is it important to the project how these expectations are determined? There are many ways of learning the expectations including an interview, form, JAD sessions, or more elaborate statistical research.

The project manager must determine whether it is critical to the project that a particular approach be taken to learn the expectations of stakeholders. If so, then additional subtasks should be identified in the project plan. If not, then subtasks are not necessary. The resource can use discretion to perform the task.

Another strategy to consider when trying to identify tasks for a project is to adopt a formal project development methodology. A project development methodology is a roadmap that guides you through the entire project development cycle. Using a combination of project development methodology and your reasoning assures that critical tasks are identified in your project.

SCHEDULING

Project scheduling deals with the planning of timetables and the establishment of dates during which various resources, such as equipment and personnel, will perform the activities required to complete the project. Schedules are the cornerstone of the planning and control system, and because of their importance, are often written into the contract by the customer.

The scheduling activity integrates information on several aspects of the project, including the estimated duration of activities, the technological precedence relations among activities, constraints imposed by the availability of resources and the budget, and if applicable, due-date requirements. This information is processed into an acceptable schedule by appropriate models, most often of the network type. The aim is to answer the following questions:

1. If each of the activities goes according to plan, when will the project be completed?
2. Which tasks are most critical to ensure the timely completion of the project?
3. Which tasks can be delayed, if necessary, without delaying project completion, and by how much?
4. More specifically, at what times should each activity begin and end?
5. At any given time during the project, what is the range of dollars that should have been spent?
6. Is it worthwhile to incur extra costs to accelerate some of the activities?

The first four questions relate to time, which is the chief concern of this section; the latter two deal with the possibility of trading off time for money.

The schedule itself can be presented in several ways, such as a timetable or a Gantt chart, which is essentially a bar chart that shows the relationship of activities over time. Different schedules can be prepared for the various participants in the project. A functional manager may be interested in a schedule of tasks performed by members of the group. The project manager may need a detailed schedule for each WBS element and a master schedule for the entire project. The vice president of finance may need a combined schedule for all projects that are underway in the organization to plan cash flows and capital requirements. Each person involved in the project may need a schedule with all the activities in which he or she is involved.

Schedules provide an essential communications and coordination link between the individuals and organizations participating in the project. They facilitate the coordination of effort among people coming from different organizations working on different elements of the WBS in different locations at different time periods. By developing a schedule the project manager is *planning* the project. By authorizing work according to the scheduled start of each task, he or she triggers execution of the project; and by comparing the actual execution dates of tasks with the scheduled dates, he or she *monitors* the project. When actual performance deviates from the plan to such an extent that corrective action must be taken, the project manager is exercising *control*.

Although schedules come in many forms and levels of detail, they should all relate to the master program schedule, which gives a time-phased picture of the principal activities and highlights the major milestones associated with the project. For large programs a modular approach that reduces the prospects of getting bogged down in the excess detail that necessarily accompanies work assignments is recommended. To implement this approach, the schedule should be partitioned according to its functions or phases and then disaggregated to reflect the various work packages. For example, consider the work breakdown structure shown in Figure 2-1 for the development of a microcomputer. One possible modular array of project schedules is depicted in Figure 2-2. The details of each module would have to be worked out by the individual project leaders and then integrated by the project manager to gain the full perspective.

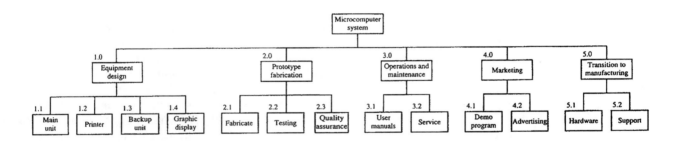

FIGURE 2-1   *Work Breakdown Structure for a Microcomputer*

Schedules are working tools for program planning, evaluation, and control. They are developed in many iterations with project team members and continuing feedback from the client. The reality of changing circumstances requires that they remain dynamic throughout the project life cycle. Every project has unique management requirements. When preparing the schedule, it is important that the dates and time allotments for the work packages be in precise agreement with those set forth in the master schedule. These times are control points for the project manager. It is his or her responsibility to insist on and maintain consistency, but the actual scheduling of tasks and work packages is usually done by those responsible for their accomplishment—after the project manager has approved the due dates. This procedure ensures that the final schedule reflects the interdependencies among all the tasks and participating units, and that it is consistent with available resources and upper management expectations.

It is worth noting that the most comprehensive schedule is not necessarily best in all situations. In fact, too much detail can impede communications and divert attention from critical activities. Nevertheless, the quality of a schedule has a major effect on the success of the project and frequently affects other projects that compete for the same resources.

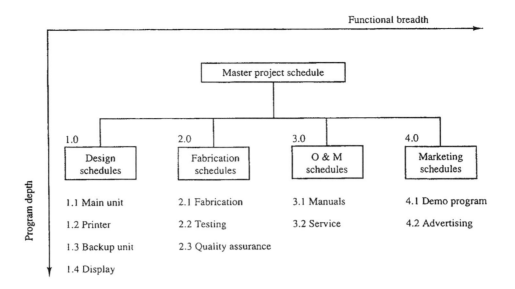

FIGURE 2-2 *Modular Array of Project Schedules (From H. J. Thamhain,* Engineering Program Management, *© 1984 by John Wiley & Sons, Inc.; reprinted by permission of the publisher.)*

■ KEY MILESTONES

A place to begin the development of any schedule is to define the major milestones for the work to be accomplished. For ease of viewing, it is often convenient to array this information on a time line depicting events and their due dates. Once agreed upon, the resultant milestone chart becomes the skeleton for the master schedule and its disaggregated components. A key milestone is defined as an important event in the project life cycle and may include, for instance, the fabrication of a prototype, the start of a new phase, a status review, a test, or the first shipment. Ideally, the completion of these milestones should be easily verifiable. But in reality, this may not be the case. Design, testing, and review tend to run together. There is always a desire to do a bit more work to correct superficial flaws or to extract a marginal improvement in performance. This blurs the demarcation points and makes project control that much more difficult.

Key milestones should be defined for all major phases of the project prior to startup. Care must be taken to arrive at an appropriate level of detail. If the milestones are spread too far apart, continuity problems in tracking and control can arise. On the other hand, too many milestones can result in unnecessary busywork, over control, confusion, and increased overhead costs. As a guideline for long-term projects, four key milestones per year seem to be sufficient for tracking without overburdening the system.

The project office, in close cooperation with the customer and the participating organizations, typically has the responsibility for defining key milestones. Selecting the right type and number is critical. Every key milestone should represent a checkpoint for a collection of activities at the completion of a major project phase. Some examples with well-defined boundaries include:

- Project kickoff
- Requirements analysis complete
- Preliminary design review
- Critical design review
- Prototype fabricated
- Integration and testing completed
- Quality assurance review

- Start volume production
- Marketing program defined
- First shipment
- Customer acceptance test complete

ESTIMATING THE DURATION OF PROJECT ACTIVITIES

A project is composed of a set of tasks. Each task is performed by one organizational unit on one WBS element. Most tasks can be broken down into activities. Each activity is characterized by its technological specifications, drawings, list of required materials, quality control requirements, and so on. The technological processes selected for each activity affect the resources required, the materials needed, and the timetable. For example, to move a heavy piece of equipment from one point to another, resources such as a crane and a tractor-trailer might be called for, as well as qualified operators. The time required to perform the activity may also be regarded as a resource. If the piece of equipment is mounted on a special fixture prior to moving, the required resources and the performance time might be affected. Thus the schedule of the project as well as its cost and resources requirements are a function of the technological decisions.

Some activities cannot be performed unless certain activities are completed beforehand. For example, if the piece of equipment to be moved is very large, it might be necessary to disassemble it or at least remove a few of its parts before loading it onto the truck. Thus the "moving" task has to be broken down into activities with precedence relationships among them.

The process of dividing a task into activities, and activities into subactivities, should be performed carefully to strike a proper balance between size and duration. The following guidelines are recommended:

1. The length of each activity should be approximately in the range of 0.5 to 2% of the length of the project. Thus if the project takes about one year, each activity should be between a day and a week.

2. Critical activities that fall below this range should be included. For example, a critical design review that is scheduled to last two days on a three-year project should be included in the activity list because of its pivotal importance.

3. If the number of activities is very large (say, above 250), the project should be divided into activities, perhaps by functional area, and individual schedules developed for each. Schedules with too many activities quickly become unwieldy and are difficult to monitor and control.

We start our discussion with techniques commonly used to estimate the length of activities. We then describe the effects that precedence relationships among activities have on the overall schedule.

Two approaches are used for estimating the length of an activity: the deterministic approach and the stochastic approach. The deterministic approach ignores uncertainty and thus results in a point estimate. The stochastic approach addresses the probabilistic elements in a project by estimating both the expected duration of each activity and its corresponding variance. Although tasks are subject to random forces and other uncertainties, the majority of project managers prefer the deterministic approach because of its simplicity and ease of understanding. A corollary benefit is that it yields satisfactory results in most situations.

■ STOCHASTIC APPROACH

Only in rare instances is the exact duration of a planned activity known in advance. Therefore, to gain an understanding of how long it will take to perform the activity, it is logical to analyze past data and to construct a frequency distribution of related activity durations. An example of such a distribution is illustrated in Figure 2-3. From the plot we observe that previously, the activity under consideration was performed 40 times, requiring anywhere from 10 to 70 hours. We also see that in three of the 40 observations the actual duration was 45 hours and that the most frequent duration was 35 hours. That is, in some eight of the 40 repetitions, the actual duration was 35 hours.

The information in Figure 2-3 can be summarized by two measures: the first is associated with the center of the distribution (commonly used measures are the mean, the mode, and the median), and the second is related to the spread of the distribution (commonly used measures are the variance, the standard deviation, and the interquartile range). The mean of the distribution in Figure 2-3 is 35.25, its mode is 35, and its median is also 35. The standard deviation is 13.3 and the variance is 176.89.

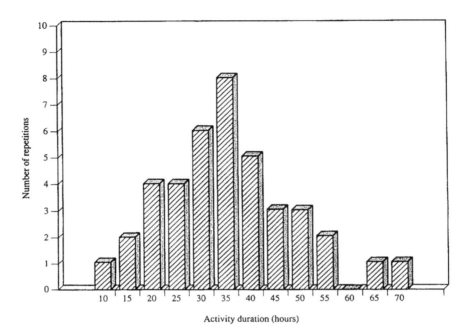

FIGURE 2-3   *Frequency Distribution of an Activity Duration (From Avraham Shtub, Jonathan F. Bard, and Shlomo Globerson,* Project Management: Engineering, Technology and Implementation, *© 1994 by Prentice-Hall, Inc.: reprinted by permission of the publisher.)*

When working with empirical data, it is often desirable to fit the data with a continuous distribution that can be represented mathematically in closed form. This approach facilitates the analysis. Figure 2-4 shows the superposition of a normal distribution with the parameters $\mu = 35.25$ and $\sigma = 13.3$ on the original data.

While the normal distribution is symmetrical and easy to work with, the distribution of activity durations is likely to be skewed. Furthermore, the normal distribution has a long left-hand tail while actual performance time cannot be negative. A better model of the distribution of activity lengths has proven to be the beta distribution, which is illustrated in Figure 2-5.

A visual comparison between Figures 2-4 and 2-5 reveals that the beta distribution provides a closer fit to the frequency data depicted in Figure 2-3. The left-hand tail of the beta distribution does not cross the zero duration point, nor is it necessarily symmetric. Nevertheless, in practice a statistical test (such as the chi-square goodness-of-fit test; Bain and Engelhardt 1987) must be used to determine whether a theoretical distribution is a valid representation of the actual data.

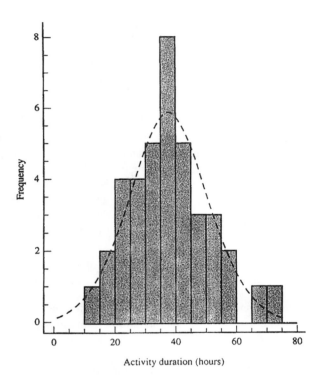

FIGURE 2-4   *Normal Distribution Fitted to the Data (From Avraham Shtub, Jonathan F. Bard, and Shlomo Globerson,* Project Management: Engineering, Technology and Implementation, *© 1994 by Prentice-Hall, Inc.: reprinted by permission of the publisher.)*

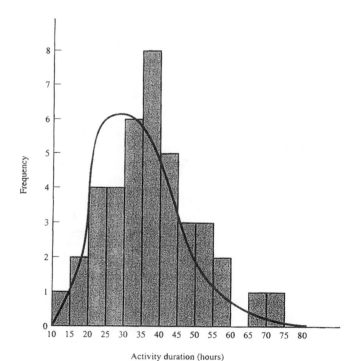

FIGURE 2-5   *Beta Distribution Fitted to the Data (From Avraham Shtub, Jonathan F. Bard, and Shlomo Globerson,* Project Management: Engineering, Technology and Implementation, *© 1994 by Prentice-Hall, Inc.: reprinted by permission of the publisher.)*

In project scheduling, probabilistic considerations are incorporated by assuming that the time estimate for each activity can be derived from three different values:

a = optimistic time, which will be required if execution goes extremely well

m = most likely time, which will be required if execution is normal

b = pessimistic time, which will be required if everything goes badly

Statistically speaking, a and b are estimates of the lower and upper bounds of the frequency distribution, respectively. If the activity is repeated a large number of times, only in about 0.5% of the cases would the duration fall below the optimistic estimate, a, or above the pessimistic estimate, b. The most likely time, m, is an estimate of the mode (the highest point) of the distribution. It need not coincide with the midpoint $(a + b)/2$ but may occur on either side.

To convert m, a, and b into estimates of the expected value $\bar{d}$ and variance (v) of the elapsed time required by the activity, two assumptions are made. The first is that the standard deviation, s (square root of the variance), equals one-sixth the range of possible outcomes; that is,

$$s = \frac{b - a}{6}$$

The rationale for this assumption is that the tails of many probability distributions (such as the normal distribution) are considered to lie about 3 standard deviations from the mean, implying a spread of about 6 standard deviations between tails. In industry, statistical quality control charts are constructed so that the spread between the upper and lower control limits is approximately 6 standard deviations (6σ). If the underlying distribution is normal, the probability is 0.9973 that $\bar{d}$ falls within $b - a$. In any case, according to Chebyshev's inequality, there is at least an 89% chance that the duration will fall within this range (see, e.g., Bain and Engelhardt 1987).

The second assumption concerns the form of the distribution and is needed to estimate the expected value, $\bar{d}$. In this regard, the definition of the three time estimates above provide an intuitive justification that the duration of an activity may follow a beta distribution with its unimodal point occurring at m and its endpoints at a and b. Figure 2-6 shows the three cases of the beta distribution: (a) symmetric, (b) skewed to the right, and (c) skewed to the left. The expected value of the activity duration is given by

$$\bar{d} = \frac{1}{3}\left[2m + \frac{1}{2}(a + b)\right] = \frac{a + 4m + b}{6}$$

Notice that $\bar{d}$ is a weighted average of the mode m and the midpoint $(a + b)/2$, where the former is given twice as much weight as the latter. Although the assumption of the beta distribution is an arbitrary one and its validity has been challenged from the start (Grubbs 1962), it serves the purpose of locating $\bar{d}$ with respect to m, a, and b in what seems to be a reasonable way (Hillier and Lieberman 1986).

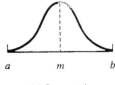

| a | m | b |

(a) Symmetric

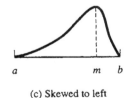

| a m | b |

(b) Skewed to right

| a | m b |

(c) Skewed to left

FIGURE 2-6   *Three Cases of the Beta Distribution: (a) Symmetric; (b) Skewed to the Right; (c) Skewed to the Left (From Avraham Shtub, Jonathan F. Bard, and Shlomo Globerson,* Project Management: Engineering, Technology and Implementation, *© 1994 by Prentice-Hall, Inc.: reprinted by permission of the publisher.)*

The following calculations are based on the data in Figure 2-3 from which we observe that $a = 10$, $b = 70$, and $m = 35$.

$$\bar{d} = \frac{10 + (4)(35) + 70}{6} = 36.6 \quad \text{and} \quad s = \frac{70 - 10}{6} = 10$$

Thus assuming that the beta distribution is appropriate, the expected time to perform the activity is 36.6 hours with an estimated standard deviation of 10 hours.

■ DETERMINISTIC APPROACH

When past data for an activity similar to the one under consideration are available and the variability in performance time is negligible, the duration of the activity may be estimated by its mean; that is, the average time it took to perform the activity in the past. A problem arises when no past data exist. This problem is common in organizations that do not have an adequate information system to collect and store past data, and in R&D projects where an activity is performed for the first time. To deal with this situation, two techniques are available: the modular technique and the benchmark job technique. Each is discussed below.

■ MODULAR TECHNIQUE

This technique is based on decomposing each activity into subactivities (or modules), estimating the performance time of each module, and then totaling the results to get an approximate performance time for the activity. As an example, consider a project to install a new flexible manufacturing system (FMS). A training program for employees has to be developed as part of the project. The associated task can be broken down into the following activities:

1. Definition of goals for the training program
2. Study of the potential participants in the program and their qualifications
3. Detailed analysis of the FMS and its operation
4. Definition of required topics to be covered
5. Preparation of a syllabus for each topic
6. Preparation of handouts, transparencies, and so on
7. Evaluation of the proposed program (a pilot study)
8. Improvements and modifications

If possible, the time required to perform each activity is estimated directly. If not, the activity is broken into modules and the time to perform each module is estimated based on past experience. Although the new training task may not be wholly identical to previous tasks undertaken by the company, the modules themselves should be common to many training programs, so historical data may be available.

■ BENCHMARK JOB TECHNIQUE

This technique is best suited for projects containing many repetitions of some standard activities. The extent to which it is used depends on the performing organization's diligence in maintaining a database of the most common activities along with estimates of their duration and resource requirements.

To see how this technique is used, consider an organization that specializes in construction projects. To estimate the time required to install an electrical system in a new building, the time required to install each component of the system would be multiplied by the number of components of that type in the new building. If, for example, the installation of an electrical outlet takes on the average 10 minutes, and there are 80 outlets in the new building, a total of $80 \times 10 = 800$ minutes is required for this type of component. After performing similar calculations for each component type or job, the total time to install the electrical system would be determined by summing the resultant times.

The benchmark job technique is most appropriate when a project is composed of a set of basic elements whose execution time is additive.

PRECEDENCE RELATIONS AMONG ACTIVITIES

The schedule of activities is constrained by the availability of resources required to perform each activity and by technological constraints known as *precedence relations*. Several types of precedence relations exist among activities. The most common, termed "start to end," requires that an activity can start only after its predecessor has been completed. For example, it is possible to lift a piece of equipment by a crane only after the equipment is secured to the hoist.

A "start to start" relationship exists when an activity can start only after a specified activity has already begun. For example, in projects where concurrent engineering is applied, logistic support analysis starts as soon as the detailed design phase begins. The "end to start" connection occurs when an activity cannot end until another activity has begun. This would be the case in a project of building a nuclear reactor and charging it with fuel, where one industrial robot transfers radioactive material to another. The first robot can release the material only after the second robot achieves a tight enough grip. The "end to end" connection is used when an activity cannot terminate unless another activity is completed. Quality control efforts, for example, cannot terminate before production ceases, although the two activities can be performed at the same time.

A lag or time delay can be added to any of these connections. In the case of the "end to end" arrangement, there might be a need to spend two days on testing and quality control after production shuts down. In the case of the "start to end" connection, a fixed setup may be required between the two activities. In some situations the relationship between activities is subject to uncertainty. For example, after testing a printed circuit board that is to be part of a prototype communications system, the succeeding activity might be either to install the board on its rack, to repair any defects found, or to scrap the board if it fails the functionality test.

We will concentrate on the analysis of "start to end" connections, the most commonly used. The analysis of other types of connections, as well as the effect of uncertainty on precedence relations (probabilistic networks), are discussed in Wiest and Levy (1977). The large number of precedence relations among activities makes it difficult to rely on verbal descriptions alone to convey the effect of technological constraints on scheduling, so graphical representations are frequently used. A number of such representations are illustrated with the help of an example project. Table 2.1 contains the relevant activity data.

TABLE 2.1
Data for Example Project

Activity	Immediate predecessors	Duration (weeks)
A	—	5
B	—	3
C	A	8
D	A,B	7
E	—	7
F	C,E,D	4
G	F	5

In this project, only "start to end" precedence relations are considered. From the table we see that activities A, B, and E do not have any predecessors and thus can start at any time. Activity C, however, can start only after A finishes, while D can start after the completion of

A and B. Further examination reveals that F can start only after C, E, and D are finished, and that G must follow F. Because activity A precedes C, and C precedes F, A must also precede F by transitivity. Nevertheless, when using a network representation, it is only necessary to list immediate or direct precedence relations; implied relations are taken care of automatically.

The three models used to analyze precedence relations and their effect on the schedule are the Gantt chart, the critical path method, and the program evaluation and review technique. As mentioned, the latter two are based on network techniques in which the activities are placed either on the nodes or on the arrows, depending on which is more intuitive for the analyst.

■ GANTT CHART

The most widely used management tool for project scheduling and control is a version of the bar chart developed during World War I by Henry L. Gantt. The Gantt chart, as it is called, enumerates the activities to be performed on the vertical axis and their corresponding duration on the horizontal axis. It is possible to schedule activities by either early start or late start logic. In the early start approach, each activity is initiated as early as possible without violating the precedence relations. In the late start approach, each activity is delayed as much as possible as long as the earliest finish time of the project is not compromised.

A range of schedules is generated on the Gantt chart if a combination of early and late starts is applied. The early start schedule is performed first and yields the earliest finish time of the project. That time is then used as the required finish time for the late start schedule. Figure 2-7 depicts the early start Gantt chart schedule for the example above. The bars denote the activities; their location with respect to the time axis indicates the time over which the corresponding activity is performed. For example, activity D can start only after activities A and B finish, which happens at the end of week 5. A direct output of this schedule is the earliest finish time for the project (22 weeks for the example).

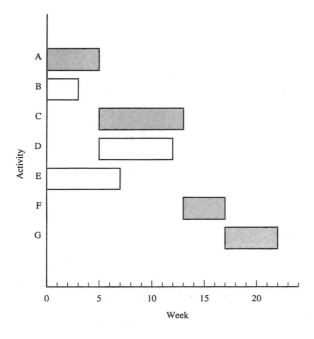

FIGURE 2-7　　*Gantt Chart for an Early Start Schedule (From Avraham Shtub, Jonathan F. Bard, and Shlomo Globerson,* Project Management: Engineering, Technology and Implementation, *© 1994 by Prentice-Hall, Inc.: reprinted by permission of the publisher.)*

Based on the earliest finish time, the late start schedule can be generated. This is done by shifting each activity to the right as much as possible while still starting the project at time zero and completing it in 22 weeks. The resultant schedule is depicted in Figure 2-8. The difference between the start (or the end) times of an activity on the two schedules is called the slack (or float) of the activity. Activities that do not have any slack are denoted by a black bar and are termed *critical*. The sequence of critical activities connecting the start and end points of the project is known as the *critical path*, which logically turns out to be the *longest path* in the network. A delay in any activity along the critical path delays the entire project. Put another way, the sum of durations for critical activities represents the *shortest* possible time to complete the project.

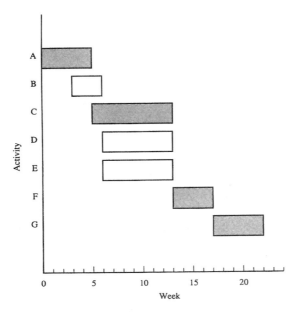

FIGURE 2-8 *Gantt Chart for a Late Start Schedule (From Avraham Shtub, Jonathan F. Bard, and Shlomo Globerson,* Project Management: Engineering, Technology and Implementation, *© 1994 by Prentice-Hall, Inc.: reprinted by permission of the publisher.)*

Gantt charts are simple to generate and interpret. In the construction there should be a one-to-one correspondence between the listed tasks and the work breakdown structure and its numbering scheme. As shown in Figure 2-9, which depicts the Gantt chart for the microcomputer development project, a separate column can be added for this purpose. In fact, the schedule should not contain any tasks that do not appear in the WBS. Often, however, the Gantt chart includes milestones such as project kickoff and design review, which are listed along with the tasks.

In addition to showing the critical path, Gantt charts can be modified to indicate project and activity status. In Figure 2-9, a bold border is used to identify a critical activity, and a shaded area to indicate the approximate completion status at the August review. Accordingly, we see that tasks 2, 5, and 8 are critical, falling on the longest path. Task 2 is 100% complete, task 4 is 65% complete, task 7 is 50% complete, while tasks 5, 6, and 8 have not yet been started.

Gantt charts can be modified further to show budget status by adding a column that lists planned and actual expenditures for each task. Many variations of the original bar graph have been developed to provide more detailed information for the project manager. One commonly used variation is shown in Figure 2-10, which replaces the bars with lines and triangles to indicate project status and revision points. To explain the features, let us examine No. 2, equipment design. According to the code given in the lower left-hand corner of the figure, this task has been rescheduled three times, finally starting in February, and was completed by the end of June.

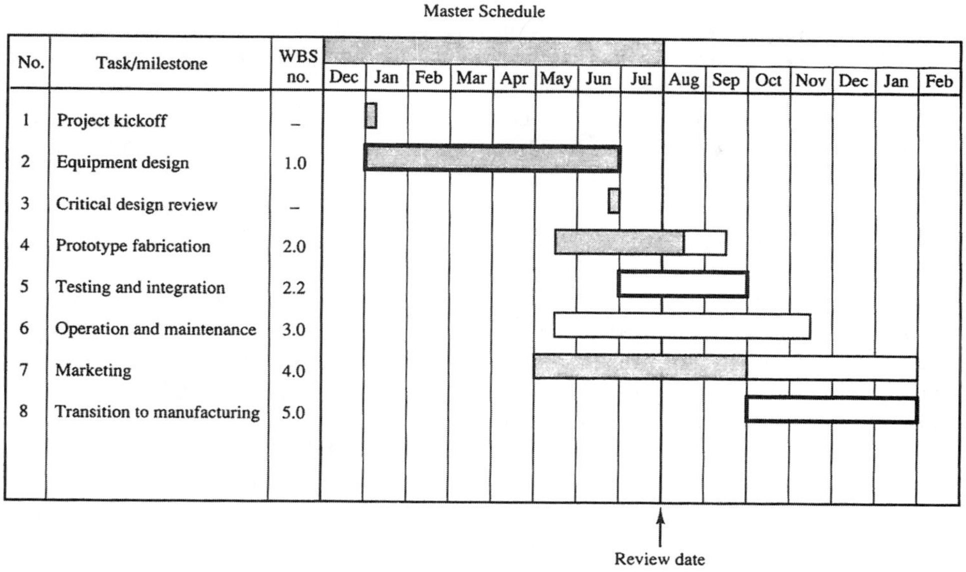

FIGURE 2-9 *Gantt Chart for the Microcomputer Development Example (From H. J. Thamhain,* Engineering Program Management, *© 1984 by John Wiley & Sons, Inc.; reprinted by permission of the publisher.)*

The problem with adding features to the bar graph is that they take away from the clarity and simplicity of the basic form. Nevertheless, the additional information conveyed to the user may offset the additional effort required in generating and interpreting the data. A common modification of the analysis is the case when a milestone has a contractual due date. Consider, for example, activity 8 (WBS No. 5.0) in Figure 2-10. If management decides that the required due date for the termination of this activity is the end of February (instead of the

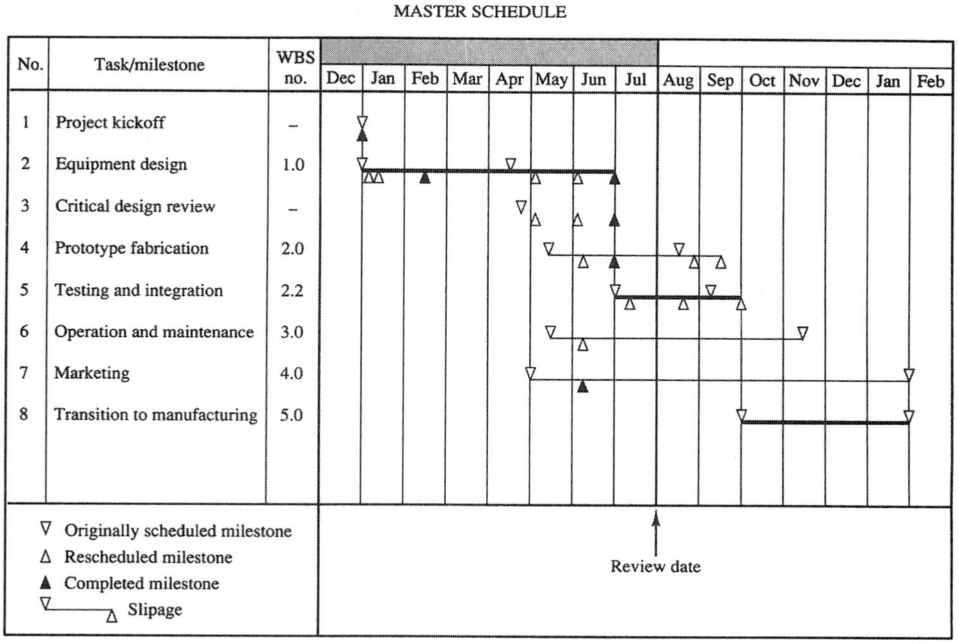

FIGURE 2-10 *Extended Gantt Chart with Task Details (From H. J. Thamhain,* Engineering Program Management, *© 1984 by John Wiley & Sons, Inc.; reprinted by permission of the publisher.)*

end of January), a slack of one month will be added to each activity in the project. If, however, the due date of activity 8 is the end of December, the schedule in Figure 2-10 is no longer feasible because the sequence of activities 2, 5, and 8 (the critical sequence) cannot be completed by the end of December.

The major limitation of bar graph schedules is their inability to show task dependencies and time–resource trade-offs. Network techniques are often used in parallel with Gantt charts to compensate for these shortcomings.

■ NETWORK TECHNIQUES

The basic approach to all project scheduling is to form an actual or implied network that graphically portrays the relationships between the tasks and milestones in the project. Several techniques evolved in the late 1950s for organizing and representing this basic information. Best known today are PERT (program evaluation and review technique) and CPM (critical path method). PERT was developed by Booz, Allen & Hamilton in conjunction with the U.S. Navy in 1958 as a tool for coordinating the activities of over 11,000 contractors involved with the Polaris missile program. CPM was the result of a joint effort by DuPont and the UNIVAC division of Remington Rand to develop a procedure for scheduling maintenance shutdowns in chemical processing plants. The major difference between the two is that CPM assumes that activity times are deterministic, while PERT views the time to complete an activity as a random variable that can be characterized by an optimistic, a pessimistic, and a mostly likely estimate of its durations. Over the years a host of variants has arisen, mainly to address specific aspects of the tracking and control problem, such as budget fluctuations, complex intertask dependencies, and the multitude of uncertainties found in the R&D environment.

PERT/CPM is based on a diagram that represents the entire project as a network of arrows and nodes. The two most popular approaches are either to place the activities on the arrows (AOA) and have the nodes signify milestones, or to place activities on the nodes (AON) and let the arrows show precedence relations among activities. A precedence relation states that, for example, activity X must be completed before activity Y can begin, or that X and Y must end at the same time. It allows tasks that must precede or follow other tasks to be clearly identified, in time as well as function. The resulting diagram can be used to identify potential scheduling difficulties, to estimate the time needed to finish the entire project, and to improve coordination among the participants.

To apply PERT/CPM, a thorough understanding of the project's requirements and structure is needed. The effort spent in identifying activity relationships and constraints yields valuable insights. In particular, four questions must be answered to begin the modeling process:

1. What are the chief project activities?
2. What are the sequencing requirements or constraints for these activities?
3. Which activities can be conducted simultaneously?
4. What are the estimated time requirements for each activity?

PERT/CPM networks are an integral component of project management and have been shown to provide the following benefits (Clark and Fujimoto 1989, Meredith and Mantel 1989):

- They furnish a consistent framework for planning, scheduling, monitoring, and controlling projects.
- They illustrate the interdependencies of all tasks, work packages, and work units.
- They aid in setting up the proper communications channels between participating organizations and points of authority.
- They can be used to estimate the expected project completion dates as well as the probability that the project will be completed by a specific date.
- They identify so-called critical activities which, if delayed, will delay the completion of the entire project.

- They also identify activities with slack that can be delayed for specific periods of time without penalty, or from which resources may temporarily be borrowed without negative consequences.

- They determine the dates on which tasks may be started, or must be started, if the project is to stay on schedule.

- They illustrate which tasks must be coordinated to avoid resource or timing conflicts.

- They also indicate which tasks may be run, or must be run, in parallel to achieve the predetermined completion date.

As we will see, PERT and CPM are easy to understand and use. And while computerized versions are available for both small and large projects, manual calculation is quite suitable for many everyday situations. Unfortunately, though, some managers have placed too much reliance on these techniques at the expense of good management practice (Vazsonyi 1970). For example, when activities are scheduled for a designated time slot, there is a tendency to meet the schedule at all costs. This may divert resources from other activities and cause much more serious problems downstream, the effects of which may not be felt until a near-catastrophe has set in. If tests are shortened or eliminated as a result of time pressure, design flaws may be discovered much later in the project. As a consequence, a project that appeared to be under control is suddenly several months behind schedule and substantially over budget. When this happens, it is convenient to blame PERT/CPM even though the real cause is poor management.

■ CRITICAL PATH METHOD (CPM)

The critical path method (CPM) is a way of looking at the project plan to determine the impact a task or subtask has on the duration of the project. Tasks are interrelated: that is, some tasks must be completed before another task can begin. The sum of the duration of all dependent tasks determines the *duration of the project.* This is the critical path for the project.

The duration of a task that is on the critical path impacts the duration of the project. If the actual duration is shorter than the estimated duration, then the project's estimated completion date is earlier than the original forecast. Likewise, a task on the critical path that exceeds the estimated duration lengthens the duration of the project.

Tasks that don't fall on the critical path are tasks that are performed concurrently with a task on the critical path. The duration of a task not on the critical path may not shorten or extend the duration of the project, depending on the duration of tasks that are being performed concurrently.

Let's say there are four tasks:

1. Identify data used for the point-of-sale system (three-week duration).
2. Design the screen for the point-of-sale system (two-week duration).
3. Design the database for the point-of-sale system (one-week duration).
4. Test the screen and database for the point-of-sale system (three-week duration).

Tasks 1, 2 and 4 constitute the critical path. Task 1 must be completed before task 2 begins and task 4 cannot begin until task 2 and task 3 are completed. The duration for this project segment is the sum of the duration of tasks 1, 2, and 4, which is eight weeks. A delay in tasks 1, 2 or 4 delays the completion of the entire project segment.

Task 3 is dependent upon completion of task 1 because data for the system must be known before a database design can be developed. Likewise, task 4 is dependent upon the completion of task 3. That is, you cannot test the screen and the database without the database design.

There is no dependency between task 2, screen design, and task 3, database design. Both can occur concurrently. Notice that task 2 will take two weeks to finish and task 3 one week. Therefore, the database design will be complete a week before the next dependency—task 4—begins.

Therefore, a delay in completing task 3 won't delay the project as long as the delay does not exceed one week. This is why task 3 is not on the critical path.

The duration between the end of a task and the beginning of the next dependent task is called the *slack time*. The slack time between task 3 and task 4 is a week. However, if the duration of task 3 is extended a week or more, then task 3 becomes part of the critical path. Further delays in finishing task 3 will then extend the duration of the project.

The critical path method is the tool project managers use to assist in making scheduling decisions about the project. For example, the critical path method helps to answer questions such as, "Can a resource assigned to this task be temporarily reassigned to another task?"

Let's assume two resources are used in the previous example. One designs the screen and the other designs the database. Furthermore, let's assume these resources have the skills to perform both tasks.

If it appears the screen design task is falling behind schedule, the project manager can consult the critical path and reassign the resource from the database design to the screen design task. In this way, the project manager is making use of the database-design task slack time.

PROJECT MANAGEMENT TOOLS

A project consists of hundreds of tasks and subtasks, each having duration and dependencies. Numerous resources are required to complete these tasks on time. It is the project manager's responsibility to identify tasks, subtasks, duration, dependencies, and resources, and then to manage the development of the project.

The complexity of any project can overwhelm any project manager unless proper controls are used to track the project. A control is a method that:

- Identifies factors of a project such as tasks, duration, resources, and cost.
- Reports on the status of each factor during project development.
- Forecasts possible outcomes such as start and end dates based on estimates and actual data.

Project management software is the tool used to control a project. There are several project management software tools available in the marketplace. A commonly used package is Microsoft Project, which is used throughout this book to illustrate the techniques for controlling a project.

Microsoft Project requires specific information about the project, which is used to automatically determine the project schedule, resource schedule, the critical path, and an assortment of reports that show different views of the project plan. In addition, Microsoft Project is capable of tracking resource costs.

■ TASKS, SUBTASKS AND ROLLUPS

A project task is likely to be divided into subtasks and subtasks might be divided further into lower-level subtasks. The task list for a project can easily become unruly because it is difficult to visually comprehend the relationships among tasks and subtasks. Microsoft Project simplifies the relationship by organizing project tasks and displaying just the level of task you want to view.

Begin using Microsoft Project by entering tasks into the Gantt chart, which is the first chart shown when you start Microsoft Project. See *Hint 1 How to enter tasks* for instructions for entering tasks. You'll also need to enter the duration for each task (see *Hint 2 How to enter duration*).

You can establish the level of each task by the order in which you enter the task and by the indentation of the name of the task on the Gantt chart (see *Hint 3 Assigning task levels*). Let's say a top-level task is to develop the point-of-sale system, which is a functional component of a much larger system.

Enter as the first task on the Gantt chart, "Develop the point-of-sales system." Next is a second level task to "Determine the data to display to the customer." This is followed by a third level task, "Determine Stakeholders' Expectations." As shown in Figure 2-11, each of these tasks is indented to indicate its level.

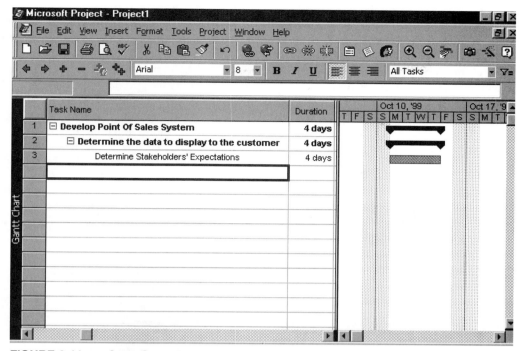

FIGURE 2-11   *Gantt Chart: Task Levels Displayed*

Task levels form a tree in which each level is another branch. An indicator to the left of the task name indicates that the task contains subtasks. A plus sign means a subtask exists but is not shown, while a minus sign indicates that all subtasks are displayed.

Microsoft Project automatically hides or shows subtasks, enabling the project manager to view the project at various levels of detail (see *Hint 4 Hide and view subtasks*). This is called a *rollup of tasks*. Figure 2-12 shows the Gantt chart where subtasks are hidden.

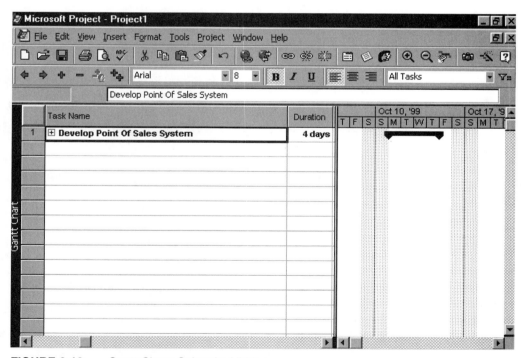

FIGURE 2-12   *Gantt Chart: Subtasks Hidden*

■ DEPENDENCIES AND RESOURCES

Once tasks are entered into the Gantt chart, you can indicate the dependencies of the tasks, if any exist (see *Hint 5 How to set dependencies*). Microsoft Project automatically adjusts the Gantt chart to reflect the dependencies. Tasks that are represented by a bar are moved on the Gantt chart to reflect the end date of the predecessor task, and a line connects the two dependent task bars. Likewise, adjustments are made to other charts, graphs, and reports automatically.

Figure 2-13 contains tasks used to illustrate the critical path method described earlier in this section. The Gantt chart contains the top-level task of Develop The Point Of Sales System. Beneath this task are four subtasks. No dependencies are established for the subtasks; therefore, Microsoft Project assumes all the subtasks are performed concurrently. The duration of the task is set to the duration of the longest subtask, which is 15 days.

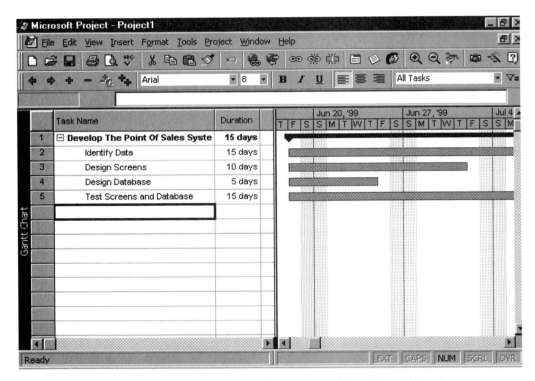

FIGURE 2-13 *Gantt Chart: Tasks Used to Illustrate the Critical Path Method*

Figure 2-14 reflects the tasks once dependencies are set for the subtasks. Task bars on the Gantt chart are repositioned to show the relationships among tasks. Lines connect task bars showing dependencies, and concurrent tasks are shown as parallel task bars.

The duration of the high-level task is automatically recalculated to reflect the length of the critical path, which consists of tasks 2, 3, and 5. Task 4 is performed concurrently with task 3, so the duration of task 3 does not affect the critical path.

When the task, subtasks, and dependencies have been entered into Microsoft Project, the next step is to enter resources required to complete each subtask (see *Hint 6 How to set up resources*). Resources are entered onto the resource sheet, as shown in Figure 2-15.

Resources consist of personnel and anything else required for the project. In this example, personnel resources are identified by position, such as programmer-1. Once staff is hired for those positions, the title can be replaced by the person's name. Numbering the titles enables you to identify similar positions such as programmer-2 and programmer-3. Also on the resource sheet are two servers that will be used for the project. These are called network server-1 and database server-1.

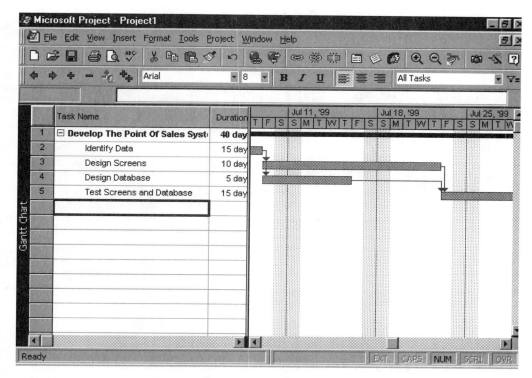

FIGURE 2-14   *Gantt Chart Reflecting Tasks Once Dependencies Are Set for Subtasks*

All resources are entered into the resource sheet before they can be assigned to a task. In addition to the name of the resource, you can include a unit cost of the resource such as the hourly rate and overtime rate. We'll explore more about resources and costing in the next section.

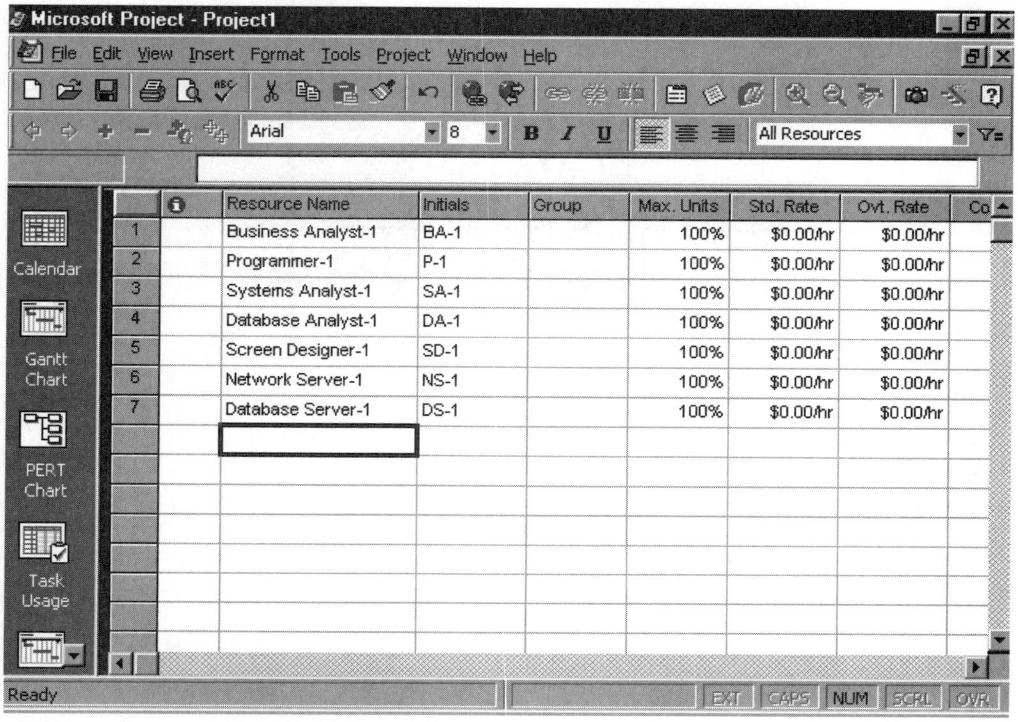

FIGURE 2-15   *Resource Sheet*

After resources are entered into the resource sheet, you can return to the Gantt chart and assign resources to subtasks (see *Hint 7 Assigning resources to subtasks*). In Figure 2-16 the database analyst is assigned to the Identify Data subtask.

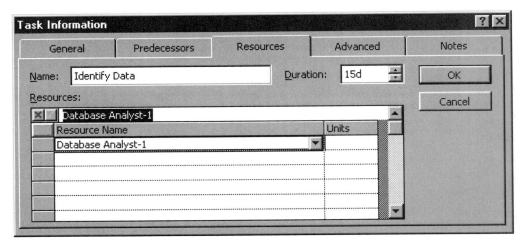

FIGURE 2-16   *Database Analyst Assigned to the Identify Data Subtask*

■ PERT CHART AND THE CALENDAR

The PERT chart, shown in Figure 2-17 (see *Hint 8 Displaying the PERT chart*), depicts the project in a network diagram. Each box is called a *node,* and contains information about a task or subtask. The critical path is illustrated by a bold frame around the box, which displays in red on the computer screen. Non-critical path tasks and subtasks are shown with a thin frame and in black.

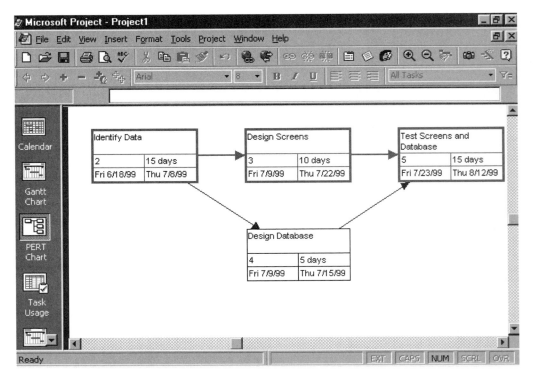

FIGURE 2-17   *The PERT Chart*

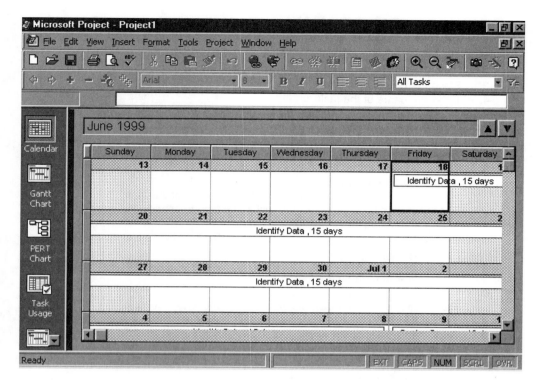

FIGURE 2-18   *Monthly Calendar*

Microsoft Project also displays tasks on a monthly calendar, as shown in Figure 2-18 (see *Hint 9 Displaying the calendar*). This is useful whenever an overview of the entire month is necessary.

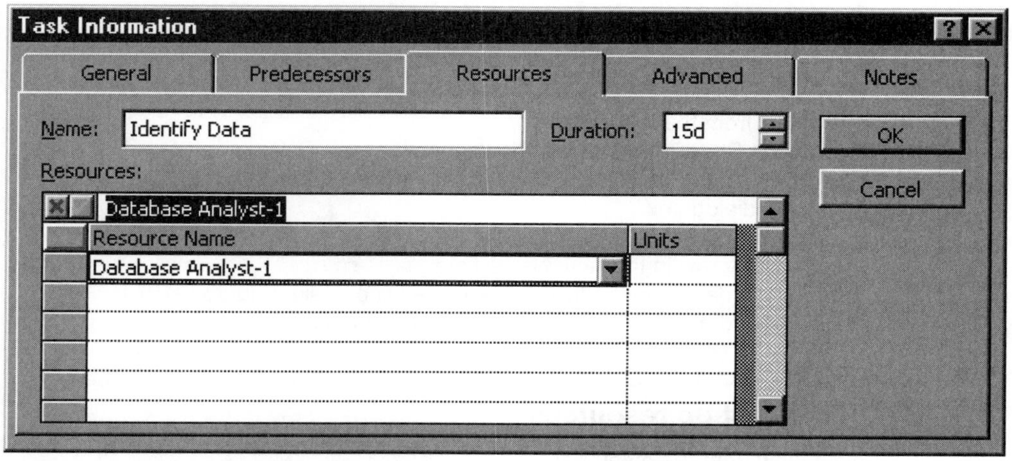

FIGURE 2-19   *Task Information*

Hint 1 How to enter tasks

1. Select View from the menu bar.
2. Select Gantt Chart from the drop-down menu.
3. Place the cursor in an empty Task name cell called the Task Name field.
4. Enter the name of the task.

Hint 2 How to enter duration

1. Select View from the menu bar.
2. Select Gantt Chart from the drop-down menu.
3. Locate the task for which you want to set the duration.
4. Place the cursor in the Duration field along the side of the task.
5. Either click the up or down arrows within the field to change the duration, or enter the duration into the field.

Hint 3 Assigning task levels

1. Select View from the menu bar.
2. Select Gantt Chart from the drop-down menu.
3. Place the cursor in the task that you want to move to a subtask.
4. Click the indent arrow (right arrow) on the toolbar and the task will be indented.
5. Click the reverse indent arrow (left arrow) on the toolbar and the indented task will be moved to the left.

Hint 4 Hide and view subtasks

1. Select View from the menu bar.
2. Select Gantt Chart from the drop-down menu.
3. Hide subtasks by clicking the minus sign appearing to the left of a task (Figure 2-11). The subtasks are removed from view on the Gantt chart and the minus sign changes to a plus sign.
4. View subtasks by clicking the plus sign appearing to the left of a task (Figure 2-12). The subtasks are displayed on the Gantt chart and the plus sign changes to a minus sign.

Hint 5 How to set dependencies

1. Select View from the menu bar.
2. Select Gantt Chart from the drop-down menu.
3. Double-click on the task that is dependent on other tasks to display the Task Information dialog box.
4. Click the Predecessors Tab.
5. Click an empty row in the Task Name field.
6. Click the down arrow in the field to display a list of tasks (Figure 2-19).
7. Click the task that must be completed prior to your selected task.
8. Click OK.

Hint 6 How to set up resources

1. Select View from the menu bar.
2. Select Resource Sheet from the drop-down menu.
3. Enter the name of the resource in the Resource Name Field (Figure 2-15).

Hint 7 Assigning resources to subtasks

1. Select View from the menu bar.
2. Select Gantt Chart from the drop-down menu.
3. Double-click on the task that is dependent on other tasks to display the Task Information dialog box.
4. Click the Resources Tab.
5. Click an empty row in the Resource Name field.
6. Click the down arrow in the field to display a list of resources (Figure 2-16).
7. Click the resource to be assigned to the task.
8. Click OK.

Hint 8 Displaying the PERT chart

1. Select View from the menu bar.
2. Select PERT Chart from the drop-down menu (Figure 2-17).

Hint 9 Displaying the Calendar

1. Select View from the menu bar.
2. Select Calendar from the drop-down menu (Figure 2-18).

SUMMARY

The project manager begins development of the project plan by reviewing the request for proposal (RFP). A request for proposal describes in general terms the nature of the project from the viewpoint of the project sponsors.

An RFP should be considered a discussion document whose details must be carefully examined to determine aspects of the request that are achievable and those that are not achievable. The project manager cannot assume that every facet mentioned in the RFP can be delivered.

The rationale for excluding aspects of the project must be presented to the project sponsor in an effort to modify the scope of the project. Once there is an agreement, the project manager must identify the functional components of the project. A functional component is a piece of the project that can be developed and implemented independently of the other functional components. Each functional component is divided into sub-functional components.

The project manager must then develop a project plan that will deliver the project, on time, within cost, and in perfect working condition. The project plan consists of an executive summary and supporting exhibits. The executive summary provides the project sponsor with a complete, high-level overview of key factors of the project. These factors include:

- A statement of the business case.
- The *analysis of the request for proposal* and subsequent factors relating to the project.
- A solution statement that explains the solution proposed by the project manager.
- A *statement of assumptions* that lists the premises used as the basis for the project manager's proposed solution.
- A *statement of limitations* that identifies the constraints within which the project manager must deliver the project.
- A brief *history of the project.*
- A *high-level organization of the project* that divides the project into functional components and identifies components as phases of the project.

- Delivery date for the project and for each phase.
- Staffing requirements for the project and for each phase.
- A *statement of major acquisitions* for the entire project and for each phase.
- A *summarization of the cost* of the project and for each phase.
- A statement of return on investment.
- A cash flow analysis.

The project manager must determine the milestones of the project—typically, its phases. Likewise, all deliverables must be identified. A deliverable is a piece of the project that shows progress.

Sub-functional components of the project need to be divided into tasks and tasks divided into subtasks. The project manager must ask him- or herself what steps need to be performed to complete a task or to develop a sub-functional component. Answers to these questions help to identify tasks and subtasks. A formal project methodology, explained in Section 1, can also be used as a guide for this purpose.

Each task must be assigned duration. There are five common techniques used for this purpose. These are the Stochastic Approach, Deterministic Approach, the Modular Technique, and Benchmark Job Technique.

The project manager must determine the precedence of tasks and subtasks. Simply stated, he or she must establish which tasks are dependent upon the completion of other tasks. The duration of all dependent tasks determines the duration of the project, also referred to as the critical path.

The duration of a task or subtask on the critical path has a direct impact on the duration of the entire project. A delay in a critical path task delays the entire project. A delay in the performance of a task or subtask that is performed concurrently with a task on the critical path may not affect the duration of the project. A concurrent task or subtask typically has a shorter duration than its concurrent task or subtask. The shorter duration is considered built-in slack time. If the delay exceeds the slack time, then the concurrent task is on the critical path and the duration affects the duration of the project.

An exhibit of the project plan contains details of highlighted information that appear in the executive summary. Exhibits can take on many formats, such as a Gantt chart, a PERT chart, and other kinds of reports.

The project manager must be able to control all the facets of the project plan, especially as changes are made to it during the development of the project. The most efficient way to control the project plan is by using a project management tool such as Microsoft Project. A project manager tool automatically calculates the schedule of the project, helps manage resources, and identifies costs based on basic information supplied by the project manager. In addition, the project management tool provides a wealth of standard and customized reports that can be used as exhibits for the executive summary.

RESOURCES AND PROJECT FINANCING

Two critical components of every project are the resources necessary to complete the project and the finances of the project. A resource is anything required to complete the project's tasks and subtasks. Finances are the funds to underwrite the project—money to pay resources. A project manager must make sure all the project's resources and financial needs are included in the project plan. Overlooking a key resource or a financial matter can defeat the project before it is launched.

It is the project manager's responsibility to identify all the resources necessary to complete the project, and then to develop a project budget that forecasts the project cost. Not all projects are good investments for an organization. The cost of the project, for example, may exceed the benefit it provides to the organization, and in such a case the project must be scrapped. The project manager has the job of analyzing the project budget and deciding whether the project is a worthwhile venture.

In this section, you'll learn the methods used to identify resources for a project. You'll also explore ways to develop a project budget and to determine whether a financial investment in the project is in the best interest of the organization.

RESOURCES

A *resource* is a person or thing that is required to complete a task or a subtask. There are *human resources*—people who will perform the tasks—and *non-human resources*—things used to perform the task.

The project manager identifies resources for the project by analyzing the project task list. The *project task list* contains all the tasks and subtasks necessary to complete the project.

The project manager must focus on the lowest-level tasks. A *low-level task* is one that contains no subtasks. For example, the job of building front steps for a house is a task that has many subtasks, such as ordering bricks. The subtask, "ordering bricks" is a low-level task because it has no subtasks. Resources are assigned to low-level tasks.

■ HUMAN RESOURCES

Once a low-level task is identified, the project manager must ask, "what skills are required to perform this task?" In answer to this question, he or she creates a skill set that is used to develop a job description for the resource. A *skill set* is a list of skills that a human resource must possess to perform a task.

At times, a project manager may lack the insight necessary to define the skill set. In such cases, he or she must ask for input from experts who have experience performing the task.

This type of input from experts is crucial; otherwise a critical skill might not be included, and an incorrect resource may be hired for the project.

It is also important that the project manager describe a resource in objective rather than subjective terms to assure the proper selection is made for the project team. Let's say, for example, there is a task to create a data entry screen.

Intuitively, a project manager can identify the resource as a programmer. However, while it is true that a programmer is the resource who will perform the task, the title "programmer" can have many different definitions. The title's vagueness can lead to the wrong programmer being assigned to the task. A better approach is to use specific terms to describe the resource, such as "a Powerbuilder programmer who has experience building data entry screens."

Be sure to include in the skill set the experience factor of the resource. The *experience factor* describes the necessary level of experience the resource has in performing the task.

For example, if the project requires the design of a computer network, a Microsoft Certified Network Engineer might be a likely resource. However, certification implies the resource has passed a series of tests, but did not need to have experience performing the task. Experience is not a requirement for certification.

The project manager must state whether the resource who will design the network should be someone who, although trained, has little or no experience; someone who has experience assisting a network designer; or someone who has designed a network for a similar-sized organization.

Once the skill set is determined for every low-level task, those skills are grouped into resources and placed on the resource list. A *resource list* is the list of resources required to complete the project.

Human resources are customarily identified by job title, just as a project team is organized in traditional roles and responsibilities that are identified by job titles. A review of the skill sets enables the project manager to slot the skills with the appropriate titles on the project team. Titles depend on the nature of the project and might be different on each project. For example, a construction project has different job titles than a computer systems project.

■ NON-HUMAN RESOURCES

A non-human resource is a thing necessary to complete the task, such as a desk. The project manager determines the non-human resources required for a low-level task by asking, "what does the human resource require to perform this task?"

The answer in some cases is obvious, such as desk space and a computer for a programmer resource. Other needs are not so obvious, such as the software required to build the data entry screen. The project manager must consult with experts who can identify technical non-human resources. He or she must be sure all information about a task is known before identifying non-human resources; otherwise a critical resource could be overlooked.

For example, the project manager knows that a business analyst must interview stakeholders to determine their expectations about the project. Obvious non-human resources for this task include a desk and telephone. However, airline tickets and hotel rooms might also be necessary if stakeholders are located around the country. Overlooking this factor will exclude substantial travel resources from the project budget.

Once the non-human resources are identified, they are placed on the resource list. All resources, regardless of whether they are human or non-human, are included on the same list.

NUMBER OF RESOURCES

Allocating resources to a project involves understanding low-level tasks, and then assigning to each task the correct number of human and non-human resources from the resource list. A low-level task has duration, which is the estimated time required to complete the task. It is the responsibility of the project manager to decide the number of resources that are required to perform the task within the duration.

The number of resources to allocate to a task is dependent on two factors: time constraints and previous allocation of the same resources.

Time constraint is the duration within which the task must be completed. Whether or not one human resource can complete the task within that time constraint depends on the amount of work he or she can perform. Performance is measured in person-days. A *person-day* is eight hours of work provided by a human resource.

Let's return to the task of interviewing stakeholders mentioned previously. Assume there are five stakeholders who need to be interviewed. Consider that 10 person-days (two weeks) are required to arrange and plan for a single interview, conduct the interview, and document the results.

Therefore it will take a business analyst 50 person-days (10 weeks) to complete the task. The duration might fit well into the project plan. However, the time could be cut in half, if necessary, by assigning two business analysts to the task.

A word of caution: assigning more than one human resource to a task can actually extend the duration of the task or have no impact on reducing the duration. The project manager must ask, "does it make sense to increase the number of resources on a task?" The answer depends on the nature of the task. Take the project that requires that a busload of workers be driven to the work site. The duration of the task is an hour. Assigning two bus drivers to the task doesn't cut the duration. Likewise, assigning two programmers to build the same screen might take longer than planned because this is a one-programmer job. Two programmers tend to get into each other's way.

Previous allocation of a resource must also be considered when assigning a resource to a task. *Previous allocation of a resource* requires the project manager to consider the current assignments of the resource before allocating the resource to another task. Without considering a resource's schedule, a project manager could assign the same resource to concurrent tasks, resulting in the resource being over-allocated.

For example, a business analyst could be assigned to interview stakeholders and to review the flow of the existing system, both scheduled for the same time in the project plan. 200% of the business analyst's time is allocated, making him or her over-allocated by 100%.

A project management tool such as Microsoft Project is able to identify resource over-allocation by using a resource graph. A *resource graph* (see Figure 3-1) shows a bar graph representing the percentage a resource is allocated per workday.

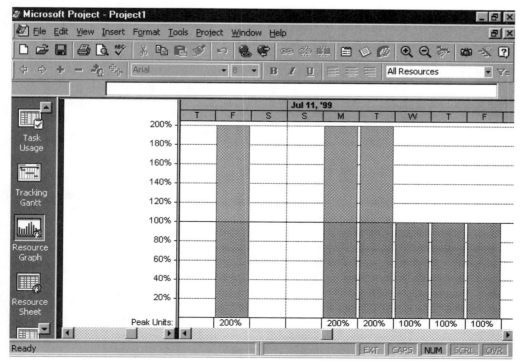

FIGURE 3-1   *Resource Graph*

No resource should be over-allocated. Simply said, a resource cannot do two things at the same time. Over-allocation can be eliminated by assigning another resource, redefining the task, or beginning the task at a different time.

RESOURCES INCREASE THE TASKS LIST

Earlier in *Project Planning and Implementation* you were introduced to the concept of zero-based staffing. Zero-based staffing requires a project manager to identify tasks for a project before considering resources. Once resources are assigned to the project, the project manager must again review the task list to determine whether all the tasks are included in the project plan.

The review of the task list is critical, because the inclusion of resources increases the number of tasks for the project. Let's say that you assign a business analyst to a task along with the tools required to perform the task (e.g., computers, office space). You must ask yourself, what tasks are necessary to acquire these resources?

In this example, a job description must be written, candidates must be recruited, a description of the computer must be written and the computer must be ordered. Likewise, the amount of office space must be decided and acquired. These are just a few of the tasks that have to be completed before the business analyst can start work on the task.

Each task required to acquire a resource has duration. In some cases, that duration can substantially increase the duration of the project. This is especially true with acquiring a non-human resource such as facilities or a human resource such as hiring the project team. Obtaining facilities for your project team could take six months by the time all the approvals are received and the office space acquired and outfitted for the project team. This is six months added to the beginning of the project.

In addition, you may expect to search three months or more before enticing a skilled technician to join your organization. Anticipate another month after the candidate accepts before he or she comes on board, and still another few weeks before the technician comes up to speed on the project.

Availability of resources also plays a critical role. Specialty hardware such as machinery or a network server may require substantial lead time. *Lead time* is the elapsed time from when the resource is ordered to when it is received. Lead time for facilities might be six months, while resources that are in demand by the industry could have longer lead times.

It is critical for a project manager to carefully investigate the impact that task and the duration for acquiring resources have on the project's delivery date. A common error made in project planning is to underestimate the time required to acquire resources—and this type of error typically isn't discovered until the project is well underway.

Once the error appears, the project manager unreasonably adjusts the duration of other tasks to compensate. These maneuvers compound the error, since they shorten the time the project team has to complete the project. Team members then are rushed into mistakes, reducing the quality of the entire project.

After identifying additional tasks necessary to acquire resources for the project, the project manager must again review the resource list. New resources must be assigned to new tasks. For example, personnel agencies that will help with the recruitment process must be located, which adds yet more tasks to the project. Finding and negotiating with personnel agencies is a task that must be performed by—you guessed it—a resource.

PRIORITIZING RESOURCES AND USING SCARCE RESOURCES

After several iterations of assigning resources to the project, it is a good practice to prioritize resources. This exercise groups resources into two categories: those that are critical to the project and those that are nice to have, but not necessary.

For example, let's say you plan for each team member to have a printer. Although this is an ideal, you could achieve similar results by connecting a few printers to a network and having the staff share printers.

Resources that are not critical to the project shouldn't prevent any task from being started or completed. For example, you could shorten the duration of the project by eliminating any resource that has a long lead time and that is not critical to the project.

In prioritizing resources, a project manager must be prepared to limit the use of scarce resources. A *scarce resource* is a person or thing that is in great demand in the industry or within the organization and may not be available full-time on the project.

Scarce resources are common when a project requires technicians with specialized skills or equipment that must be shared with other projects within the organization. Typically, project managers are required to formally request a scarce resource from the manager in charge of that resource. The request may not be met if the resource is already allocated to another project for that period.

For example, a database designer is likely to work for the database group in the Information Technology department of the organization. A project manager who requires the services of a database designer must make such a request to the manager of the database group.

The database group manager reviews all such requests and prioritizes them based on the needs of the entire organization. Even though the database designer is critical to the project, other requests may overshadow the project.

A project manager must be prepared to work around limited access to scarce resources. In the case of the database designer, the project manager could assign another team member familiar with database design to create the preliminary design. The database designer is then needed to fine-tune the design rather than develop it from scratch—that is, another resource could handle 80% of the job and the scarce resource 20%.

■ RECRUITING RESOURCES

Identifying a human resource for a project is easier than recruiting the person to join your project team. Although you might think your project is better to work on than a moon shot, you must be prepared to convey your enthusiasm to a prospective candidate.

There are several ways to recruit a person. These are: to transfer a current employee of the organization to your project, to enlist the organization's personnel department to locate candidates outside the organization, and to supplement your project team with an outside consultant.

The best approach is to identify a current employee whose background and experience complements your needs. The employee is already on staff and has proven that he or she blends with the style and culture of the organization, and delivers quality work on time.

The difficulty of filling a position from within is competition from other project managers. The employee is likely to be a key contributor to an existing project and the rival project manager may not be eager to release him or her to work on your project.

Hiring a person outside the organization expands the talent pool beyond the skills already on staff. You have the opportunity to acquire expertise that might be missing from the organization. However, recruiting from the outside is fraught with risk. The interviewing process and background checks cannot guarantee the candidate will fit within the organization's culture and the project team. It will take three months after the person joins the team to determine if he or she is the proper resource for the job.

Bringing in a consultant is another way to expand the skill set of the team. The consultant is an outside contractor who uses his or her experience to complete your tasks. The consultant leaves the project once the job is finished.

There are three kinds of consultants: independent consultants; consultants provided by consultant service firms; and those from a consulting firm.

An independent consultant is a person who offers his expertise in exchange for an hourly or daily fee. He or she works for him- or herself.

A consultant service finds candidates to fill your positions. Your organization contracts with and pays the consultant service to provide a person for your project team. The consultant service then hires the candidate as its own employee. Once the contract expires, the person leaves the project team and might leave the employ of the consultant service.

Using such a service has the advantage of being able to utilize an independent consultant without tax implications. Organizations must pay employer taxes for each employee on staff. This tax can be avoided by hiring a consultant rather than an employee. However, the IRS has a strict definition of an employee, which tends to consider independent consultants as employees of the organization. A consultant who is an employee of a consultant service is clearly not an employee of your organization. The consultant service, rather than your organization, pays the employer tax.

The drawback of using a consultant service is that the consultant can become a disgruntled employee and there is little you can do to change the situation. There have been cases when the consultant service does not pay the consultant for weeks, even though the organization has paid the consultant service on time. The project manager feels the brunt of the consultant's anger, but is helpless to change the situation.

A consulting firm is an organization that can take over any or all aspects of the project. Such a firm has its own employees and methodologies to address any problems that might arise during the development of the project.

The consulting firm has a wide selection of skilled staff consultants ready to come into any organization as well-oiled machines. Their purpose is to expand their roles within the organization. While addressing your task, consultants are also scouting your organization for other consulting opportunities.

In addition, some consulting firms charge a premium price for junior talent. It is not at all uncommon for a consulting firm to staff your project with employees fresh out of college with little practical experience.

CLASSIFICATION OF RESOURCES USED IN PROJECTS

Project resources can be classified in several ways. One approach is based on accounting principles, which distinguish between labor costs (human resources), material costs, and other "production" costs, such as subcontracting and borrowing. This classification scheme is very useful for budgeting and accounting. Its major drawbacks are that it does not specifically include the cost of the less tangible resources such as information (blueprints, databases), and it does not capture the main aspect of project resource management (i.e., the availability of resources).

A second approach is based on resource availability. Some resources are available at the same level every time period (e.g., a fixed workforce). These are *renewable* resources. A second class consists of resources that come in a lump sum at the beginning of the project and are used up over time. These are *depletable* resources such as material or computer time. A third class of resources is available in limited quantities each period. However, their total availability throughout the project is also circumscribed. These are called *doubly constrained* resources. The cash available for a project is a typical example of a doubly constrained resource.

A third classification scheme is similarly based on resource availability. The first class includes all "nonconstrained" resources—those available in unlimited quantities for a cost. A typical example is untrained labor or general-purpose equipment. The second class includes resources that are very expensive or impossible to obtain within the time span of the project. Special facilities such as a test range that is open only four hours a day, or technical experts who work on many projects, are two such examples. This class also includes resources of which a given quantity is available for the whole project, such as a rare type of material that has a long lead time. The quantity ordered at the beginning of the project must last throughout, due to its limited supply.

This scheme is characteristic of an ABC inventory management system. Resources of the first class (C category) are available in unlimited quantities and so do not require continuous monitoring. Nevertheless, they still might be expensive, so their efficient use will contribute to the cost-effectiveness of the project. Resources in the second class (A category) have high priority and should be monitored closely because shortages might significantly affect the project schedule.

In general, depletable resources, and those limited by periodic availability, should be considered individually during the planning process. This means that project schedules should be designed to ensure efficient use of nonconstrained resources, and that tight controls should be placed on the consumption of constrained resources.

In addition to availability considerations, the cost of resources should be weighed when developing project schedules. This is very important whenever activities can be performed by different sources. The combination of resources (often called the "mode") assigned to activities affects both the schedule and the cost of the project.

Quite often, it is not possible to allocate resources to activities accurately at the early stages of a project. This is because of the underlying uncertainty that initially shrouds resource requirements. Therefore, resource planning is a continuous process that takes place throughout the life cycle of the project.

In a multiproject environment the specific resource alternative selected also affects other ongoing projects. It is common wisdom to start the planning process by assuming that each activity is performed by the minimum cost resource alternative. To identify this alternative, the following points should be considered:

- The selection of resources should be designed for maximum flexibility so that resources not essential for one project can be used simultaneously on other projects. This flexibility can be achieved by buying general-purpose equipment and by broadly training employees.

- Up to a certain point, the more of a particular resource used, the less expensive it is per period of time (due to savings in setup cost, greater learning, and economies of scale).

- The marginal contribution of a resource decreases with usage. Frequently, when increasing the quantity of a resource type assigned to an activity, a point is reached where additional resources do not shorten the activity's duration. That is, inefficiencies and diminishing returns set in.

- Some resources are discrete. When this is the case, decreasing resource levels, necessarily in integer quantities, could result in a sharp decline in productivity and efficiency.

- Resources are organizational assets. Resource planning should take into consideration not only what is best for an individual project, but what is best for the organization as a whole.

- The organization has better control over its own resources. When the choice of acquiring or subcontracting for a resource exists, the degree of availability and control should be weighed against cost considerations.

The output of each resource is measured by its capacity, which is commonly defined in either one of two ways:

1. *Nominal capacity*: maximum output achieved under ideal conditions. The nominal capacity of equipment is usually contained in its technical manual. Nominal capacity of labor can be estimated with standard work measurement techniques commonly used by industrial engineers.

2. *Effective capacity*: maximum output taking into account the mixture of activities assigned, scheduling and sequencing constraints, maintenance aspects, the operating environment, and other resources used in combination.

Resource planning is relatively easy when a single resource is used in a single project. When the coordinate use of multiple resources is called for, planning and scheduling become more complicated, especially when dependencies exist among several projects. In some cases it is justified to use excessive levels of inexpensive resources to maximize the utilization of resources that are expensive or in limited supply.

The life cycle of a project affects its resource requirements. In the early stages, the focus is on design. Thus highly trained personnel such as system analysts, design engineers, and financial planners are needed. In subsequent stages, execution becomes dominant, and machines and material requirements increase. A graph of resource requirements as a function of time is called a *profile*. An example of labor and material profiles as a function of a project's life-cycle stages is presented in Figure 3-2. Curve (a) depicts the requirements for engineers as a function of time. As can be seen, demand peaks during the advanced development phase of the project. Curve (b) displays the requirements for technicians. In this case, the maximum is reached during the detailed design and production phases. This is also true for material requirements, as shown in curve (c).

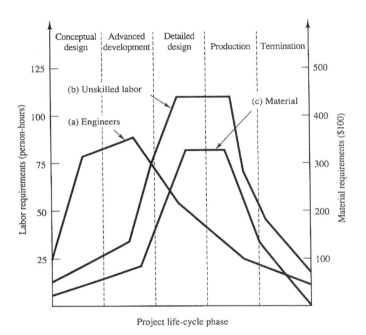

FIGURE 3-2   *Typical Resource Requirement Profiles (From Avraham Shtub, Jonathan F. Bard, and Shlomo Globerson,* Project Management: Engineering, Technology and Implementation, *© 1994 by Prentice-Hall, Inc.: reprinted by permission of the publisher.)*

The general shape of the profiles depicted in Figure 3-2 can be modified somewhat by careful planning and control. Slack management is one way to reshape resource requirements. Because it is always possible to start an activity within the range defined by its early and late start schedules, it may be possible to achieve higher resource utilization and lower costs by exploring different assignment patterns. In some projects, limited resource availability forces the delay of activities beyond their late start. When this happens, project delays are inevitable unless corrective action can be taken immediately.

RESOURCE LEVELING SUBJECT TO PROJECT DUE-DATE CONSTRAINTS

To discuss the relationship between resource requirements and the scheduling of activities, consider our example project. Assuming that only a single resource is used (unskilled labor) in the project, Table 3.1 lists the resource requirements for each of the seven activities.

The data in Table 3.1 are based on the assumption that performing an activity requires that the resource be used at a constant rate. Thus activity A requires eight unskilled labor-

TABLE 3.1
Resource Requirements for the Example Project

Activity	Duration (weeks)	Required labor days per week	Total labor days required
A	5	8	40
B	3	4	12
C	8	3	24
D	7	2	14
E	7	5	35
F	4	9	36
G	5	7	35

days in each of its five weeks. When the usage rate is not constant, resource requirements should be specified for each time period (a week in our example).

The Gantt chart for the early start schedule is shown in Figure 3-3a; the corresponding resource requirement profile is depicted in Figure 3-3b. As can be seen, the early start schedule produces a high level of resource use at the early stages of the project. During the first 3 weeks there is a need for 17 labor-days each week. Assuming 5 working days per week, the requirement during the first 3 weeks is 17/5 = 3.4 unskilled workers per day. The fractional component of demand can be met with overtime, second-shift, or part-time workers. The lowest resource requirements occur in week 13, where only 3 labor-days are needed. Thus the

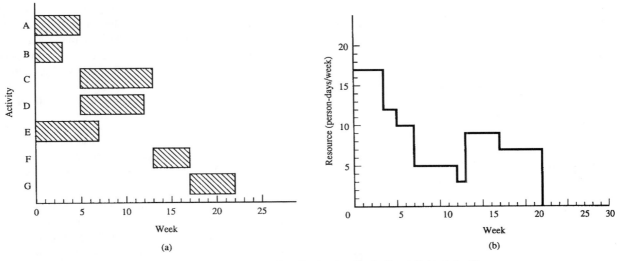

(a)   (b)

FIGURE 3-3   *(a) Gantt Chart and (b) Resource Profile for the Early Start Schedule (From Avraham Shtub, Jonathan F. Bard, and Shlomo Globerson,* Project Management: Engineering, Technology and Implementation, *© 1994 by Prentice-Hall, Inc.: reprinted by permission of the publisher.)*

early start schedule generates a widely varying profile, with a high of 17 labor-days per week and low of 3 labor-days per week; the range is 17 − 3 = 14.

The Gantt chart and resource requirement profile associated with the late start schedule are illustrated in Figure 3-4. Due to the effects that scheduling decisions have on resource requirements, there is a difference between the profiles associated with the late start and early start schedules. In the example, the late start schedule moves the maximum resource usage from weeks 1 through 3 to weeks 3 through 5. Furthermore, maximum usage is reduced from 17 labor-days per week to 12 labor-days per week, giving a range of 12 − 3 = 9. It is important to note that the reduction in range while moving from the early start to the late start schedule is not necessarily uniform over the intermediate cases.

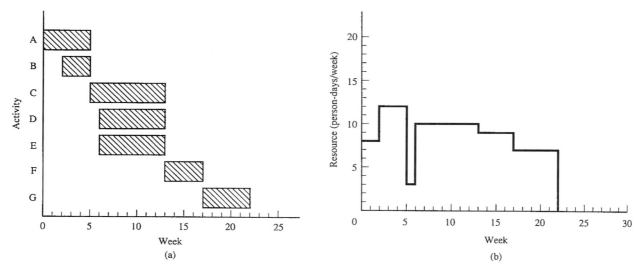

FIGURE 3-4   *(a) Gantt Chart and (b) Resource Profile for the Late Start Schedule (From Avraham Shtub, Jonathan F. Bard, and Shlomo Globerson,* Project Management: Engineering, Technology and Implementation, *© 1994 by Prentice-Hall, Inc.: reprinted by permission of the publisher.)*

Resource leveling can be defined as the reallocation of total or free slack in activities to minimize fluctuations in the resource requirement profile. It is assumed that a more steady usage rate leads to lower resource costs. For labor, this assumption is based on the proposition that costs increase with the need to hire, fire, and train personnel. For materials, it is assumed that fluctuating consumption rates mean an increase in storage requirement (perhaps to accommodate the maximum expected inventory), and more effort invested in material planning and control.

Resource leveling can be performed in a variety of ways. A generic resource-leveling procedure is illustrated next and used to solve the example project.

1. Calculate the *average* number of resource-days per period (e.g., week). In the example, a total of 196 resource-days or labor-days are required. Since the project duration is 22 weeks, 196/22 = 8.9 or about 9 labor-days per week are required on the average.

2. With reference to the early start schedule and noncritical activities, gradually delay activities one at a time, starting with those activities that have the largest free slack. Check the emerging resource requirement profile after each delay. Select the schedule that minimizes resource fluctuations by generating daily resource requirements close to the calculated average.

Continuing with the example, we see that activity E has the largest free slack (6 weeks). The first step is to delay the start of E by 3 weeks until the end of activity B. This reduces resource requirements in weeks 1 through 3 by 5 units. The emerging resource profile is:

Week	1	2	3	4	5	6	7	8	9	10	11
Load	12	12	12	13	13	10	10	10	10	10	5

Week	12	13	14	15	16	17	18	19	20	21	22
Load	5	3	9	9	9	9	7	7	7	7	7

This profile has a maximum of 13 and a minimum of 3 labor-days per week. Since the maximum occurs in weeks 4 and 5 and activity E can be delayed further, consider a schedule where E starts after A is finished (after week 5). The resource requirements profile in this case is:

Week	1	2	3	4	5	6	7	8	9	10	11
Load	12	12	12	8	8	10	10	10	10	10	10

Week	12	13	14	15	16	17	18	19	20	21	22
Load	10	3	9	9	9	9	7	7	7	7	7

The maximum resource requirement is now 12 and occurs in weeks 1 through 3. The minimum is still 3, giving a range of $12 - 3 = 9$. The next candidate for adjustment is activity B, with a free slack of 2 weeks. However, delaying B by 1 or 2 weeks will only increase the load in weeks 4 and 5 from 8 to 12, yielding a net gain of zero. Therefore, we turn to the last activity with a positive free slack—activity D, which is scheduled to start at week 5. Delaying D by 1 week results in the following resource requirement profile:

Week	1	2	3	4	5	6	7	8	9	10	11
Load	12	12	12	8	8	8	10	10	10	10	10

Week	12	13	14	15	16	17	18	19	20	21	22
Load	10	5	9	9	9	9	7	7	7	7	7

The corresponding graph and Gantt chart are depicted in Figure 3-5. Note that this profile has a range of $12 - 5 = 7$, which is smaller than that associated with any of the other candidates, including the early start and late start schedules. This is as far as we can go in minimizing fluctuations without causing a delay in the entire project.

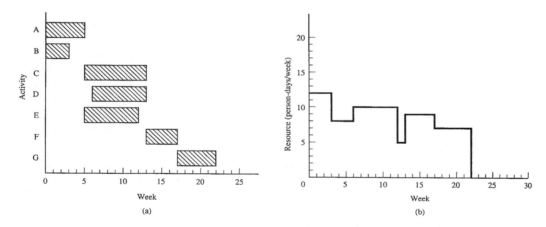

FIGURE 3-5   *(a) Gantt Chart and (b) Leveled Resource Profile for the Example Project (From Avraham Shtub, Jonathan F. Bard, and Shlomo Globerson,* Project Management: Engineering, Technology and Implementation, *© 1994 by Prentice-Hall, Inc.: reprinted by permission of the publisher.)*

For small projects, the foregoing procedure works well but cannot always be relied upon to find the optimal profile. To improve on the results, a similar procedure can be activated by starting with the late start schedule and checking the effect of moving activities with slack toward the start of the project. In some projects the objective may be to keep the maximum resource utilization below a certain ceiling rather than merely leveling the resources. If this objective cannot be met by rescheduling the critical activities, one or more of them would have to be expanded to reduce the daily resource requirements.

The analysis is more complicated when several types of resources are used, the number of activities is large, and several projects share the same resources. Sophisticated heuristic procedures have been developed for these cases. Most project management software packages employ such procedures for resource leveling.

RESOURCE ALLOCATION SUBJECT TO RESOURCE AVAILABILITY CONSTRAINTS

Most projects are subject to resource availability constraints. This is common when resources are limited and good substitutes cannot be found. As a consequence, any delay or disruption in an activity may render the original project schedule infeasible. Cash flow difficulties may cause limited availability of all resource types: renewable, depletable, and nonconstrained. Some resources may be available in unlimited quantities, but due to cash flow problems, their use may have to be cut back in a specific project or over a specific period of time.

Under resource availability constraints, the project completion date calculated in the critical path analysis may not be achieved. This is the case when the resources required exceed the available resources in one or more time periods, and the slack of noncritical activities is not sufficient to solve the problem.

Of course, resource availability constraints are not always binding on the schedule. This can be illustrated with the example project. If 17 or more labor-days are available every week, then either an early start or a late start schedule can be employed to complete the project within 22 weeks. The leveled resource profile derived above requires at most 12 labor-days per week. Therefore, as long as this number is available, no delays will be experienced. If fewer resources are available in some weeks, however, the project may have to be extended beyond its earliest completion date. Activities A and B require a total of 12 labor-days per week when performed in parallel. To avoid an extension, despite a low resource availability, the project manager can try using one or more of the following techniques:

1. *Performing activities at a lower rate using available resource levels.* This technique is effective only if the duration of an activity can be extended by performing it with fewer resources. Consider activity B in the example. Assuming that only 11 labor-days are available each week and activity A (which is critical) is scheduled to be performed using 8 of those days, only 3 days a week are left for activity B. Since B requires a total of (3 weeks) × (4 labor-days per week) = 12 labor-days of the resource, it may be possible to schedule B 3 days per week for 4 weeks. If this is not satisfactory, extending B to 5 weeks at 3 days per week may provide the solution.

   This technique may not be applicable if a minimum level of resources is required each period (week) in which the activity is performed. Such a requirement might result from technological or safety considerations.

2. *Activity splitting.* It might be possible to split some activities into subactivities without significantly altering the original precedence relations. For example, consider splitting activity A into two subactivities: A_1, which is performed during weeks 1 and 2, and A_2, which is performed after a break of 4 weeks. It is possible then to complete the project within 22 weeks, using only 11 labor-days each week. This technique is attractive whenever an activity can be split, the setup time after the break is relatively short, and the activities succeeding the first subactivity can be performed in accordance with the original plan, that is, the second subactivity has no effect on the original precedence relations.

3. *Modifying the network.* Whenever the network is based solely on end-to-start precedence relations, the introduction of other types of precedence relations might help manage the constrained resources. For example, if an end-to-start connection on the critical path is replaced by a start-to-start connection, the delay caused by lack of resources may be eliminated. By considering the real precedence constraints among activities and modeling these constraints using all types of precedence relations, some conflicts can be resolved.

4. *Use of alternative resources.* This option is available for some resources. Subcontractors or personnel agencies, for example, are possible sources of additional labor. However, the corresponding costs may be relatively high, so a cost overrun versus a schedule overrun trade-off analysis may be appropriate.

If these techniques cannot solve the problem, one or more activities will have to be delayed beyond their total slack, causing a delay in the completion of the project. To illustrate, consider the example project under a resource constraint of 11 labor-days per week. Because activity A requires 8 of these 11 days, activity B can start only when A finishes. The precedence relations force a delay of activity D—the successor of B, as well as F and G. The new schedule and resource profile are depicted in Figure 3-6.

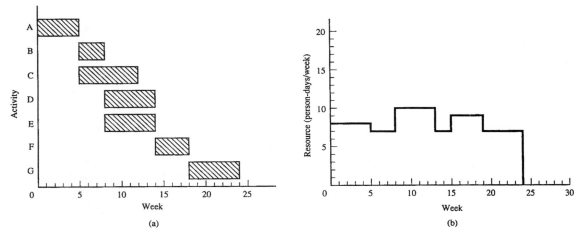

FIGURE 3-6   *Scheduling under the 11 Resource Days/Week Constraint: (a) Gantt Chart; (b) Resource Profile (From Avraham Shtub, Jonathan F. Bard, and Shlomo Globerson,* Project Management: Engineering, Technology and Implementation, *© 1994 by Prentice-Hall, Inc.: reprinted by permission of the publisher.)*

It is interesting to note that the maximum level of resources used in the new schedule is 10 labor-days. Thus in the example project, a reduction of the available resource level from 11 to 10 labor-days per week does not result in a change in the schedule. A further reduction to 9 labor-days each week will cause a further delay of the project since the concurrent scheduling of activities C, D, and E requires a total of 10 resource-days. A feasible schedule in this case and the accompanying resource profile are shown in Figure 3-7.

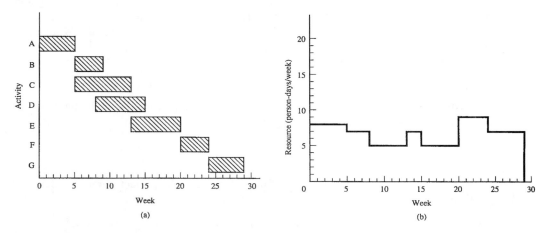

FIGURE 3-7   *Scheduling under the 9 Resource Days/Week Constraint: (a) Gantt Chart; (b) Resource Profile (From Avraham Shtub, Jonathan F. Bard, and Shlomo Globerson,* Project Management: Engineering, Technology and Implementation, *© 1994 by Prentice-Hall, Inc.: reprinted by permission of the publisher.)*

It is impossible to reduce the resource level below 9 labor-days per week since activity F must be performed at that level. Table 3.2 summarizes the relationship between the resource level available and the project duration.

TABLE 3.2
Implications of Resource Availability

Resource availability (work days/week)	Project duration (weeks)	Resource utilization
12	22	0.74
11	24	0.74
10	24	0.82
9	29	0.75

Resource utilization is defined as the proportion of time that a resource is used. For example, if 12 labor-days are available each week and the project duration is 22 weeks, a total of $12 \times 22 = 254$ resource days are available. Because only 196 days are used to perform all the project's activities, the utilization of this resource is $196/254 = 0.74$. Resource utilization is an important performance measure, particularly in a multiproject environment. Resource leveling and resource allocation techniques can be used to achieve high levels of utilization over all projects and resources. Matrix organizational structures help organizations achieve high utilization by taking advantage of pooled resources.

The analysis of multiple projects where several types of resources are used in each is a complicated scheduling problem. In most real-life applications the problem is solved with heuristics, using priority rules to make the allocations among activities. Some of these rules are discussed in the following section.

PRIORITY RULES FOR RESOURCE ALLOCATION

A common approach to resource allocation is to begin with a simple critical path analysis assuming unlimited resource availability. Next, a check is made to see if the resultant schedule is infeasible. This would be the case whenever a resource requirement exceeds its availability. Infeasibilities are addressed one at a time, starting with the first activity in the precedence graph, and making a forward pass toward the last. A priority measure is calculated for each activity competing for a scarce resource. The activity with the lowest priority is delayed until sufficient resources are available. This procedure is used to resolve each infeasibility.

Examples of common priority rules are:

- Activity with the smallest slack
- Activity with minimum late finish time (as determined by critical path analysis)
- Activity that requires the greatest number of resource units (or the smallest number of resource units)
- Shorter activities (or longer activities)

A priority rule based on the late start of the activity and the project duration calculated by a critical path analysis is also possible. For example, define:

CPT = earliest completion time of the project (based on critical path analysis)

$LS(i)$ = late start of activity i (based on critical path analysis)

$PT(i)$ = priority of activity i, where $PT(i) = CPT - LS(i)$

This rule gives high priority to activities that should start early in the project life cycle. In the case of multiple-project scheduling, the value of CPT is calculated for each project.

Next, we look at a priority rule based on each activity's resource requirements. Let

$AT(i)$ = duration of activity i

$R(i,k)$ = level of resource k required per unit of time for activity i

$PR(i,k)$ = priority of activity i with respect to resource type k, where

$$PR(i,k) \equiv AT(i) \times R(i,k)$$

In this rule, high priority is given to the activity that requires the maximum use of resource k.

A rule based on aggregated resources is used when some activities require more than a single resource. Define

$PSUMR(i)$ = priority of activity i based on all its required resources

$\equiv AT(i) \sum_k R(i,k)$

To operationalize this rule, it is necessary to define a common resource unit such as a resource-day.

A weighted time-resource requirement priority rule can be fashioned from two of the previous rules; for example, let

ω = weight between 0 and 1

$PTR(i)$ = weighted priority of activity i, where $PTR(i) \equiv \omega PT(i) + (1 - \omega) PSUMR(i)$

By controlling the value of ω, emphasis can be shifted from the time dimension, $PT(i)$, to the resource dimension, $PSUMR(i)$.

Many of the priority rules above can be modified to take into account a variety of additional factors, including:

- Slack of the activity (total slack, free slack)
- Early start, late start, early finish, and late finish of the activity
- Duration of the activity
- Number of succeeding/preceding activities
- Length of the longest sequence of activities containing the activity
- Maximum resource requirement sequence of activities containing the activity

PROJECT MANAGEMENT BY CONSTRAINTS

The notion of bottlenecks used in job-shop and flow-shop scheduling can be extended to project resource management. Bottleneck resources delay activities due to their limited availability. In a multiresource project, bottlenecks whose capacity is relatively inexpensive to increase may cause low utilization of expensive or scarce resources. For example, a leased crane is an expensive resource that might be idle if an operator is not available. This is because to perform an activity, both resources are required simultaneously. From an economic point of view, it is preferable to maximize the utilization of the expensive resource at the risk of under-utilizing the inexpensive one. Therefore, if the leased crane is available and needed 14 hours each day but an operator can only work between eight and 10 hours a day, it would be advisable to hire two operators for a total of 16 hours a day, allowing for two hours of operator idle time.

Of course, idle resources signal inefficiencies that should be brought to the attention of management to see if they can be put to alternative use. Resource utilization is a key factor, sharing center stage with cost and on-time performance during project evaluation. Each of these factors figures prominently in the planning and review process.

BUDGET AND FINANCIALS

Allocation of resources to project tasks enables the project manager to address financial issues. Financial issues determine how much the project will cost the organization, when those costs will be incurred, how they will be absorbed within the organization, and whether or not the project is a good financial investment for the organization.

In accounting terms, these issues are the project's budget, cash flow, charge back, and return on investment. Each of these falls within the responsibility of the project manager. In many organizations, the accounting department provides the resources to assist the project manager with the financial aspects of the project.

It is important that the project manager be familiar with financial terms and concepts, which this section explores.

■ THE PROJECT BUDGET

Uppermost in the mind of the project sponsor is the question, "how much will the project cost the organization?" The project sponsor looks to the project manager to answer this question. The cost of the project is considered the project's budget.

The project's budget is divided into two categories of expenses: the development cost and the cost of maintaining the system once it is implemented. The same technique is used to develop both segments of the budget.

A *project's budget* is the total cost of resources. Costs are divided into three areas: variable cost, fixed cost, and overhead cost. *Variable costs* are expenses that vary depending upon the use of the resource. For example, a mason who builds a foundation is paid an hourly wage. The number of hours worked depends on the duration of tasks he or she is assigned to perform. The cost of this resource varies depending upon hours worked; it is considered a variable cost.

Fixed costs are resources that don't vary with usage. Let's say an inventory system requires a database server. The server is a fixed cost because, regardless of the usage, the organization's expenses remain unchanged.

Overhead costs are resources not directly related to a project task that are allocated to the project. These expenses include a proportion of the cost of building services, insurance, electricity, and other resources shared throughout the organization.

■ ESTIMATING THE BUDGET

The project manager is responsible for developing an estimated budget. An *estimated budget* is a best guess of the cost of the project. Estimates are not perfect, but should provide a reasonable expectation of the final cost. The definition of reasonableness is subjective and varies with each organization. Some accountants expect the estimated budget to be within +/–10% of the actual expense.

A common approach used to arrive at an estimated budget is to determine the cost of each task—the lowest segment of the project that is assigned resources. Resources are assigned a cost factor, such as an hourly wage. Tallying the cost of resources for a task determines the *cost of the task*.

There are drawbacks with this method, especially when it comes to fixed-cost resources that are shared among multiple tasks. Let's say 10 tasks require the database server. The database server is a fixed cost resource. How is this cost allocated to the 10 tasks?

Accountants advise project managers to use various methods to account for shared fixed-cost items. For example, the cost can be assigned to the entire project, or to a higher-level task if only related subtasks used the fixed-cost resource; or a proportion of the cost may be allocated to each task. In the case of the database server, the total cost of the server can be divided by 10 and allocated to the 10 tasks that require the server.

Developing an estimated budget can become tricky. Later we'll explore various techniques you can used to create an estimated budget.

Budgets are organized to mirror phases of a project. A *phase* is a functional component of the project that can be developed and implemented without other functional components. Each phase has a development and an ongoing budget, which enables the project sponsor to cancel any phase that is not economical for the organization to develop.

The *total estimated cost of a phase* is the sum of the variable cost, fixed cost and overhead cost for all tasks in the phase. You'll find it easier to arrive at an estimated budget at the phase level of the project than at the task level, because fixed cost and overhead resources are assigned to the phase as a whole rather than proportioned to each task. The *total estimated cost of the project* is the sum of the total estimated cost of the phases of the project.

■ CASH FLOW

The organization needs to know when budget expenses will be incurred so the accounting department can plan to have funds available to pay the cost. The efficient use of cash is critical to every organization. Cash can be used to earn revenue in the form of interest or be invested into a project in the form of payment for an expense. The treasurer of the organization manages the organization's cash position and determines the most efficient use of the cash for the organization.

Cash is received by the organization in the form of revenue from sales or grants, and of donations in the case of non-profit organizations. Ideally, the flow of revenue into the organization complements payment of expenses; that is, there is always enough cash on hand to pay the bills.

However, this is not necessarily true in every situation. Over the course of a year enough revenue is generated to cover expenses in a healthy organization, but the revenue flow does not normally parallel the expenses.

The project manager needs to forecast when expenses will be incurred. This is called the project's *cash flow*. The cash flow is the basis for the treasurer to develop a funding plan for the project. A *funding plan* identifies the source of revenue needed to meet expenses.

There are two sources of revenue. These include the organization's various forms of income, such as sales, and funds loaned by lenders. If the organization's revenues fall short in a particular month and are insufficient to meet project expenses, the treasurer must borrow the funds from a lender, which is typically a bank. The *cost of borrowing* is the interest paid to the lender for use of the money. This cost becomes an overhead expense to the organization.

However, if sufficient revenue is generated to cover the monthly project cost, then cash generated by the revenue flow is used to pay the project's expenses. Excess cash is lent to financial institutions to generate interest revenue for the organization. *Excess cash* is the difference between monthly revenue and expenses.

As can be seen, the project manager's cash flow forecast can have a crucial impact on the financial well-being of the organization.

■ CHARGE BACK

The purpose of a project is either to help the organization generate more revenue or to reduce expenses. In either case, the project will increase profitability. The method used to relate an expense with revenue is called a charge back system. A *charge back system* is a means for controlling expenses by directly relating an expense to a revenue flow.

Organizations are grouped into profit centers. A *profit center* has the responsibility to produce a profit for the organization by incurring expenses used to generate a revenue flow. The profit center is expected to generate more revenue than expense. The difference between revenue and expenses is called *profit*.

A profit center manager who might be the project sponsor determines that a complete project will either allow the profit center to generate more revenue, reduce current expenses, or generate a greater profit. The project is then positively indicated. The project is assigned a cost center associated with the profit center. A *cost center* is an accounting item identified by a cost center number that is used to relate an expense to a profit center. The cost center is similar to a bank account for the project. The estimated budget is the opening balance. Expenses are deducted from the balance as they are incurred.

The flow of expenses to a cost center has a different purpose than the project's cash flow. The concept of profit and cost centers is a way of controlling expense. Cash flow is a way of forecasting the cash needs of the organization.

Let's say the organization sells three products. A product manager who is responsible for generating profit manages each product by designing, developing, manufacturing, and selling the product. The product manager will incur expenses to build and sell the product, which offset the revenue from the sales of the product. Excess revenue becomes profit for the organization and excess expenses become a loss. The product is a profit center for the organization, and assigned to the profit center are one or more cost centers. Expenses are allocated to a cost center.

A product manager determines there is a business advantage to undertake a project. Based on the project manager's estimated budget, the product manager can forecast an increase in profit once the project is implemented.

Expenses incurred by the project can be direct expenditures or allocated expenditures. A *direct expense* is a purchase of goods or services directly for the project, such as wages for a consultant. An *allocated expense* is a monthly charge for the proportion of a fixed asset or shared resource used for the project and other projects throughout the organization.

For example, the project is charged a monthly facilities fee to cover office space, lighting, and other services. This charge is based on the square footage used to house the project team. Likewise, the cost of computers, servers, and other fixed assets are proportionally allocated to the project monthly. The project manager pays for only the time the asset is used by the project team.

The monthly charge for a fixed asset is determined by amortizing the cost of the asset over the life of the asset. *Amortization* is the allocation of an asset's cost over the life of the asset. Standard accounting rules establish the life of an asset and the appropriate amortization method to allocate cost.

Let's say a computer cost $1,000 and has a life of five years. The monthly cost is about $42. The project's cost center is charged $42 each month the project team uses the computer.

It is important for the project manager to realize that the monthly cost allocated to the project is different than the cash flow demands of the project. For example, the $1,000 computer costs the organization $1,000 the day the computer is purchased. That is, the treasurer must plan to have $1,000 available when the computer is bought for the project. Cost allocation is the amount deducted from the project's budget each month.

THE PROJECT BUDGET

An organization's budget (usually expressed in dollars) represents management's long-range, mid-range, and short-range plans. The budget should contain a statement of prospective investments, management goals, resources necessary to achieve those goals, and a timetable. Its structure should match that of the organization. In particular, a functional structure shows an organization's investments and expenditures grouped three ways: (1) development of new products (engineering), (2) production of existing products (manufacturing), and (3) campaigns for new or existing products (advertising, marketing). A project-oriented structure, on the other hand, reveals the organization's planned costs and expected revenues for each project, while a matrix structure partially supports both the functional and project-based component of an organization's budget. This is explained presently.

The budget of any specific project is tied to the organizational budget. In some organizations, a project budget includes only expenditures (e.g., government agencies such as the Department of Defense are engaged in projects strictly as clients). In other organizations, the project budget includes both income and expenditures (e.g., contractors whose expenditures for labor, materials, and subcontracting are covered by their clients). When an organization is involved in several projects, the budgets of these projects are coordinated centrally. It is important to combine the budget of each project to avoid the risk of steering the organization into financial difficulties. This issue should be considered when selecting new projects because it provides a hard constraint in the decision-making process.

In a matrix organization, the budget links the functional units to the projects. On a specific project the cost of resources invested by the functional unit is charged against the project's budget. This link is one of the interfaces between the functional structure and the project aspect of the matrix organization.

A well-designed budget is an efficient communication channel for management. Through the budget, managers (at all levels) are advised of their organizational goals and the resources allocated to their units. A detailed budget defines expected costs and expenditures, thus setting the framework of constraints within which each manager is expected to operate. These constraints represent organizational policy and goals. The well-structured budget is a yardstick that can be used to measure the performance of organizational units and their managers. Managers who participate in the budget development process commit themselves, their subordinates, and their unit's resources to the goals specified in the budget as well as the constraints implied by the negotiated funding levels. A successful manager is one who can achieve the budget goals with the resources allocated to his or her project, that is, one who can successfully execute the organization's policy. The well-structured budget is also a useful tool for identifying deviations from plans, the magnitude of these deviations, and their source. Therefore, it is part of the baseline for cost and schedule control systems. In addition, the budget's structure depends on the organizational structure, while its level of detail depends on the planning horizon for which it was prepared.

The *long-range,* or *strategic,* budget defines an aggregate level of activity for the organization over a period of several months to several years. For example, in a functional organization this budget might define a goal of selling 100,000 units in the coming year with a 15% increase in sales in each of the following four years. The expected marketing cost in the budget is $50,000 for the first year with 8% increases in each subsequent year. In an organization with a project structure, the strategic budget will define the total budget for each project. For example, assume that for project X the design stage has a one-year completion due date and a $500,000 budget. A critical design review is scheduled accordingly. In two years a prototype will be tested in the lab. The associated budget is $600,000. The final product will be tested in the third year for a cost of $550,000. The long-range budget is typically updated annually.

By using the budgeting process, management establishes long-range goals, schedules to achieve these goals, and the available resources. When the actual expenditures, income and results are compared to the original budget, management can monitor the organization's performance. Also, when necessary, management can change the budget to control both goal setting and resource allocation.

A *mid-range, tactical* budget is a detailed presentation of the long-range budget and covers 12 to 24 months. It is updated quarterly. The tasks to be performed provide the basis of the entries. A rolling planning horizon is used so that every time (e.g., quarterly) the mid-range budget is updated, a budget for the ensuing quarter is added while the budget for the recently completed quarter is deleted. The tactical budget details the monthly expected costs of labor, materials, and overhead for each task. In a functional organization, the tactical budget projects the expected costs and revenues of each product family and the expected costs of each functional department.

A *short-range* or *operational* budget lists specific activities and their costs. This budget spans a period up to one year and covers the costs of resources (such as labor and material) required to perform each activity. For example, the short-range budget of a project might specify that the design of a prototype be done on a $10,000 CAD system which runs on a $5,000 piece of equipment. Lead times are three and two weeks, respectively, for the hardware and software. Installation starts as soon as both items are delivered. The expected cost of installation and training is $2,000. This short-term (operational) budget relates project costs to project activities through the project's lower-level network model.

A project's budget contains several dimensions. The first relates to the tasks and activities to be performed. The primary effort is to establish the relationship between cost and time for scheduled tasks and activities. The second dimension is based on the organizational breakdown structure. Each task is assigned to an organizational unit in the OBS. The third dimension is the work breakdown structure. Each task is assigned to a WBS element in the lowest level of the hierarchy. Over time, however, they are distributed among the WBS elements at their corresponding levels.

As each organization develops its own budgeting procedures, several points can help make the budget an efficient vehicle for planning, as well as a standard channel of communication:

- The budget should present management's objectives stated in terms of measurable outputs: for example, the successful completion of a test or the development of a new software module. These outputs should be presented with their budgetary constraints. Thus the budget presents available resources and the goals to be achieved using these resources. The presentation can be based on a functional structure, a project's organizational structure, or a combination of the two if a matrix structure is assumed.

- The budget should be presented quantitatively (e.g., in monetary units or sometimes in person-hours) as a function of time. The presentation should facilitate a periodic and cumulative comparison between actual and planned performance levels.

- The budget should be divided into long-range (strategic), mid-range (tactical), and short-range (operational) levels. Each level should contain a detailed breakdown of the budget at the preceding level for the planning horizon. A rolling horizon approach should be used in developing the budgets of new periods and in updating the budgets of previous periods.

Management reserve may be included at strategic and tactical levels. This reserve acts as a buffer against uncertainty and should be consumed by transforming it into specific line items in the mid- and short-range budgets.

PROJECT BUDGET AND ORGANIZATIONAL GOALS

The budget of an organization reflects management's goals. These goals and organizational constraints determine decisions on project selection, resource allocation, and the desired rate of progress for each project. The budget depends on the perceived organizational mission and the sector to which the organization belongs (private, government, or nonprofit). It also depends on internal and external environmental factors. The following are seven common factors affecting project selection and budget structure:

1. *Competition.* Most organizations in the private sector need a competitive edge to survive. External challenges force continued improvement within the organization and occur in various ways, such as the following:
   • *Time-based competition.* Spurs the implementation of concurrent engineering with the goal of shortening new product development cycles and improving customer service. It is also instrumental in reducing customer lead times. A major emphasis is on achieving project milestones and goals in a timely manner.
   • *Cost-based competition.* In a cost-based environment, the project budget includes smaller, tightly controlled reserves.
   • *Quality-based competition.* Total quality management is emphasized.

2. *Profit.* The ability to generate profits in the short and long run is essential to most organizations in the private sector. Selection decisions are frequently

based on a project's expected profits. A project can be tentatively evaluated by techniques such as net present value, internal rate of return, and payback period.

3. *Cash flow.* The organizational cash flow is an aggregate of all routine activities combined with other ongoing projects. When unexpected cash flow problems arise, projects that generate quick cash become high-priority items in the budget allocation process. In some cases an organization may prefer projects that begin to produce revenues immediately, albeit small, over projects that generate a slow cash flow and higher profits in the distant future. In the short run, to improve the cash position of the firm, activities that generate income (like payment milestones) may be budgeted earlier than other activities that have the same or an even shorter slack.

4. *Risk.* Uncertainty and risk may influence budgetary decisions. An organization that tries to avoid the risk of delays may budget its projects according to an early start schedule. This, in turn, may lead to early expenditures and cash flow problems. Organizations that try to minimize the risk of cost overruns sometime budget each activity at its lowest level. If a longer activity duration occurs, the lowered risk of a cost overrun can translate into an increased risk of delays.

   The selection of new projects may also be influenced by risk assessment. In this case, the project's portfolio, to which the organization is committed, is affected by the organization's perceived risk level.

5. *Technological ability.* Some organizations in the public sector are willing to budget high-tech projects in order to acquire new, more advanced technologies. In the private sector (including such industries as computers, microelectronics, and aerospace), an organization's technological ability is an important aspect of its competitive edge. To outdistance competitors, technologically advanced projects are selected and budgeted to assure progress.

6. *Resources.* Each project's budget is a monetary representation of the value of resources allocated to perform that project. If adequate resources are not available, little can be accomplished, so whatever effort is expended will have negligible effect. Therefore, it is important to classify and track resources according to their availability.

   In the long- and mid-range budgets, organizational plans for acquiring new resources are put forth. The short-range budget addresses plans to use these resources. In preparatory stages of a project, it is important to remember that some resources may not be available even if budgeted adequately. Therefore, in preparing the budget, resource availability (both inside and external to the organization) needs to be coordinated with the planned costs of these resources.

7. *Perceived needs.* Project selection and budgeting depend largely on organizational goals. In the government sector, especially in defense, perceived needs (or new threats) are a driving force. Cost and risk considerations might be secondary when national security or public health are considered.

These seven factors link organizational goals and the internal and external aspects of the operational environment with each project's budget. Clearly, developing an organizational budget and a budget for each project requires a coordinated effort among management, accounting, marketing, and the other functional areas.

PREPARING THE BUDGET

Budget preparation is the process by which organizational goals are translated into a plan that specifies the allocated resources, the selected processes, and the desired schedule for achieving these goals. The budget must integrate information and objectives from all functional levels of the organization with information and objectives from the various project leaders. Although upper management sets the long-range (strategic) objectives, lower-level management is responsible for establishing the detailed (operational) plans and must clearly articulate and understand the short-range objectives before executing the budget.

In a project or a matrix organization, lower-level managers, who are concerned primarily with the daily operations, should be most knowledgeable in the technical details regarding the most appropriate way to perform each project. They should also be intimately familiar with expected activity durations and costs. Thus it is important to integrate upper-level management input with the knowledge of the functional and project managers.

The organizational budget consists of both ongoing activities, such as the production and marketing of existing products, and one-time efforts or projects. It is easier to budget ongoing activities, since past budgets for these activities can serve as a reference point for planning. By adjusting for anticipated demand, the expected inflation rate, and the effect of learning, the financial planners can develop the new budget based on past information. Project budgeting is more difficult, though, since previous budgets are often unavailable. Cost estimation, the project schedule, and the effect of resource availability should be considered in developing the project budget.

The building blocks of the project's budget are the work packages in which tasks performed on the lowest-level WBS elements are assigned to organizational units at the lowest level of the OBS. A budget is developed for each work package. Budgets are then developed for each WBS element at each level in the hierarchy and for each organizational unit at each OBS level.

Thus the process of integrating single project budgets and the budgets of ongoing activities into an acceptable organizational budget requires planning and coordination. The final budget should embody sound, workable programs for each functional area, and coordinate the efforts of functional units and project managers to achieve their goals. Three procedures are commonly used in budgeting: the top-down approach, the bottom-up approach, and the iterative-mixed approach.

■ TOP-DOWN BUDGETING

The trigger for the budgeting process is the strategic long-range plan that is developed by top management based on its experience and perception of the organization's goals and constraints. The long-range plan is then passed to the functional unit managers and the project managers who develop the tactical (mid-range) and detailed operational (short-range) budgets, respectively.

One problem with top-down budgeting is the translation of long-range budgets into short-range budgets. The former can be spread in any number of ways over the budgets of projects and functional units. The best combination yielding the most efficient schedule for each of the projects involved is not easy to construct given the constraints imposed by the long-range budget. Therefore, the question is how to schedule projects in a "suboptimal way" to meet the strategic goals. This suboptimality is a result of top management's limited knowledge of the specifics of each project, task, and activity, knowledge that is unavailable when preparing the long-range budget using the top-down approach.

A second problem with this approach is the competition for funds among lower-level managers who try to secure adequate funding for their operations. But since top management fixes the total budget, the only way for lower-level managers to gain an advantage is to undercut their counterparts. Such a situation does not promote cooperation and understanding and does not guarantee the optimal allocation of funds. Table 3.3 illustrates the top-down budgeting process.

■ BOTTOM-UP BUDGETING

To overcome the disaggregation problem of top-down budgeting, many organizations adopt a budgeting approach starting at the project manager level. Each project manager is asked to prepare a budget proposal that supports efficient and on-schedule project execution. Based on these proposals, functional managers prepare the budgets for their units, considering the resources

TABLE 3.3
Top-Down Approach to Budget Preparation

Step	Organizational level	Budget prepared at each step
1	Top management	Strategic budget based on organizational goals, constraints, and policies
2	Functional management	Tactical budget for each functional unit
3	Project managers	Detailed budgets for each project, including the cost of labor, material, subcontracting, overhead, etc.

required in each period. Finally, top management streamlines and integrates the individual project and functional unit budgets into a strategic long-range organizational budget.

The advantages of this approach are the clear flow of information and the use of detailed data available at the project management level as the basic source of cost, schedule, and resource requirement information. The disadvantage of the approach is that top management has limited influence over the budgeting process, since the functional and project managers prepare most of the short- and mid-range budgets. However, top management can influence the outcome by issuing a statement to the lower-level managers, as they prepare the short- and mid-range budgets, outlining organizational policies and goals. Also, top management can steer the budgeting process by selecting projects based on its perception of organizational needs and goals. Table 3.4 illustrates the bottom-up budgeting process.

TABLE 3.4
Bottom-Up Approach to Budget Preparation

Step	Organizational level	Budget prepared at each step
1	Top management	Setting goals and selection of projects (a framework for budget)
2	Project management	Detailed budget proposals for projects including costs of material, labor, subcontracting, etc.
3	Functional management	Mid-range budget for each functional unit
4	Top management	Adjustments and approval of the aggregate long plan budget resulting from the process

As stated, the major problem with the bottom-up approach is the reduced level of control it offers top management. Since the aggregate budget is developed based on input obtained from the project and functional unit managers, the gap between strategic and operational objectives may be wide. This creates a need to fine-tune the organizational budget. The process is carried out iteratively through adjustment and review until a satisfactory compromise is achieved.

■ ITERATIVE BUDGETING

The two budgeting approaches presented above are "pure" in that the process flows in one direction, either bottom-up or top-down. Some of the shortcomings of these approaches can be eliminated by combining the information flows in an iterative fashion. A typical iterative approach starts with top management setting a budget framework for each year of a strategic plan. This framework then directs the selection of new projects and serves as a guideline for project managers as they prepare their budgets. Detailed project budgets are aggregated into functional unit budgets and, finally, into an organizational budget that top management reviews and, if necessary, modifies. Based on the approved budget, functional unit and project managers modify their respective budgets. The process may undergo several iterations until convergence takes place at the strategic, tactical, and operational levels.

This process is based on input from all levels of management and usually produces better coordination between the different budgets (functional versus project and long-range versus short- and mid-range). Major disadvantages center on the relatively long duration needed for agreement and the excessive use of management time.

The process of adjusting a project budget to the framework of the organizational budget is based on the internal relationship between schedule, resources, and cost. This relationship can be exploited in several ways.

TECHNIQUES FOR MANAGING THE BUDGET

The budget of a project represents scheduled expenditures and scheduled revenue as a function of time. The simplest approach to budgeting is to estimate the expected costs and income associated with each activity, task, and milestone. Based on the project schedule, these costs are assigned specific dates and a budget is generated; however, it may be only a partial budget because some of the indirect costs are usually not included at the preliminary stage. Typical indirect costs are those for management, facilities, and quality control and are not always related to specific activities. Adding these costs results in a more complete project budget. The product of this effort can serve as the basis for the decision-making process needed to develop a detailed, comprehensive budget. The development of detailed project budgets based on schedule and resource considerations is the first step in an iterative approach. The next step is to integrate them into an acceptable organizational budget.

■ SLACK MANAGEMENT

One approach to integrating these projects is to change activity timing and the associated expenditure or income, an approach known as slack management. Noncritical activities that have free slack are usually the first candidates for this type of rescheduling. Activities with total slack are the next choices, and the final choices are critical activities that can be delayed only at the cost of delays in project completion time. Rescheduling activities makes the integration of single project budgets into an acceptable organizational budget easier.

To illustrate the relationship between a project's cash flow and its schedule, let us return to the example project. The length of the critical path in the project is 22 weeks. Critical activities are A, C, F, and G, while activities B, E, and D have either free or total slack that can be used for budget planning. Table 3.5 depicts the costs and durations of the project's activities.

An early start schedule results in relatively high expenditures in the project's earlier stages, while a late start schedule results in relatively high expenditures in the later stages. Table 3.6 presents this project's cash flow for the early start schedule assuming, for budgeting purposes, that the cost of each activity is evenly distributed throughout its duration. Table 3.7 enumerates the cash flow of the project for the late start case.

TABLE 3.5
Project Activity Durations and Costs

Activity	Duration (weeks)	Cost ($1,000)
A	5	1.5
B	3	3.0
C	8	3.3
D	7	4.2
E	7	5.7
F	4	6.1
G	5	7.2
		31.0

TABLE 3.6
Cash Flow of an Early Start Schedule

Week	A	B	C	D	E	F	G	Weekly cost	Cumulative cost
1	300	1,000			814.3			2,114	2,114
2	300	1,000			814.3			2,114	4,229
3	300	1,000			814.3			2,114	6,343
4	300				814.3			1,114	7,457
5	300				814.3			1,114	8,571
6			412.5	600	814.3			1,827	10,398
7			412.5	600	814.3			827	12,225
8			412.5	600				1,013	13,238
9			412.5	600				1,013	14,250
10			412.5	600				1,013	15,263
11			412.5	600				1,013	16,275
12			412.5	600				1,013	17,288
13			412.5					412	17,700
14						1,525		1,525	19,225
15						1,525		1,525	20,750
16						1,525		1,525	22,275
17						1,525		1,525	23,800
18							1,440	1,440	25,240
19							1,440	1,440	26,680
20							1,440	1,440	28,120
21							1,440	1,440	29,560
22							1,440	1,440	31,000
	1,500	3,000	3,300	4,200	5,700	6,100	7,200	31,000	

Figure 3-8 depicts the cash flows for the early and late start schedules; Figure 3-9 depicts their cumulative cash flows. From Figure 3-9 we see that if the strategic long-range organizational budget allocates only $4,913 to the project for weeks 1 through 5, then during this period only a late start schedule is feasible. Also, increasing the project's budget over $10,398 for the first five weeks makes an early start schedule feasible. Any budget in between will force a delay of noncritical activities.

The choice between an early and a late start schedule affects the risk level associated with the project's on-time completion. Using a late start schedule means that all the activities are started as late as possible without any slack to buffer against uncertainty, increasing the probability of delays. Therefore, the budgeting process should resolve the conflict between a project budget that supports the organizational budgeting requirements versus the higher risk of a schedule overrun.

Projects with large numbers of activities tend to have a large choice of schedules with associated budgets. For example, in Figure 3-8, any schedule that falls between the early and late start budget lines would be feasible from the point of view of meeting the critical milestones on time.

■ CRASHING

In addition to using slack management as part of the budgeting process, another option may be available: change activity duration by selecting different technologies to perform the activity and by adding or deleting the necessary resources. So far we have assumed that each activity is performed in the most economical way. Thus the combination of resources assigned to each activity is assumed to be selected to minimize the total cost of performing that activity.

TABLE 3.7
Cash Flow of the Late Start Schedule

Week	Activity A	B	C	D	E	F	G	Weekly cost	Cumulative cost
1	300							300	300
2	300							300	600
3	300	1,000						1,300	1,900
4	300	1,000						1,300	3,200
5	300	1,000						1,300	4,500
6			412.5					412	4,913
7			412.5	600	814.3			1,827	6,739
8			412.5	600	814.3			1,827	8,566
9			412.5	600	814.3			1,827	10,393
10			412.5	600	814.3			1,827	12,220
11			412.5	600	814.3			1,827	14,046
12			412.5	600	814.3			1,827	15,873
13			412.5	600	814.3			1,827	17,700
14						1,525		1,525	19,225
15						1,525		1,525	20,750
16						1,525		1,525	22,275
17						1,525		1,525	23,800
18							1,440	1,440	25,240
19							1,440	1,440	26,680
20							1,440	1,440	28,120
21							1,440	1,440	29,560
22							1,440	1,440	31,000
	1,500	3,000	3,300	4,200	5,700	6,100	7,200	31,000	

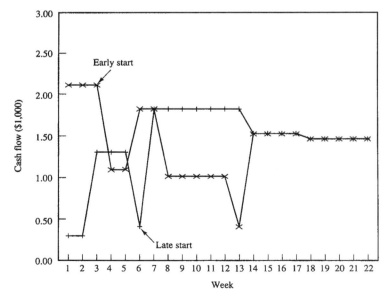

FIGURE 3-8 *Cash Flow for Early Start and Late Start Schedules (From Avraham Shtub, Jonathan F. Bard, and Shlomo Globerson,* Project Management: Engineering, Technology and Implementation, *© 1994 by Prentice-Hall, Inc.: reprinted by permission of the publisher.)*

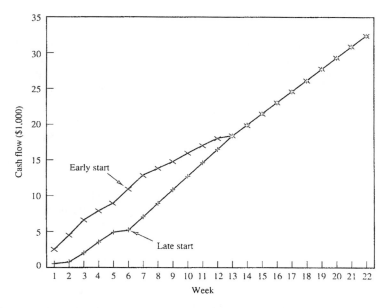

FIGURE 3-9   *Cumulative Cash Flow for Early Start and Late Start Schedules (From Avra-ham Shtub, Jonathan F. Bard, and Shlomo Globerson,* Project Management: Engineering, Technology and Implementation, *© 1994 by Prentice-Hall, Inc.: reprinted by permission of the publisher.)*

However, in many cases it is possible to reduce an activity's duration by spending more money. Thus trade-offs exist between the minimum cost–longest duration option at one extreme and any other option that reduces an activity's duration at a higher cost.

This is the essence of the original version of CPM, which places equal emphasis on time and cost. The emphasis is achieved by constructing a time-cost curve for each activity. This curve plots the relationship between the direct cost for the activity and its resulting duration. In its simplest form, the plot is typically based on two points: the *normal* point and the *crash* point. The former gives the cost and time involved when the activity is performed in the normal way without extra resources such as overtime, special materials, or improved equipment that could speed things up. By contrast, the crash point gives the time and cost when the activity is fully expedited; that is, no cost is spared to reduce its duration as much as possible. As an approximation, it is then assumed that all intermediate time-cost trade-offs are possible and that they lie on the line segment between these two points. Thus the only estimates needed are the cost and time for normal and crash points.

Consider, for example, a manual painting operation requiring 4 days at $400 per day. With a special compressed airflow system, however, two workers can complete the job in 2 days for $1,000 per day. Thus the activity can be performed in 4 days for $400 × 4 = $1,600 or in 2 days for $1,000 × 2 = $2,000. The normal duration is associated with the lowest-cost option for the activity. This value is used in a CPM analysis and in the preparation of the initial budget.

More formally, the normal duration of an activity is the duration that minimizes the direct cost. In some instances a schedule based on normal durations may produce high indirect costs, for example, when a project due date is given and a penalty is charged for completion after the due date. Even when the due date can initially be met by a normal schedule, uncertainty during the project execution may cause schedule overruns. The resultant penalties must be traded off with the cost of shortening the duration of some activities to minimize (or avoid completely) these late charges.

A similar situation occurs when a fixed overhead is charged for a project's duration. Rent for facilities would be such an example. In this case, management might consider shortening some activities to reduce the project's duration and hence save on indirect costs.

PRESENTING THE BUDGET

The project budget is a communications channel that must serve both internal and organizational planning and control needs. Two dimensions are used to measure the quality of a project's budget: the budget's ability (1) to advance organizational goals within the imposed constraints, and (2) to communicate the proposed plan to the project team and organization, and sometimes to subcontractors and the client.

The budget is easier to understand and use if it is presented clearly and concisely. Consider the following recommendations when preparing and presenting a project's budget:

1. Incorporate a schedule indicating the time that expenditures and revenues are expected to be realized.

2. Present the budget in quantitative, measurable units such as dollars or person-hours. If you use different units in the same budget, clearly define the conversion between units.

3. Make an effort to define milestones corresponding to the achievement of measurable goals. Typical milestones for R&D projects are system design review, preliminary design review, critical design review, and the passing of prototype performance tests. In contractor-client projects, the achievement of such milestones can serve as the basis for client payments. It is important to budget milestones according to the costs of activities leading up to them. In the example project, if event 3 is defined as a milestone representing the completion of activities A and B, its budget is based on the costs of activities A and B ($4,500). Assuming an early start schedule, these activities are scheduled to terminate five weeks after the project initiation. Assuming a $2,500 overhead (or $500 per week), the total payment of this milestone is likely to be above $4,500 and close to $7,000.

4. Use the budget as a baseline for progress monitoring and control. If a weekly progress report is required, plan the budget at the weekly level. On the other hand, if weekly progress reports are issued but the budget is prepared on a monthly basis, a meaningful comparison between planned progress and actual progress is possible only once every four progress reports. Similarly, break down the budget to enable a direct comparison with the progress reports. The cost breakdown used in preparing the budget should be the same as the breakdown used to collect and analyze data for both the project and organizational control systems.

5. The budget should translate short-range objectives into work orders, purchasing orders, and so on. This links the design and development phases to the production phase through the budgeting and work authorization processes.

6. Break down the budget by the organizational units responsible for its execution and the work content assigned to such units. For example, Table 3.8 itemizes the activities by assigned departments of the example project.

7. Whenever you use a specific standard in budgeting, reference it. For example, suppose that activity C is welding the pressure tank of a submarine and is budgeted at $3,300. This figure might have been derived from the company standard, which says that it costs $300 per inch to perform a weld. The estimated welding length is 11 inches. Such information should be referenced in the budget. By referencing the standard used, you can later trace any deviations in actual cost to the deviation's source (i.e., the cost per inch or the length of the welding) and, if necessary, update the standard.

TABLE 3.8
Breakdown of the Budget by Organizational Units

Activity	Department 1	Department 2
A		$1,500
B		3,000
C	$3,300	
D	4,200	
E		5,700
F	6,100	
G	7,200	
Department total	$20,800	$10,200

8. Include five components in the short-term (operational) budget:
   (a) *Work packages of discrete effort.* Each work package defines the organizational element responsible for a task and the task's WBS element. Identifying the work package this way allows you to present the budget along WBS and OBS lines. Such an identification also serves as a baseline for a control system capable of tracing the sources of deviations between planned and actual progress.
   (b) *Level of effort.* This category, which includes the cost of efforts related to more than one work package, occurs as the activities progress over time.
   (c) *Apportioned effort.* This category includes the cost of efforts based on a factor of a discrete effort (work package) as exemplified by such activities as inspection and quality control.
   (d) *Cost of material.* These costs include the WBS element for which it will be used and the OBS element that will use it.
   (e) *Other costs.* Costs such as those associated with subcontracting must be included.

9. Budget planners should try to define most of the project's effort in discrete terms as part of the work packages. These packages present units of work at levels where the work is performed and where the effort is assignable to a single organizational element.

10. Budget overhead costs for each organizational element with a clear definition of the procedures used for allocating these costs. One option is to include a management reserve in the long- and mid-range budgets as a buffer against uncertainty. The level of management reserve depends on the amount of uncertainty involved in estimating the actual cost, timing, and technological maturity of the effort required. This reserve should be factored into the budget, once again in discrete terms, as work progresses and information becomes available.

11. Define a target budget at completion as the total budget costs plus management reserve and undistributed monies.

Following this list of recommendations will make it easier to prepare and use the budget. Much can be gained by presenting a financial plan quantitatively in terms that relate the required effort to cost, timing, responsible organizational elements, and project components. Nevertheless, each organization has its own guidelines for budget preparation and presentation, so the recommendations above should be used advisedly to supplement such guidelines in areas where they are unclear or incomplete.

PROJECT EXECUTION: CONSUMING THE BUDGET

During the project's production phase, three processes occur simultaneously:

1. The short-range budget is translated into work and purchasing authorizations. This process generates work orders, purchase orders, and contracts with suppliers and subcontractors. It requires a feedback system that facilitates a comparison between actual progress and the original plans, and compares the actual cost of the effort performed with the budgeted cost. The exact structure of a feedback system used for project control depends on the project's structure and the organization's needs.

2. The tactical (mid-range) budget is translated into a short-range budget through a rolling horizon mechanism. Cost estimates and schedules are accumulated into cost accounts as well as into apportioned effort and level of effort. This is a multistage process since the tactical budget for each period contains several short-range (operational) budget periods. Developing a new, realistic short-range budget requires detailed planning involving the integration of original project plans with reports on actual progress. The short-range budget should detail the mid-range budget and in case of cost or schedule deviations, present a detailed plan for corrective action. Thus development of the operational budget is based on knowledge regarding the planned execution of activities and the project's actual status.

3. The long-range budget is gradually converted into the mid-range budget. This process involves the distribution of accumulated funds, the allocation of management reserves to specific work packages, and the handling of engineering changes. Such changes are frequent in long projects. During the project execution phase, new market requirements (client needs) or new technological developments may call for modifications in the project's technological aspects. The configuration management system handles all these change requests. This system keeps track of change requests and the steps followed that lead to approval or rejection. An approved technological change may have both cost and schedule consequences. Thus the process of translating long-range budgets into mid-range budgets should address all approved technological changes and their impact on the project.

Management reserve, designed to buffer uncertainty, should be consumed as soon as the results of tests and studies are available. Such results provide the basis for developing a detailed project plan translating management reserve budgets into work packages, thus reducing the level of uncertainty.

The budgeting process is ongoing. Long-term plans are translated into detailed short-term budgets, and short-term budgets are translated into work orders, purchase orders, and contracts with subcontractors and suppliers.

IMPORTANT POINTS IN THE BUDGETING PROCESS

The budgeting process provides an interface between organizational goals as perceived by top management, and the project managers' actions to achieve those goals. The techniques for budget preparation link the project's schedule, required resources, and net present value. The outcome provides an action framework for each organizational element. This framework integrates the budgets of the individual functional units and projects, as well as those of routine, ongoing activities into the total organizational budget.

Each project's budget is important in transforming goals into both plans and actions while providing guidelines for integration across the organizational and work breakdown structures. Management uses the budget as a communications channel to inform organizational elements of resource allocation decisions and the level of performance that is expected of them over time. This channel should be designed with rapid response in mind so that approved changes and deviations from the plan can be communicated quickly. The clearer the budget presentation, the easier it is for management at all levels to win over resistant elements in the organization. Thus not only is the quality of the budget important but also the planning that goes into its presentation.

■ MANAGING THE BUDGET

The estimated budget is called the *baseline budget*, and is used to gauge whether or not the project's forecasted cost is on target with actual expenditures. An estimated budget is the project manger's best guess of what the project will cost the organization. Although some organizations allow for a 10% deviation, it is critical that the project manager keeps the project as close to the estimate as possible. The project is part of an overall scheme to increase profits for the organization, and a project that comes in over budget will affect the organization's profitability.

Each month during the development of the project the project manager must compare the actual costs with the projected costs shown in the estimated budget. That is, the project manager must compare the actual cost against the baseline budget. Deviations between the actual and baseline budget should be minor when costs are aggregated to a monthly total, since the excess cost of a task could be offset by a reduced cost for another task during that month.

Let's say that there are 10 tasks performed in a month. Actual cost for three tasks are 20% higher than the baseline budget. Three other tasks are 20% lower than the baseline budget. The remaining tasks mirror the baseline budget. Therefore, actual average costs for all 10 tasks stay within the baseline budget estimate because those lower than the estimate offset those that are higher. However, the project manager must react swiftly if the actual average cost is more than 10% above the estimate since this is an indication that the estimated budget is lower than actual cost. If this condition is left unchecked, the cost of the project will exceed the estimated budget and could have a serious impact on the profitability of the organization.

An inaccurate estimate is caused by several factors:

- A resource or task is overlooked.
- An error in arithmetic is made.
- An estimating technique is used incorrectly.
- An assumption used as the foundation for the estimate changes.

Regardless of what caused the deviation to occur, the project manager needs to alter the project plan so actual costs fall in line with the estimated budget. The project manager can:

- Redefine tasks.
- Replace an expensive resource with a less costly one.
- Redefine the scope of the project.

JUSTIFYING INVESTMENT IN THE PROJECT

The project sponsor and his or her financial advisors use the estimated budget to determine whether the project is a good investment for the organization. The project costs the organization money that could be used for other purposes. Therefore, the project sponsor, with the help of the project manager, must justify using the money to develop the project.

An investment made by an organization has many of the same characteristics that you may find in your own investments. Each investment has risks and rewards. The project sponsor must identify all the investment opportunities for the organization, weigh the risks and rewards of each, and then determine which investment is in the best interests of the organization.

Let's say you receive $100. You can place the money under the mattress. The risks are the money could be lost or stolen and you lose earning power because the money is not earning you interest. The reward is that the money is always available.

You could place the money in the bank. The risk is you must wait to access your money according to bank rules. The rewards are that the money is insured and earns you 5% interest.

You could buy stock. The risk is that you can lose the money and the reward is that the investment might appreciate 15% annually.

You could buy boxes of cereal similar to those sold in a grocery store. The risk is that you may not be able to sell all the boxes and the reward is that you may sell all the boxes in one day and earn 50% on your investment.

An organization has practically the same choices as you, except that instead of cereal the organization invests in its product or service. The question the project sponsor and project manager must answer is: why should the organization invest money in a particular project?

■ COST BENEFIT ANALYSIS

A *cost benefit analysis* is the process of comparing the expense of the project to the benefits the project will have to the organization. The cost benefit analysis is a process performed by the accounting department to help the project sponsor determine whether the project is a worthwhile venture.

The initial step is to determine various alternatives the organization has to solve a problem. Let's say the organization needs to replace an existing manual accounts payable system with a new system that takes full advantage of discounts offered by suppliers. An accounts payable system is the way an organization pays bills. Assume also that it is common for suppliers to offer a 2% discount on an outstanding invoice if the organization pays the invoice within 10 days rather than waiting the traditional 30-day period.

There are four alternatives:

- Do nothing: leave the existing system alone.
- Hire more staff and continue with the manual system.
- Purchase accounts payable software from an outside supplier.
- Develop a new accounts payable system in-house.

Costs and benefits must be determined for each alternative. *Cost* is categorized as one-time and annual costs. The *benefit* is the annual savings or increase in revenue realized if the alternative is adopted. The difference between the total cost and the benefit is the *net benefit* of the option.

Let's continue with our example. The first option is to do nothing. There is no one-time cost and the annual cost is $40,000 used to compensate the accounts-payable clerk. The annual benefit is −$75,000 because the current system loses the opportunity to realize a savings of $75,000 in supplier discounts.

The second alternative is to hire two additional accounts-payable clerks. This will result in a staff of three accounts-payable clerks at which time the organization will realize the benefit. The annual cost is $120,000 (See Table 3.9). There is no one-time cost. The benefit is $75,000 in savings by realizing the supplier discount.

TABLE 3.9
Alternative Two Costs

Cost Category	Item		Cost
One-time cost	None		N/A
		Total	$0
Annual cost	1 Accounts-Payable Clerk		$40,000
	2 Additional Clerks		$80,000
		Total	$120,000

The third alternative is to buy an accounts-payable system from a vendor. Table 3.10 lists the one-time cost to acquire the software. There is also an annual cost of $42,000, which includes upgrades, maintenance, and the original accounts-payable clerk. The benefit of this expense is $75,000 annually in savings.

TABLE 3.10
Alternative Three

Cost Category	Item		Cost
One-time Cost	Purchase software		$ 7,500
	Modifications to software		$ 9,200
	Purchase two PCs		$ 5,000
	Train staff		$ 1,250
		Total	$22,950
Annual Cost	Annual software update		$ 2,000
	1 Accounts-Payable Clerk		$40,000
		Total	$42,000

The fourth alternative is to develop the software in-house. Table 3.11 shows the expenses for undertaking this option.

TABLE 3.11
Alternative Four

Cost Category	Item		Cost
One-time Cost	System design		$ 5,000
	Programming		$24,000
	Training, installation, and migration		$ 1,200
	Equipment		$ 2,000
		Total	$32,200
Annual Cost	Annual software maintenance		$ 900
	1 Accounts-Payable Clerk		$40,000
		Total	$40,900

A comparison must be made among all four options. This comparison is called a cost benefit analysis, where the total cost of each option is compared to the benefit. An alternative showing a positive net benefit is a viable option.

Table 3.12 shows the cost benefit analysis for our example. The annual benefit is subtracted from the total cost of the alternatives to determine the annual net benefit. The first alternative, which is to do nothing, has a cost of $40,000 and a negative benefit of $35,000. That is, the organization loses the opportunity to earn $75,000 annually because their current operations fail to take advantage of supplier discounts.

TABLE 3.12
Cost/Benefit Analysis

	1	2	3	4
Costs	Do nothing	Hire staff	Buy software	Write software
One-time cost	0	0	−$22,950	−$32,200
Annual cost	−$40,000	−$120,000	−$42,000	−$40,900
Annual benefit	−$75,000	$ 75,000	$75,000	$75,000
Annual net benefit (excluding one-time cost)	−$115,000	−$45,000	$33,000	$34,100

Keep in mind that none of the alternatives will produce a positive net benefit in the first year. This could indicate that none of the options is a good investment. This is not necessarily true because some alternatives will absorb all the cost and realize an annual benefit at some period in the future. The project sponsor needs to determine the future date when the cost of each alternative is fully absorbed. The technique used to determine this date is called the break-even analysis.

■ BREAK-EVEN ANALYSIS

The *break-even analysis* identifies the break-even point, which is the time at which all the cost of an alternative is offset by the benefits gained from its implementation. Not all alternatives have a break-even point, as is illustrated in Table 3.13, which provides the break-even analysis for the accounts payable example.

TABLE 3.13
Break-Even Analysis

Year	Alternative 2 Hire Staff			Alternative 3 Buy Software			Alternative 4 Write Software		
	Cost	Benefit	Net Benefit	Cost	Benefit	Net Benefit	Cost	Benefit	Net Benefit
1	$120,000	$75,000	−$45,000	$62,950	−$75,000	−$137,950	$72,200	−$75,000	−$147,200
2	$240,000	$150,000	−$90,000	$104,950	0	−$104,950	$113,100	0	−$113,100
3	$360,000	$225,000	−$135,000	$146,950	$75,000	−$71,950	$154,000	$75,000	−$79,000
4	$480,000	$300,000	−$180,000	$188,950	$150,000	−$38,950	$194,900	$150,000	−$44,900
5	$600,000	$375,000	−$225,000	$230,950	$225,000	−$5,950	$235,800	$225,000	−$10,800
6	$720,000	$450,000	−$270,000	$272,950	$300,000	$27,050	$276,700	$300,000	$23,300

A break-even analysis requires the project sponsor to project the total cost and benefits of an alternative over a period of time, which might be months or years. Costs and benefits are shown as cumulative to reflect the organization's complete investment and return. The project sponsor's objective is to find the alternative with the shortest break-even point.

Before beginning the break-even analysis, the project sponsor reviews the results of the cost benefit analysis and identifies alternatives that have no hope of returning a benefit to the organization. Those alternatives are eliminated from the break-even analysis.

Let's continue with our example. Reviewing the cost benefit analysis (Table 3.12) it becomes obvious that the first alternative will never return a positive benefit. Therefore, alternative 1 is not included in the break-even analysis.

The cost and benefits for the remaining alternatives can be forecast over a six-year period— one year of development and five years of operation. Notice that the cost of alternative 2 always exceeds the benefits; therefore alternative 2 can be discarded. Alternatives 3 and 4 provide a brighter picture. The organization realizes $75,000 savings each year if either of these alternatives is in operation. However, in the first year when both alternatives are being developed the organization loses the opportunity to save $75,000. This is denoted as a −$75,000 in the break-even analysis.

During the second year, which is the first year both alternatives are in operation, the cumulative benefit is zero because the savings of $75,000 is offset by the loss in the first year. Both alternatives provide a positive net benefit in the sixth year. This is the break-even point.

■ RETURN ON INVESTMENT

The project is an investment for the organization similar to an investment in stock, in a manufacturing plant, or the purchase of a certificate of deposit. Each investment opportunity has a return value and a level of risk. The return value and the risk of an investment are related in that the higher the return-value the greater will be the risk of investment. The *return on investment* (ROI) is the amount realized beyond the initial investment.

The project sponsor must convince the organization's executive committee that the project will return a value better than other investment opportunities. Calculating the return on investment for the project provides the supporting data to justify investing in the project. This assumes, of course, that the return on investment in the project is sufficient compared to the risk. The *project's risk* is the risk of failure if the project is unable to deliver the benefit promised when the project was launched.

The return on investment is calculated using data from the break-even analysis. Figure 3-10 contains the return on investment formula. Table 3.14 shows the return on investment for alternatives 3 and 4 for each year the system is in operation. Alternative 2 was determined not to be a viable alternative because its cost would never be offset by the benefit according to the break-even analysis.

TABLE 3.14
Return on Investment

| Year | Alternative 3 Buy Software | | | Alternative 4 Write Software | | |
	Cost	Benefit	Return on Investment	Cost	Benefit	Return on Investment
1	$62,950	−$75,000	0	$72,200	−$75,000	0
2	$104,950	0	0	$113,100	0	0
3	$146,950	$75,000	0	$154,000	$75,000	0
4	$188,950	$150,000	0	$194,900	$150,000	0
5	$230,950	$225,000	0	$235,800	$225,000	0
6	$272,950	$300,000	9.9%	$276,700	$300,000	8.4%

$$\text{Return on Investment} = \frac{(\text{Benefit} - \text{Cost})}{\text{Cost}}$$

FIGURE 3-10 *Return on Investment Formula*

■ TRACKING COST USING MICROSOFT PROJECT

Developing a budget for any project is fraught with problems, since a project manager must account for all fixed and variable costs associated with every aspect of the project. If a key facet is overlooked or an estimate is lacking the proper foundation, then the project could be over budget. Over budget means the cost estimate is exceeded.

Microsoft Project, like other project management software tools, can calculate the cost of each task and tally these costs to forecast the cost of the project. Calculations are based on factors such as standard rate, overtime rate and fixed rates for resources assigned to tasks. The project manager determines the rates and enters them into Microsoft Project.

For example, a consultant may charge a standard hourly rate for a normal workday and another hourly rate for overtime. Both rates can be entered separately into Microsoft Project (see Hint 1 and Hint 2). When the project manager assigns the consultant to a task, Microsoft Project uses the duration and the percentage of time to which the resource is allocated to the task to calculate the cost of the resource. The *standard rate* is applied to allocations up to and including 100%. The *overtime rate* is applied to allocations over 100%.

A resource can charge the project manager a fixed amount, as in the case of a flat rate for installing a piece of machinery. That fixed cost can be directly assigned to a task (see Hint 3). Microsoft Project includes the fixed cost when calculating the total cost for the task.

Microsoft Project is also able to account for resources that have a standard rate, overtime rate, and a fixed cost. Let's say that software purchased from a vendor comes with a fixed installation charge and an hourly charge for custom modifications. There is also an overtime charge if the modifications require longer than an eight-hour-day to complete. All three charges can be assigned to the task and will be included in cost calculations.

Some material resources, such as concrete, are sold as a unit cost. A *unit cost* is a price for a predefined measure of the resource such as per yard. The total cost for the resource is based on the number of units required to complete the task. Microsoft Project enables the project manager to define the unit cost of a resource and the number of units required for the task; then Microsoft Project calculates the estimated cost for using the resource.

It is common for a resource to be multi-skilled and able to perform more than one job. For example, a systems analyst might also fill in as a business analyst.. Each job has a different rate of pay, so the project manager must be able to pay the resource based upon the job performed.

Microsoft Project has a feature that defines 25 different rates, using one of five cost tables. The project manager enters the various rate information (see Hint 4), then tells Microsoft Project to apply the appropriate rate when the resource is assigned to a task.

There are also situations in which there is a fixed cost that needs to be assigned directly to a task. This is the case when a permit is required to complete the task. The charge for the permit is applied at the task level (see Hint 5).

Hints 6 through 8 illustrate the way to display the cost of a task, resource, and the entire project using Microsoft Project.

Hint 1 Assign a standard rate to a resource.

1. Select View from the menu bar.
2. Select Resource Sheet.
3. Enter hour rate in the Std. Rate field (Figure 3-11).

Hint 2 Assign an overtime rate to a resource.

1. Select View from the menu bar.
2. Select Resource Sheet.
3. Enter hour rate in the Ovt. Rate field (Figure 3-11).

Hint 3 Assign a fixed cost to a resource.

1. Select View from the menu bar.
2. Select Resource Sheet.
3. Enter hour rate in the Cost/Use field (Figure 3-11).

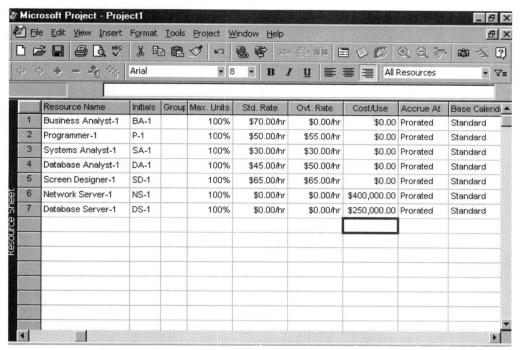

FIGURE 3-11   *Assigning Rates to a Resource*

Hint 4 Assign different pay rates for the same resource.

1. Select View from the menu bar.
2. Select Resource Sheet.
3. Double-click on the resource name to display the Resource Information screen.
4. Select the Costs tab.
5. Select a cost-rate-table and enter the rate. Cost rate table A is the default cost rate table (Figure 3-12).

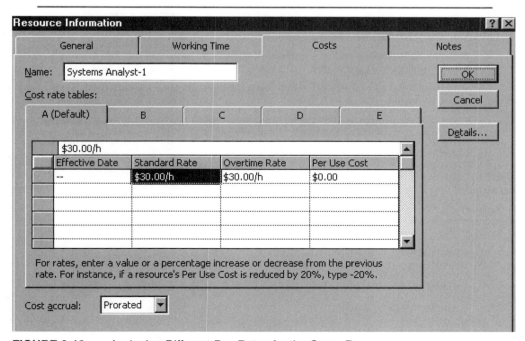

FIGURE 3-12   *Assigning Different Pay Rates for the Same Resource*

Hint 5 Assign a fixed cost to a task.

1.   Select View from the menu bar.
2.   Select Gantt Chart.
3.   Select View from the menu bar.
4.   Select Table.
5.   Select Cost.
6.   Enter the cost in the Fixed Cost field (Figure 3-13).

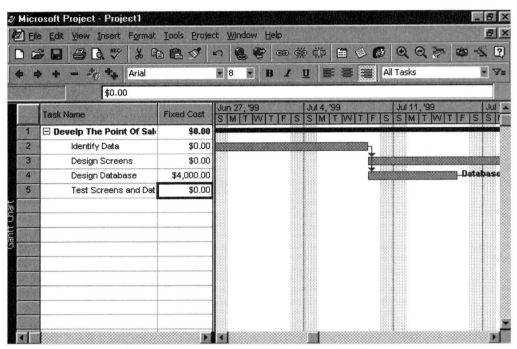

FIGURE 3-13   *Assigning a Fixed Cost to a Task*

Hint 6 View cost per task

1.   Select View from the menu bar.
2.   Select Gantt Chart.
3.   Select View from the menu bar.
4.   Select Table.
5.   Select Cost.
6.   Scroll right to view costs for the task (Figure 3-14).

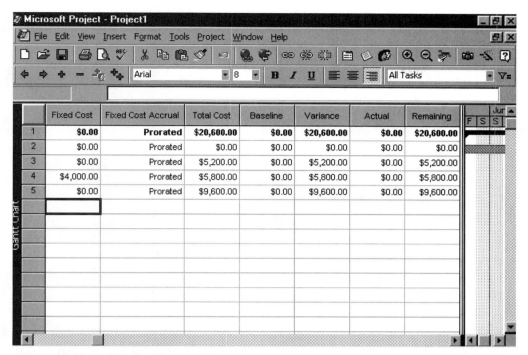

FIGURE 3-14   *Viewing Cost per Task*

Hint 7 View cost per resource

1.   Select View from the menu bar.
2.   Select Resource Sheet.
3.   Select View from the menu bar.
4.   Select Table.
5.   Select Cost (Figure 3-15).

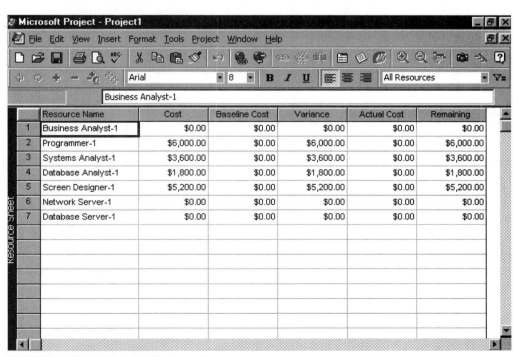

FIGURE 3-15   *Viewing Cost per Resource*

Hint 8 View the project cost

1. Select Project from the menu bar.
2. Select Project Information.
3. Select Statistics (Figure 3-16).

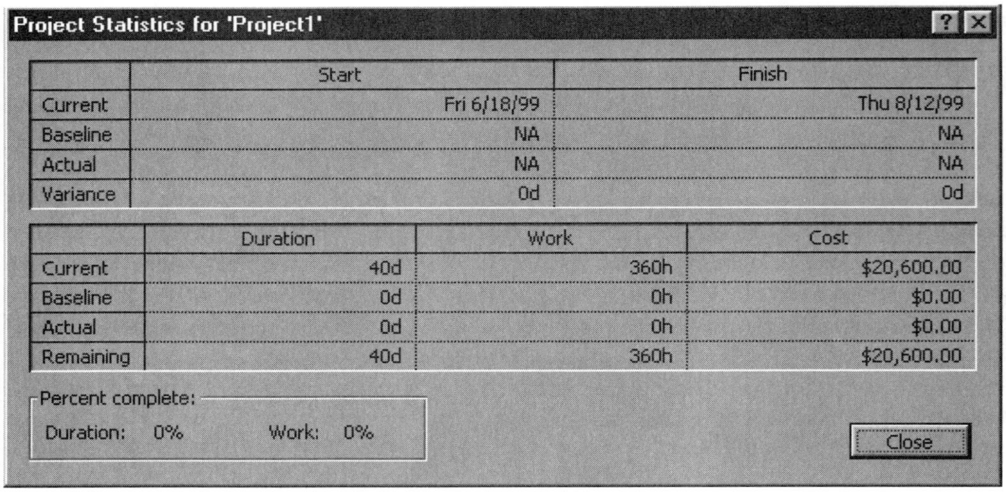

Project Statistics for 'Project1'			? X
	Start		Finish
Current	Fri 6/18/99		Thu 8/12/99
Baseline	NA		NA
Actual	NA		NA
Variance	0d		0d

	Duration	Work	Cost
Current	40d	360h	$20,600.00
Baseline	0d	0h	$0.00
Actual	0d	0h	$0.00
Remaining	40d	360h	$20,600.00

Percent complete:
Duration: 0%   Work: 0%

Close

FIGURE 3-16 *Viewing Project Cost*

SUMMARY

A project manager must identify the resources necessary to complete a task and the finances required to underwrite the project. Overlooking a key resource or a financial matter can defeat the project before it is launched.

Review low-level tasks on the project task list to identify resources. Only low-level tasks are assigned resources since higher-level tasks are composed of subtasks. For each low-level task, the project manager must ask, "what skills are required to perform this task?" In answer to this question, the project manager creates a skill set that is a list of skills that a resource must possess to perform the particular task.

A resource must be described in detail rather than in subjective terms to assure the proper resource is selected for the project team. Be sure to include in the skill set the *experience factor* of the resource, which is the level of experience the resource has in performing the task. Once the skill set is determined for every low-level task, those skills are grouped into resources and placed on the resource list.

Resources are divided into two categories: human resources, who are the people needed to complete the task, and non-human resources, which are things necessary to complete the task, such as a desk. The project manager determines the non-human resources for a low-level task by asking, "what does the human resource require to perform this task?"

Resources are allocated from the resource list to low-level tasks. This is called allocating resources. The project manager must identify the number of resources required to complete a task within the specified duration. The number of resources to allocate to a task is dependent on two factors: time constraints and previous allocation of the same resources.

The project manager must determine the number of person-days needed to complete the task within the time constraint, which is the duration of the task. Likewise, the project manager must consider the previous allocation of a resource when assigning a resource to a task. He or she must avoid assigning a resource to concurrent tasks, since this will over-allocate that resource.

Once resources are identified the project manager must ask, "what tasks are necessary to acquire these resources?" Additional tasks are added to the project to acquire the resources. Careful attention must be paid to the lead time necessary to acquire the resource, because lead time extends the duration of the project. Additional tasks to acquire resources will also require new resources.

Every project is an investment of the organization's funds into a venture that is expected to increase profit. The project sponsor must determine whether the project is a worthwhile investment, based on the estimated project budget developed by the project manager.

The estimated project budget is divided into three areas: variable cost, fixed cost, and overhead cost. Variable costs are expenses that vary depending upon the use of the resource. Fixed costs are resources that don't vary with usage. Overhead costs are resources that are not directly related to a project task but are still allocated to the project.

An estimated budget is determined by tallying the cost of resources for each low-level task. Tasks for each phase of the project are summed to determine the estimated cost of the phase and the totals for all the project's phases are tallied to determine the total estimated cost of the project.

The project manager must provide the treasurer of the organization with a cash flow analysis that identifies when costs will be incurred. The treasurer uses this cash flow analysis to determine the amount of cash the organization requires to meet its expenses.

An organization relates expenses directly to a profit center by using a charge back system. Each project is assigned a cost center to which the cost of the project is charged. The cost center is directly associated with a profit center in the company.

The estimated budget for the project is the opening balance in the cost center—as if the profit center manager, who is the project sponsor, has given the project manager money to develop the project. Each month the project manager draws down from that balance to pay expenses. The estimated budget is called the baseline budget; it is used to gauge whether or not the project's forecast cost is on target with actual expenditures.

The chosen project is just one of several alternatives for addressing a situation. The project sponsor must compare alternatives by performing a cost benefit analysis. A cost benefit analysis determines the net benefit of each alternative.

A break-even analysis must be performed to determine when in the future the benefits of an alternative will offset the cost. This is called the break-even point. An alternative having a short break-even point is a viable option.

The project sponsor must determine the return on investment for each viable alternative. The return is the net benefit of the accumulated cost and benefit over a period of time, such as six years. The return on investment is measured as a percentage and must be annualized by dividing the return by the period of time of the investment. The annualized return for each alternative is compared, and the alternative with the highest return on investment is considered an attractive investment.

4

PROJECT CONTROL AND EVALUATION

Months of planning, estimating, and guessing are summed up in a project plan that is expected to make the project sponsor's idea a reality. Once the project sponsor accepts the plan, project development begins.

It is the time to execute the project plan and determine whether estimates compare to actual duration and costs, all the tasks and subtasks are identified, and all the resources are available to work on the project.

The clock is ticking and stakeholders are carefully waiting for the project team to present the first deliverable on time, within cost, and in perfect working condition; and it is the responsibility of the project manager to make sure he or she delivers on that promise.

Managing the project is one of the most challenging aspects of the project manager's job. It is like planning a moon shot. There are many known and unknown facts. The project manager did his or her best to identify all the known facts, to estimate unknown facts, and to prepare to deal with uncertainty once the project is launched.

Anything can happen after the project sponsor approves the project plan. Estimates could be inaccurate; the need for the project may dissipate; tasks may have been overlooked; and resources may be unavailable. The list of things that can go wrong is endless.

The project manager cannot eliminate all risk factors, but he or she can use techniques to minimize their impact by carefully controlling the project. Project control involves:

- Tracking all facets of the project.
- Reporting progress and problems to appropriate levels of management.
- Handling changes to the project plan once development is underway.
- Adjusting the project plan to compensate for errors in estimates.
- Calling for outside help to strengthen the project team.
- Carefully testing the project before it is implemented.

TRACKING THE PROJECT

The progress of the project must be carefully monitored to assure that tasks are performed and completed on time and within budget. You cannot assume that project development will occur exactly as planned. A project plan is an estimate of how to approach the development of a project. Real-life situations such as a change in a premise of the plan can alter conditions and make a portion of the plan invalid. Regardless of the adversities, the project can remain on course if the project manager remains in total control.

A project manager must institute ways to control every aspect of the project. A *control* is a checks-and-balances technique that compares a planned activity against what has actually occurred. Deviations between the plan and execution of the plan are noted and used to determine if corrective action is necessary.

■ PROJECT PLAN

A control takes many different forms, depending on the aspect of the project that is being controlled. The project plan is a control used to monitor the progress of the project. The original project plan is called the *baseline plan*, which is compared to the execution of the plan.

Let's say the project plan includes a task to interview project stakeholders to determine their expectations on how the completed system will function. This task has a 10-week duration and is scheduled to begin on a particular date.

On the date that the task is scheduled to begin, the project manager reviews the project's progress to determine whether the interviews actually began. If they did, then the project manager monitors the subtasks for that task until the task is completed. If the task did not start on time, the project manager determines the cause, takes corrective action, and if necessary adjusts the project plan going forth.

■ MONTHLY RESOURCE SCHEDULE

Monthly schedules are also controls used by the project manager to determine the availability of resources for current and upcoming tasks. A *monthly resource schedule* lists the allocation of resources for the month. It contains assignments to tasks and times when a particular resource is unavailable.

For example, a human resource may be on vacation or an extended sick leave. A non-human resource may be needed for another project that is behind schedule, or may be undergoing emergency maintenance.

By comparing the monthly resource schedule against the resource assignment schedule for the project, the project manager will identify schedule conflicts. A *schedule conflict* occurs when a resource is assigned to two activities at the same time, such as an extended sick leave and a project task. Schedule conflicts can be remedied by reassigning resources or rescheduling tasks.

■ BUDGET CONTROL

Budget controls must be instituted at the start of the project. A *budget control* is a way of comparing the estimated budget for the project, called a *baseline budget*, to actual expenses. The project manager prepares the baseline budget as a component of the project plan. Once the project is launched, the accounting department uses the baseline budget as the basis for a monthly budget status report. The *monthly budget status report* lists:

- Funds allocated to the project (baseline budget).
- Actual expenses.
- Amortized expenses and available funds.

Funds allocated to the project is the aggregate approved estimated budget. This is similar to the opening balance in your bank account. *Actual expenses* are funds paid, similar to withdrawals from the bank account. *Amortized funds* are reserved funds designated for anticipated expenses such as paying for resources assigned to future tasks. This is like reserving funds in your bank account for your monthly rent for the rest of the year. *Available funds* are the funds that haven't been allocated for future expenses and that can be used for any expense, similar to your bank balance after you have paid all your bills for the month.

A word of caution: budget controls are not necessarily accurate. For example, actual expenses reflect an expense paid by the "as of date" of the report and do not necessarily reflect an up-to-date status.

Let's say the "as of date" of the report is June 30th, but the report is distributed to you July 15th. It took two weeks to prepare the report. Therefore, you must realize the available funds stated in the report do not include expenses paid between June 30th and July 15th.

The monthly budget status report is informative, but may not directly correspond to the budget component of the project plan. The project plan identifies costs per task while the monthly budget status report identifies cost as an expense item.

For example, the project plan states that a particular task might cost $10,000. The monthly budget status report might show $2,000 being paid to a consultant, $3,000 to an employee's salary account, and $5,000 for facilities.

It is the responsibility of the project manager to correlate both the project plan and the monthly budget status report to be sure the per-task costs are on track.

In addition, the project manager must review each expense item in the monthly budget status report to determine whether each expense was actually incurred by the project. It is common for expenses associated with other projects to be charged to your project's cost center. Unless such an error is identified and corrected by the accounting department, the project could exceed its budget.

■ RESPONSIBILITY FOR MONITORING

The project manager has the responsibility for monitoring controls to assure that the project is going along as planned. However, the project sponsor and other stakeholders will also be monitoring the project using reports from sources other than the project manager, such as the monthly budget status report.

A control is like a newspaper in many regards. It reports facts, but it doesn't provide information to interpret those facts. Stakeholders can inadvertently be misinformed about the project, which can have far-reaching ramifications.

Let's say the monthly budget status report shows that the project is 30% over the estimated budget. This can happen if the available funds are in the negative due to an erroneous charge against the project's cost center. Stakeholders, including the project sponsor, could feel the project is in trouble based on the report long before the project manager realizes the error.

Therefore, the project manager must be proactive. It is imperative that all reports on the project that are generated by someone other than the project manager be carefully reviewed and validated immediately by the project manager. Any discrepancies must be thoroughly investigated and the results forwarded to the project sponsor and, if appropriate, to any stakeholder who received the report.

The project manager must pay particular attention to any control monitored only by a member of the project team. It is common for a project manager to delegate the task of monitoring a control to a subordinate, as in the case of the monthly budget status report. The subordinate is responsible for reviewing the details and identifying and resolving discrepancies in the report. A summary of the status is supplied to the project manager and the project manager handles any exceptions the subordinate cannot resolve.

Delegating authority frees the project manager to deal with non-routine issues. However, there is a risk that the project manager might not be presented with an accurate picture of the situation if the subordinate misinterprets facts or considers a major issue a minor one.

The ultimate responsibility for accurately stating the project status rests with the project manager and not the subordinate. Any information provided by the subordinate must be reviewed for reasonableness and challenged for accuracy. Only when the project manager is comfortable defending the report should the information be passed along to the project sponsor or stakeholders.

PROJECT REPORTING

The role of a project manager running a project is similar to that of a ship's captain in the Navy. He or she is given a mission and expected to develop a mission plan, enlist a crew, and embark toward the destination. Although the chief of naval operations (the project sponsor) expects the mission to be completed according to plan, he or she also expects periodic status reports directly from the captain.

The same holds true for a project manager. The mission is to transfer the project sponsor's idea into reality and the mission plan is the project plan. During the development of the system, the project manager must provide the project sponsor, stakeholders, and the executive committee with progress reports.

A *progress report* communicates the current status of the project as it compares with the project plan. Beyond this brief definition, a progress report can take on a variety of formats depending on the needs and expectations of the report's audience.

The simplest form of a progress report is a brief verbal comment. The project sponsor might ask, "how are we doing?" In response the project manager might say, "on schedule." The response summarizes the status.

The most complex form of a progress report is a comparison between the baseline project plan and actual developments. This kind of progress report is likely to have too much information for the project sponsor to digest to determine whether the project is on course. However, the report has the necessary details for the project manager to monitor the project.

It is the responsibility of the project manager to determine the kinds of progress reports that will be used throughout the development of the project. For each report, the project manager must identify the audience, the type of information necessary for the report, and the timeliness of the report.

The *audience for a report* consists of the people who will read the report. The project manager must ask who needs to monitor the progress of the project. A list of stakeholders will come to mind and should be noted.

The type of information necessary for each report determines the type of data presented and the level of detail required by the audience. For example, the project team requires a report that shows the resource schedule for the month. However, the project sponsor might require higher-level detail, such as a count of proposed and actual low-level tasks scheduled for the month.

The project manager can determine the type of information to include in a report by reviewing the audience list. For each person on the list the project manager must ask, "what information does the person need to monitor development of the project?" It is wise to consult the project sponsor when answering this question, since he or she has insight into the needs of the stakeholders.

The project manager must determine the level of detail required by each person on the list. It is critical to provide just the level of detail required for the person to perform his or her job. Too few details might not give the person a comfortable feeling about the project, while too many details can lead to questions left better addressed by a lower-level manager.

For example, presenting the monthly resource schedule to the project sponsor invites the project sponsor to evaluate how the project manager is managing resources. Let's say the project manager permits a resource to take a day off before a task is completed. The project sponsor might challenge that approval and probe further with questions that take the focus off the bigger picture. Resources might be reassigned to answer these questions, diminishing productive work on the project.

Timeliness of report determines the frequency of the report. Typically the project sponsor requires monthly budget reports while the project manager should maintain a daily or weekly budget report. It is critical for the project manager to limit the number and frequencies of reports to the minimum required by stakeholders, since otherwise most of the project manager's day will be spent generating reports and responding to questions.

■ AGREEMENT ON REPORTS

Once the project plan is approved, the project manager must meet with stakeholders and identify the reports necessary to monitor the progress of the project. In addition to deciding on the information contained in reports and the frequency of reports, the project manager must also determine other factors. These include:

- Report format.
- Distribution method.
- The method for asking and responding to questions.
- How to handle changes to the report.

The *report format* addresses the layout of the information. Information should be presented in an easy-to-read format in terms and presentation methods the reader can understand. If the project sponsor needs to see the task schedule for the month, the project manager could present the Gantt chart or a calendar of tasks. A Gantt chart is confusing for many people to read; in comparison, the calendar is easier.

Make sure that the format is easily reproducible. Ideally, the report should be automatically generated by Microsoft Project or whatever project management software tools are used for the project. If these standard reports will not suffice, then a template of the report should be created in a word processor or a spreadsheet. A *template* contains text that appears on every copy of the report. Spaces are left empty where updated information can be quickly inserted into the report.

Distribution method is the way the report will be sent to stakeholders. There are a number of common distribution methods. These include:

- Sent by interoffice mail.
- Sent by e-mail.
- Distributed at regular meetings.
- Personally distributed by the project manager or a member of the project team.

The choice of distribution method is dependent on the nature of the report and the audience. For example, the project sponsor might accept receipt through e-mail while the executive committee requires printed copies distributed by a member of the project. Reports to the steering committee might be handed out at weekly meetings.

Methods for asking and responding to questions is the protocol for providing information to a stakeholder that is either not contained or unclear in the report. It is crucial that such a protocol be established immediately, since otherwise inquiries could delay progress.

In some organizations it is common for the project sponsor to bypass the project manager and ask questions directly of a member of the project team. While the informality meets the immediate needs of the project sponsor, it reduces the time the team member has to perform assigned tasks.

The chain of command within the organization should be used as the protocol for inquiries. For example, an executive committee member should ask a question of the project sponsor. The project sponsor and other stakeholders should address inquiries only to the project manager or his or her designate.

■ HOW TO RESPOND TO INQUIRIES

Each report distributed by the project manager is likely to generate a variety of inquiries, ranging from serious concerns to ridiculous questions. It is important that each request be taken seriously, since the manner in which you respond to the inquiry reflects on the perceived quality of the project.

Procedures should be established for responding to questions to assure uniformity. Here are steps that are used by many project managers:

- Log every inquiry, regardless of whether the request is verbal or made in writing. Note the person's name, telephone number, location, date, and the nature of the request.

- Confirm the facts of the request by reading back to the person your understanding of the question.

- Determine the time you have to respond by asking the person for a deadline.

- Tell the person how long it will take you to respond. This is especially important if you must research the question. Don't be intimidated. The person is seeking a correct response, which could require a timely investigation.

- Make it known if priorities must shift to respond to the inquiry. The project team is allocated to development tasks. One or more tasks might need to be put aside to answer the question.

- Make sure proper approvals are received before reallocating resources to respond to the inquiry. The person making the request may not be empowered to change priorities.

- Respond to all inquiries in writing to prevent any misunderstanding.

- Respond on time. If you don't have an answer by the agreed-upon deadline, then provide the person with a status report and a new deadline.

- Restate the question in your response, give your response, and list any assumptions used as the basis for your response.

- Retain a copy of your response for future reference.

■ ROLLUP REPORTS

The number of different reports required to keep stakeholders updated can seem overwhelming at times. However, careful examination will show that all reports are related. The relationship is the source of information.

Raw data about the project are collected and presented in a detailed report. A Gantt chart is a detailed report because it contains tasks, subtasks, resource allocation, and cost for every aspect of the project.

Project reports use the concept called rollup reports to generate the detail required for each stakeholder to monitor the project. *Rollup reports* consist of several reports, each containing a lower level of details than the previous report. A report of the lowest level, such as the Gantt chart, has the fine details of the project. A higher-level report, such as the monthly budget status report, contains a summary of the lowest-level report. Therefore, it can be said that the expense portion of the Gantt chart rolls up to the monthly budget status report.

■ REVIEWING REPORTS BEFORE DISTRIBUTION

A progress report is the project manager's way of letting stakeholders know how well the project is being managed. The report reveals the project manager's triumphs and mistakes. It is critical that the project manager carefully review each report before the report is distributed. The objective is to make sure information in the report reasonably reflects the status of the project.

The project manager must review the report from the viewpoint of each stakeholder. Here are factors that should be considered:

- Compare data contained in previous reports with the current report. You can expect stakeholders to do the same in an effort to determine whether changes in data are reasonable.

- Pay careful attention to values presented in reports. Progress reports tend to be cumulative. For example, the current report shows the current month and previous month's expenses. Make sure the values that appear on previous reports are carried forward in subsequent reports.

- Identify discrepancies, such as a change in data from one month to the next, that are out of line with the project plan. Stakeholders will likely pick up any material discrepancy.

- Address discrepancies in the first page of the report or in a cover letter. It is wise to point out any discrepancy and provide the rationale before stakeholders notice it. In this way, you give the impression of being forthright and reduce the number of inquiries that would be generated by the discrepancy.

- Be honest in all reports. If a discrepancy arose because of an error, then admit that an error has occurred and provide stakeholders with your plan to correct the problem and how you intend to prevent the error from being repeated.

■ WHAT NOT TO INCLUDE IN REPORTS

Take special care when deciding the type of information you provide in a progress report. Data should complement the stakeholders' need for the report. Avoid providing needless information; otherwise you will distract the stakeholder from the purpose of the report.

Let's say the project sponsor needs to review actual vs. estimated budget data for the project. You do not need to include the details of the budget, such as the cost of every resource assigned to every task. This is too much information and clutters the report.

Instead, provide the project sponsor with summary data. Group expenses according to categories such as fixed, variable, and overhead. You could also group expenses by human resources and non-human resources.

By grouping data, you are providing the project sponsor with meaningful information that can be used to chart the financial progress of the project. If you provide detailed information you run the risk that the project sponsor will attempt to take on your role and manage the project.

Avoid giving anyone access to detailed, raw data. Raw data such as detailed cost is meaningless and is open for interpretation. It is the project manager's responsibility to analyze raw data and interpret their meaning to stakeholders.

For example, a programmer on sick leave for a week could cause alarm by giving the impression that his assignments are not being addressed until his return. However, the project manager might have implemented a contingency plan that isn't reflected in the raw data. This seemingly important issue has little or no impact on the project.

The project manager has the job of controlling the flow of project information to stakeholders. Regardless of the demands imposed by stakeholders for data, the project manager must determine who receives which information about the project.

The objective isn't to conceal the progress of the project. Instead, it is to reduce the likelihood that data will be misinterpreted.

CHANGE CONTROL

The project plan reflects specifications based on information provided from stakeholders. However, specifications will likely be modified during the course of development because of a desire for new functionality or to work around a technical problem.

Let's say the project is to build a house. The architect has asked the homeowner for a description of what he or she would like to see in the house. These ideas have been translated into blueprints and a project plan. During excavation the contractor hits a ledge, which must be removed before the excavation is completed. The homeowner is told of the problem and given alternatives to overcome the problem. Simply said, the homeowner is told that changes must be made to the original plan.

Every change that occurs once the project plan is accepted will have a critical impact on development. The change is likely to require new tasks to be added to the project plan, and new tasks require new resources and increases in the estimated project budget.

With such ramifications, the project manager must carefully control changes to the original project specifications; otherwise the project may never be completed. It is the responsibility of the project manager to educate stakeholders on the impact changes have on the development of the project.

■ CHANGE MANAGEMENT

The task of managing changes to a project is called *change management.* Change management requires that protocols be established to initiate and approve changes. These protocols must be established before the project begins and all stakeholders must agree to abide by those rules.

Change management protocols protect the project manager and the integrity of the project from bullies. A bully is a stakeholder who, through loudness or apparent authority, forces his changes to become part of the project plan. It is common for a stakeholder to forward "improvements" to be incorporated into the project plan regardless of the impact those changes have on development. Demands and threats usually rebuff any challenge by the project manager. If the project manager gives in, then he or she has lost control and the project will be in trouble.

In contrast, change management protocols establish ground rules for addressing proposed improvements in a rational and orderly manner. The change must undergo a formal review, and then if it has merit the change is incorporated into the project plan.

■ CHANGE MANAGEMENT PROTOCOLS

Change management protocols define how changes are addressed once the project is under development. The purpose of these rules is to assure the project is not unnecessarily delayed by minor modifications while providing a way to incorporate major enhancements to the project plan.

Here are protocols that can be used to control changes to the project:

- All recommended changes must be made in writing. This begins an audit trail that ends when the recommendation is either accepted or rejected. An *audit trail* documents the sequences of events involving a change in the project plan.

- The project manager must review the recommendation, validate the request, and determine the magnitude of the change along with the advantages and disadvantages of incorporating it in the project plan. Keep in mind that a change is likely to add new tasks and resources and require new funding.

- An approval process must be established. Typically, the project sponsor or the steering committee reviews the project manager's investigation into the request and then makes the decision whether or not to include the change in the project plan.

- A decision must be made to designate someone, usually the project sponsor or the steering committee, to set priorities for the project. Although a change might be approved, it still must be inserted into the project plan. Someone must decide the order in which it is to be developed compared with other tasks.

- The project manager must confirm the decision to make the change by sending a follow-up letter to all stakeholders that identifies the change, the rationale for the change, the alternatives, the date of approval, and the new priority list. In addition, a new schedule and budget must be developed and shared with stakeholders.

CONFIGURATION CONTROL

■ CONFIGURATION MANAGEMENT

Configuration management (CM) concentrates on the management of technology by identifying and controlling the functional and physical design characteristics of a system, and its support documentation. The medium of implementation is a set of tools designed to provide accurate information on what is to be built, what is currently being built, and what has been built in the past. The mission of CM is to support concurrent engineering and to assist management in evaluating and controlling proposed technological changes. Through quality assurance activities CM ensures the integrity of the design and engineering documentation, and supports production, operation, and maintenance of the system.

In configuration management, a baseline is established in each phase of the system's life cycle with well-defined procedures for handling proposed deviations. The initial baseline, known as the *functional* (or *program requirements*) *baseline*, is prepared in the first phase of the life cycle—the conceptual design phase. This baseline contains technical data regarding functional characteristics, demonstration tests, interface and integration characteristics, and design constraints imposed by operational, environmental, and other considerations. Approval is subject to a preliminary design review (PDR).

The advanced development phase produces the second baseline, the *allocated* (or *design requirements*) *baseline*. This document contains performance specifications guiding the development of subsystems and components, including characteristics derived from the system's design. Laboratory or computer simulation may be used to demonstrate achievement of functional characteristics, interface requirements, and design constraints. This baseline is subject to a critical design review (CDR).

The *product* (or *product configuration*) *baseline* is last and includes information on the system as built, including results of acceptance tests for a prototype, supporting literature, operation and maintenance manuals, and part lists. Acceptance is subject to a physical configuration audit (PCA). In addition to these three baselines, other baselines and additional design reviews are frequently needed when complicated systems are involved. Examples are a baseline that defines the initial design and a baseline that defines the detailed design of the system. The transition from one baseline to the next is controlled by design reviews.

The configuration management system ensures smooth transition and provides updated information on the configuration of the system and all pending change requests at all times. To function properly, it should perform the tasks discussed in the following subsections.

■ CONFIGURATION IDENTIFICATION

Configuration identification sets the foundation of the CM system. It starts with the selection of configuration items (CI), both software and hardware, that have one or more of the following characteristics:

- End-use function
- New or modified design
- Technical risk or technical complexity
- Many interfaces with other items
- High rate of future design changes expected
- Logistic criticality

The selection of configuration items is a critical task of systems engineering. Too few configuration items will not provide adequate management control, and too many may overload the system, sparking a waste of time and money.

Next, a coding system is adopted and configuration identification numbers are assigned. These numbers are designed to assist in providing the following information on each configuration item or a lower-level item:

1. Technical requirements which form the basis for detail design. These are provided by *specification numbers*.

2. Identification of the equipment designed and built to the applicable specification. These are provided by *equipment numbers*.

3. Technical descriptions for the equipment and its lower-level items. These are provided by *drawing and part numbers*.

4. Description of the sequence of manufacturing the equipment and its lower-level items. These are provided by equipment and item *serialization numbers*.

5. Change documents. These are provided by *change identification numbers*.

6. Sources of manufacture at all levels. These are provided by *manufacturer's code identification numbers*.

As an example, consider configuration item 123. For this CI, the following identification numbers are defined:

Specification number	SPEC 123
Equipment number	CI 123
Drawing number	123A
Serial number	123 SN5
Manufacturer number	00375
Change identification numbers:	
Engineering change request	ECR 123 N 005
Engineering order	EO 123 N 005

To control the allocation of numbers, they should be assigned from a single point and a standard procedure established to prevent errors in identification.

■ CONFIGURATION CHANGE CONTROL

Configuration change control involves the development of procedures that govern three steps:

1. *Preparation of a change request.* This step requires that a formal change request be prepared and submitted. The initiation of a change can be internal (the project team) or external (the customer, a subcontractor, or a supplier). The change request specifies the reason for the modification and forewarns management of increases in cost, schedule, and risk, as well as changes in quality, contractual arrangements, and system performance. Each change request is assigned an identification number and is evaluated after input is received from all organizational units affected. The principal aim is to collect the relevant data on each proposed change and to assess its expected impact.

   A typical change request form will include the following information:

   • Change request number _____

   • Originator _____

   • Date issued _____

   • Contract or project number _____

   • Configuration items affected by the change _____

   • Type of changes: temporary _____ permanent _____

   • Description of change _____

   • Justification for change _____

   • From serial number _____ through serial number _____

- Priority _____
    - Effect on: Cost _____

        Schedule _____

        Resource requirements _____

        Operational aspects _____

        Timeliness _____

        Quality _____

        Reliability _____

        Compatibility _____

        Life span _____

        Simplicity _____

        Safety _____

        Commonality _____

        Maintainability _____

        Friendliness _____
    - Remarks: Engineering _____

        Marketing _____

        Manufacturing _____

        Logistics support _____

        Configuration management _____

        Other organizational units _____
    - CCB decision: Accept _____ Reject _____

        More information needed _____

        Acceptance date _____

        Rejection date _____

2. *Evaluation of a change request.* A team of experts representing the different organizational functions is responsible for the evaluation of change requests. This team, known as a change control board (CCB) or configuration management board, evaluates each proposed change based on its effect on the form, fit and function of the system, logistics (manuals, training, support equipment, spare parts, etc.), and project cost and schedule. This review leads to a decision to approve or reject the change request, or to reconsider it after more data are collected.

   Changes are classified as either permanent or temporary. A temporary change might be needed for test programs or debugging software. Approval can usually be obtained in a short time compared to a request for a permanent change.

   All information regarding each proposed change is accumulated and analyzed by the change control board, which also functions as a central repository for historical records. The CCB decision is based on cost-effectiveness and risk analysis in which the need for the change and its expected benefits are weighed against implementation and project life cycle costs, its impact on project quality and schedule, and the expected risks associated with implementation.

3. *Management of the implementation of approved changes.* Approved changes are integrated into the design. This is accomplished by preparing and distributing a change approval form or an engineering change order to all parties involved, including engineering, manufacturing, quality control, and quality assurance.

   The CCB is responsible for the pivotal task of conducting a comprehensive impact analysis of each change proposed. A well-functioning change control system assures tight control of the technological aspects of a project. In addition, it provides accurate configuration records for the smooth, coordinated implementation of changes and effective logistics support during the life cycle of the system.

■ CONFIGURATION STATUS ACCOUNTING

This task provides for the updated recording of:

- Current configuration identification, including all baselines and configuration items
- Historical baselines and the registration of approved changes
- Register and status of all pending change requests
- Status of implementation of approved changes

Configuration status accounting provides the link between different baselines of the system. It is the tool that supports the CCB in its analysis of new change requests. The effect of these changes on the current baseline must be evaluated and their relationship to all pending change requests must be determined before a decision can be taken.

■ REVIEW AND AUDITS

This configuration management task provides both the contractor and the customer with the assurance that test plans demonstrate the required performance, and that test results prove conformance to requirements. Functional configuration audit includes a review of development test plans and test results, as well as a list of required tests not performed, deviations from the plan, and waivers. In this task, the relationship between quality assurance and configuration management is established. Configuration management provides the baselines and a record of incorporated and outstanding changes. Quality assurance first checks the configuration documentation to gauge requirements; then it verifies that the system conforms to the approved configuration.

Configuration management is a tool designed to help the project team know what they are developing, producing, testing, and delivering so that the appropriate support and maintenance can be given to the product throughout its life cycle. It specifies the procedures and information required for the project to be carried out in the most cost-effective manner.

COMPRESSING THE PROJECT SCHEDULE

Changes to a project tend to extend the length of the project schedule, unless new tasks can be slotted for slack time. However, conditions beyond the control of the project manager and of the project sponsor may prohibit extending the duration of the project.

Let's say a project is designed to make the organization compliant with a new law. The law establishes a deadline after which organizations failing to comply will risk substantial fines. The project plan must be modified if a critical component was overlooked, but the additional work must be performed within the projected duration of the project.

It is the project manager's responsibility to make sure all the tasks, including new tasks, are performed on time and within budget and work perfectly. At first glance it appears that the project manager is between a rock and a hard place, especially if existing tasks are dependent on new tasks. While the organization is likely to increase funding, there is no latitude in the project schedule.

Project managers employ various compressing techniques to deal with such situations. A *compressing technique* is a method of shortening the duration of the project. When new tasks must be incorporated into the project plan, the project manager begins by determining the projected length of the project and each task.

The existing project plan is used as a baseline. Adjustments are made to the plan to include new tasks, with the assumption that the duration of the project can be extended. The duration of the adjusted plan is compared with the baseline plan to determine the increase in duration caused by the changes. The increased duration is the amount of time that must be subtracted from the adjusted project plan.

Attention must be directed to tasks on the critical path, since adjustments to these tasks affect the duration of the project. Each critical path task must be examined to determine several factors:

- Is the task critical to meet the project's objectives?
- Can the task be postponed to a later phase of the project?
- Is the duration of the task correctly calculated?
- Can the task be performed more efficiently than planned?
- Will the allocation of additional resources reduce the duration of the task?

Answers to these questions help to determine whether adjustments can be made to the task. These adjustments might be sufficient to compensate for the increased duration caused by new tasks.

A word of caution: don't shortchange the project by unnecessarily adjusting tasks. If an adjustment can be implemented without affecting the quality of the project, then adjust the project plan. Avoid making adjustments simply to compensate for the increased duration. That is, if 10 days are required to complete a critical path task, don't reduce the duration if it affects the quality of the task.

After reviewing tasks on the critical path, the project manager must review the phases of the project. A phase is typically a major functional component of the project. Phases must be redefined if a reexamination of tasks does not compensate for the increased duration of the project.

SUBCONTRACTING

An alternative to developing a project with an in-house staff is to use the services of an outside contractor. An *outside contractor* is an organization that takes over responsibility to complete all or a portion of the project.

Employing the services of an outside contractor is sometimes called *subcontracting*. A *contractor* is a person who agrees with a user, such as the project sponsor, to deliver the project within time and budget constraints. The contractor can hire a staff member or another contractor to fulfill his or her obligation to the project sponsor. A *subcontractor* is another control hired by the contractor to perform specific tasks on the project.

The role of a subcontractor is to provide resources and fulfill tasks of a project. These resources span the full breadth of skills from a technician to the full project team. Some subcontractors will also take over complete responsibility for developing and maintaining the system. This is referred to as outsourcing.

The advantage of using a subcontractor is that the project manager can delegate responsibility for the development of one or more tasks. It is the subcontractor's responsibility to develop a plan and hire resources to perform the tasks according to the specifications of the contractor. The subcontractor is paid a fee for this service.

Let's say the project requires the installation of a computer network. The contractor who is the project manager establishes specifications, then hires a subcontractor to perform the installation. Acquiring resources and managing the installation is the subcontractor's responsibility. The project manager is satisfied if the work is performed on time and according to specifications.

The disadvantage of using a subcontractor is the lack of control the project manager has over how the task is performed. This is similar to bringing your car to a car dealer for repairs.

You specify the task you want to be performed and the car dealer specifies the price you'll pay for the dealer to complete the task. You have little influence over how the car dealer repairs your car.

■ THE CONTRACT

Subcontractors formally agree to work on a project by signing a contract with the contractor, usually the organization completing the project. The *contract* is a legal document that specifies the terms of the agreement.

The terms of the agreement should clearly identify the expectations of both the contractor and the subcontractor. Any item excluded from the contract is not binding. Let's say the contractor hired a subcontractor to build front steps to a house. The contractor never specified the materials to use in the contract and the subcontractor used customary materials; that is, materials used on similar houses. The contractor is not in a position to void the contract since the subcontractor complied with the terms of the contract. *Voiding the contract* terminates the agreement based on a violation of contract terms.

Legal advice is always required when a subcontractor is hired for a project. This assures that the contract clearly identifies the needs of the project manager. Here are factors that should be in every contract:

- Specifically identify what the subcontractor is to deliver. This is the specification of the task.
- Define standards for acceptances. This factor clearly states how you will determine whether the task is completed according to specifications.
- Set the deadline for completion of the task.
- Identify milestones that show progress and set deadlines for each milestone.
- Identify any constraints within which the task must be performed.
- Identify where the work will be performed. Tasks may be completed at the subcontractor's site.
- Identify the price to be paid to the subcontractor.
- Identify the method of payment. Some subcontractors may require progress payments.
- Identify reasons the contract can be terminated, such as if one or more tasks are not performed or if the project is no longer required by the organization.
- Identify financial settlements if the contract is terminated before the task is completed. Some subcontractors expect payment for all or part of the agreed-upon price as a termination fee.
- Identify any penalties for late deliveries or for tasks that don't pass the acceptance test.
- Identify any bonus paid if the task is completed sooner than the deadline.
- Identify how disagreements are to be handled. Some subcontractors prefer to have binding arbitration rather than take legal action. *Arbitration* is a process whereby a disinterested third party, called an *arbitrator*, hears facts in a dispute, then decides a settlement. *Binding arbitration* is where both parties agree before the hearing to abide by the decision.

■ SELECTING A SUBCONTRACTOR

Selecting a subcontractor for a project is a critical decision since the project manager is turning over to the subcontractor responsibility to develop a major component of the project. If the subcontractor fails to deliver a perfectly working component on time, then the entire project is at risk.

There is no guarantee that a subcontractor will deliver according to agreed-upon terms in the contract. Each time a subcontractor is hired, the project manager takes a risk that the subcontractor will not deliver as promised.

The project manager can take steps to reduce the risk by following the procedure below for choosing a subcontractor:

- Clearly define the role of the subcontractor. Ask yourself, "what do I want the subcontractor to do?"

- Formulate a request for proposal that states the subcontractor's role in the project and any constraints within which he or she must perform.

- Develop a list of qualified subcontractors. The list should include those subcontractors whose work is known to you and the organization.

- The request for proposal should be distributed to qualified subcontractors. Be sure to establish a due date 20 days after the request is sent.

- Subcontractors will submit proposals. A proposal should be held in abeyance until the due date so all proposals can be compared.

- One or more stakeholders must evaluate each proposal. Typically, the project manager and the project sponsor review proposals and select the subcontractor based on the proposal.

- Contract terms are negotiated with the selected subcontractor.

■ EVALUATING A PROPOSAL

Each proposal must be evaluated based on objective criteria to assure that the best possible subcontractor is hired for the project. Criteria can be divided into categories:

- Overall cost. The cost of a proposal is the sum of all charges specified in the proposal. Some subcontractors purposely avoid including a total cost amount in the proposal. Instead, they provide itemized costs based on various ways in which they approach the task. This gives the subcontractor flexibility to change the final cost based on negotiations with the contractor. It is the responsibility of the project manager to establish a bottom-line cost for each proposal by clarifying issues with the subcontractor.

- Level of risk. The project manager must assess the risk of adopting the proposal. He or she must answer the question, "what is the likelihood that the subcontractor is able to fulfill promises made in the proposal?"

- Determine performance measurements. The project manager must answer the question, "how will I know if the subcontractor is fulfilling promises made in the proposal once the subcontractor is hired?"

- Responsiveness and flexibility. Is the subcontractor willing to respond to changes in the specifications of the task? A subcontractor should be a team player and be able to bend rules to meet the needs of the project manager and project sponsor. This is similar to a car dealer who is willing to squeeze your car into his schedule without you having to make an appointment.

- Accountability. Some proposals are carefully worded to relieve the subcontractor of any responsibility. It is critical that there exist clear lines of accountability in the proposal; otherwise the project manager can easily lose control over components assigned to subcontractors.

- Knowledge transfer. Skills and information about the component gathered during its development must be transferred to the project team once the subcontractor delivers the component. Subcontractors at times prefer not to transfer skills and knowledge to the project team; instead, they use this information as leverage to increase their participation in the project.

■ DUE DILIGENCE

Analysis of all the proposals submitted by subcontractors should narrow the search to one or two potential candidates. Before entering into negotiations with a subcontractor, the project manager and the project sponsor must perform due diligence. *Due diligence* is the detailed evaluation of a subcontractor.

It is at this point in the evaluation process when the project manager must decide that this is a person with whom the organization can do business. The due diligence process formally qualifies the subcontractor and determines if he or she can deliver on promises in the proposal. Not all subcontractors can fulfill their promises.

Let's say a subcontractor submits a bid to design and install a computer network. The proposal appears solid. However, the subcontractor may not have the necessary resources on staff to handle the job. This means that the project manager is taking a chance that, instead of hiring the services of a proven team of network engineers, the subcontractor will find resource in time to start the job.

The due diligence process addresses the following factors:

- Viability of the subcontractor. Is the subcontractor capable of performing the contract? The subcontractor should have been in business for at least three years and have proven experience working on similar projects and similar-sized clients. The project manager must independently verify these facts.

- Financial stability. The subcontractor must be financially sound. He or she must have sufficient funds to pay bills without depending on payment from your organization. For example, the subcontractor must be able to continue to work on the project while you are processing a progress payment. Small subcontractors may not be able to meet their payrolls without financing from the client.

- Credibility. Is the subcontractor credible? This isn't an easy question to answer. The project manager must look for clues, such as whether or not terms in the proposal are clear and straightforward. A background check can also elicit information about the credibility of a subcontractor. Every statement he or she makes must be independently verified.

- Contractual compliance. Has the subcontractor ever failed to deliver on a previous contract? If a background check proves this true, then eliminate the subcontractor from consideration.

Various resources can be used in the due diligence process. Typically the organization's financial department can review credit and bank records. The legal department searches for judgments and other legal problems the subcontractor might have faced. The project manager, project sponsor and project team members can use their industry contacts to provide background information on the subcontractor.

■ MANAGING A SUBCONTRACTOR

The project manager must establish a working relationship with the subcontractor once the agreement is signed. Ground rules must be established to assure a free flow of information between the project team and the subcontractor's team to prevent a chaotic situation that could impede the project.

In addition to opening communication channels, the project manager needs to institute project controls that enable the project manager and project sponsor to monitor the progress of the subcontractor. The contract should specify deliverables and milestones similar to those used in the project plan.

A system of deliverables and milestones is the formal method used to monitor the subcontractor. The project manager should also impose informal monitoring techniques, such as visits to the subcontractor's site.

The project manager needs to maintain a friendly but professional relationship with the subcontractor. Nothing should interfere with the project manager's objective assessment of the subcontractor's performance.

Before the first deliverable is due, the subcontractor should have established a working pattern that indicates signs of progress. Questions must be raised if the subcontractor appears disorganized or seems as if he or she is not going to meet the deadline for the deliverable. Any concern must be immediately voiced so the subcontractor has an opportunity to remedy the situation before the deadline. The project manager must keep in mind that a missed deadline by the subcontractor reflects on the project manager's ability to properly manage the project.

If the subcontractor misses a contractual deadline, the project manager needs to confer with the project sponsor to determine whether the organization should break relations with the subcontractor and institute a contingency plan. As a general rule, it is better to dismiss a subcontractor immediately than to allow substandard performance.

OUTSOURCING

There has been a widespread interest by organizations to reduce internal responsibility for the development, implementation, and maintenance of systems by using the technique of outsourcing. *Outsourcing* is the assignment of responsibility for a function of the organization to an outside organization.

Let's say a real estate investment group owns a chain of shopping malls. The group's objective is to realize a return on its investment. However, someone must manage the day-to-day operations of the mall. There are two ways to handle operations: hire a staff or outsource the responsibility to a real estate management firm.

Payroll processing is another common functionality that is outsourced by many organizations. Instead of maintaining a payroll staff and related systems, the organization sends payroll information to an outside organization.

■ ADVANTAGES OF OUTSOURCING

Outsourcing offers the organization advantages over performing the functionality with its own staff. The benefits are:

- The outside firm provides expertise that is not available in-house.
- The functionality is performed more efficiently and at times is more cost-effective because the outside firm is likely providing the same service to other customers. The organization benefits from economy of scale.
- The organization foregoes the purchase of expensive equipment needed to perform the functionality. In addition, collateral costs such as facilities and staff are not incurred.
- Upgrades to and maintenance of the operation are the responsibility of the outside firm. That is, if the operation fails for any reason, the outside firm must fix it at its own cost. The organization can focus resources on its own business operations rather than on ancillary functions such as system development.
- Cost for the function is reduced while maintaining the same level of service. The outsourcing firm is likely to have lower expenses in areas such as employee benefits than the organization.
- The functionality can be purchased on an as-needed basis. For example, a payroll service is likely to charge per payroll check. As head count is reduced, so is the need for the payroll service and thus the cost is decreased.
- An organization can implement solutions that use unproven technology without being exposed to the risk of a large investment in the new technology.
- There is no increase in staff to the organization, yet its functionality is increased.

- The cost of the functionality is fixed for a time period and is predictable.
- There is accountability based on the performance of the outside firm.
- Agreement between the organization and the outside firm can be reviewed frequently and terminated if service drops below acceptable levels.

■ DISADVANTAGES OF OUTSOURCING

Outsourcing also has drawbacks that could make using an in-house staff more advantageous to the organization than using the services of an outside firm. Here are the disadvantages of outsourcing:

- Cost of outsourcing could increase in the long term beyond the expectations of the organization. As the outside firm learns more about an organization's business, it is in the position to sell the organization more services. The objective of the outside firm is to increase revenue by taking over more of the functionality of the organization.
- Added charges beyond that specified in the outsourcing contract are likely to be incurred. Simply said, items not included in the contract will cost the organization a premium to add to the project. For example, management of the real estate investment group in the previous example can open the mall on Sunday by issuing a directive to the mall manager. However, they'd likely need to reopen negotiations with an outside management firm if management of the mall is outsourced.
- In-house staff loses expertise to perform the functionality. The outside firm is not going to train an organization's in-house staff to perform the outsourced function. This is similar to taking your car to a mechanic for repair. The mechanic will fix your car, but won't show you how to fix it.
- There is limited possibility to measure the quality of the function. Quality control rests with the outside firm. For example, you don't know if the mechanic fixed your car with used or new parts. All you know is the car was broken when you gave it to him and it worked when the car was returned.
- There is a greater risk in continuity of service. Your organization is dependent on the smooth operation of the outside firm. Let say the outsourcing firm falls on bad economic times and loses skilled staff. Service to your organization may suffer and you may have limited recourse.
- Switching to a new outside firm can be costly. The organization's records must be moved to a new firm and may require retrofitting to conform to the way the new outsourcing firm conducts business.
- Your organization may develop a morale problem. Staff members who provide the outsourced function will feel they are being replaced and their future with the organization is in doubt. Others in the organization will feel that their functionality is next to be outsourced.

■ MANAGING THE OUTSOURCING PROCESS

Organizations that decide to outsource functionality must carefully examine the advantages and disadvantages before announcing their intentions to the staff. If it is decided that outsourcing is advantageous, then a search must be conducted for an outsourcing firm. The same procedures used to select a subcontractor, mentioned earlier in this section, are used to find an outsourcing firm.

Particular attention must be given to the terms of the contract with the outside firm, for factors that are loosely defined can add to the expense of the service. Terms must be explicit and not subjective.

For example, the contract might require the outside firm to produce the same quality service that the organization currently experiences. What is the current quality of service? Managers within the organization know it when they see it, but this is insufficient for an outsourcing contract. Instead, the current quality of service must be defined in measurable terms that can be tested against the performance of the outsourcing firm.

There is a danger of being too specific in an outsourcing contract. The outside firm will explicitly meet every term in the contract. However, it is not under any obligation to meet terms that are not included in the contract.

Let's say your organization hires a building maintenance firm to maintain building facilities. The agreement calls for the firm to repair the air conditioning unit when necessary, and requires the outside firm to use only original parts for any repairs made to the unit. The air conditioning unit fails and the part is back ordered. The outside firm is unable to make the repair although a secondary market replacement part is available immediately.

■ TRANSFER EMPLOYEES

In addition to contract terms, the organization must decide how to handle the transition from providing service with an in-house staff to receiving service from the outsourcing firm. Typically, the outsourcing firm requires knowledge of your organization that is available only from your existing staff. It is in the best interest of both organizations for key members of your organization to join the outsourcing firm. It is your responsibility to make such a transfer attractive to employees. Here is a procedure that encourages a successful transfer.

- Identify in-house staff whom the outsourcing firm needs to fulfill its contract with your organization.
- Determine the current and future benefits these employee have with your organization. This should include salary, bonus, working conditions, working hours, commuting, insurance, vacations, retirement benefits and other such benefits.
- Compare those benefit with offerings of the outsourcing company.
- Determine for each employee whether the benefits of the outsourcing company are sufficient to encourage him or her to transfer to the outsourcing firm.
- Plan to include in the contract an equalization clause if benefits from your firm are better than those of the outsourcing firm. Let's say your firm offers a 20% bonus each year and the outsourcing firm does not. Your firm can reimburse the outsourcing firm for the bonus as long as your employees work on your account.
- Address all discrepancies between the benefits of both firms before publicly announcing the outsourcing agreement.
- Discuss the possibility of outsourcing on a one-to-one basis with in-house staff whom you desire to transfer to the outsourcing firm. Explain how the change will affect their livelihood and how you intend to equalize benefits. Seek out the employees' opinions on transferring to the outsourcing firm. Identify any objections.
- Devise a plan for addressing each objection.
- Ask the outsourcing firm to introduce its firm and culture to employees who are targeted to leave your firm.
- Consider asking the outsourcing firm to offer your staff a signing bonus, which is reimbursed as part of the contract.
- Make the transfer between your firm and the outsourcing firm seamless. For example, sublet facilities and equipment currently used to support the function in-house to the outsourcing firm. This makes the transfer process a paper transfer and not a physical transfer. Today those are your employees. Tomorrow the outsourcing firm employs them; however, they work at the same desk, have the same telephone number, and perform the same duties.

STANDARDS, QUALITY ASSURANCE, TESTING, DELIVERY, AND MAINTENANCE

A key to the success of any project is to establish standards before development begins, and then stringently enforce those standards throughout the life of the project. A *standard* is a rule that if followed reduces the risk of errors and increases the quality of the final project.

It is the project manager's responsibility to create standards for the project team based on his or her experience with similar projects. A standard in every project is to require that another person review each completed low-level task before the task is logged as completed on the project plan.

Let's say a surveyor stakes a building site. After he completes the job, a foreperson should examine the stake positions to double-check the accuracy of the work. The foreperson does not re-survey the site. Instead, he or she compares the stake positions to the plans and determines whether they reasonably reflect the architecture's design.

Another common standard is for a resource to verify the quality of a predecessor's task before beginning work on the new task. This helps to identify problems before they snowball into a complex maze.

For example, building a brick wall requires that cement be properly mixed before bricks can be assembled. The mason should inspect the consistency of the cement before applying it to the bricks. If the cement isn't correct, then the mason doesn't start the task and reports the problem to the resource responsible for mixing the cement. Problems with the cement could have grave repercussions if the mason proceeded with his task and used the inferior cement.

Total quality management is a philosophy that imposes the standard that everyone on the project team is responsible for the quality of the entire project. Under this philosophy, each team member must offer and accept constructive criticism.

■ TESTING

A standard required of every project is to make sure all components are well tested before the project is implemented. Testing is a tedious, time-consuming job that is seen at times to excessively delay the project. While this can be true, testing is also the task that assures that the project works perfectly.

There are various kinds of testing that must be conducted at all levels of development. The initial test is called a unit test. A *unit test* is performed by a resource to assure that a task is completed as expected. This is similar to checking your math when balancing your checkbook.

The next level of testing is an *integrated test* where related tasks that pass the unit test are tested together.

Let's say the project is to build and install new windows in a building. Two tasks are building the window and installing the window. Once the window is built, the window is tested at the factory. If it works, the window is shipped to the job site.

Likewise, at the site a carpenter builds the window frame and checks measurements to be sure it conforms to specifications. If it passes this test, then the window is installed into the window frame. The window is then tested after installation as an integrated test.

Changes to specifications can be introduced any time during development. Changes enhance the performance of the project, but also introduce new problems. A third level of testing is conducted to identify these problems. This is called regression testing. A *regression test* is a series of procedures to test every aspect of the project to be sure everything works properly after changes are made to the project.

Return to the construction site example. Let's assume the homeowner wanted a larger front door and the doorframe is widened to accommodate the change. The carpenter should retest the windows on the wall to be assured changes to the doorframe didn't have an effect on the windows.

The systems test is the next level of test that must be performed. A *systems test* requires that all components of the project be tested after they are assembled together, somewhat like a shake-down cruise for a new ship. There should be very few problems discovered by a systems test if unit testing, integrated testing, and regression testing are rigorously performed.

There are two additional tests. These are an acceptance test and a parallel test. An *acceptance test* is one in which the fully developed project is turned over to stakeholders. Until the acceptance test, all testing is conducted from the technical perspective. That is, developers are testing to determine if all specifications have been met.

An acceptance test is conducted from the user's perspective. Stakeholders simulate normal business operations using the new system. This is similar to the homeowner inspecting his new home.

A *parallel test* is where the new system runs concurrently with the existing system to assure that the results are the same. Let's say the project team developed a new way to record sales for a supermarket, using scanners and automatic price checking. The current system requires the cashier to enter prices by hand and to check prices in a pricing book.

In a parallel test, one checkout counter uses the new method and another the old method. The same basket of groceries is checked out using both registers. The results are compared to determine if discrepancies exist. If they do, an investigation is conducted to explain the differences and changes are made to the new system, if necessary.

However, if the results are the same, then the new system is ready to be migrated and to replace the existing system.

Observations from MIT

- Fixing a problem has nearly a 50% chance of causing another problem.
- Old problems that were fixed tend to reappear after enhancements are made to a system.
- New problems are identified as more people use the system.

■ ACCEPTANCE TESTING

Acceptance testing is a critical period in the project's life cycle because this is when stakeholders have an opportunity to work with the complete system. This is similar to when you are given the keys to test-drive your new car.

The project manager must take an active role in designing and implementing the acceptance test. The sole objective is to satisfy the stakeholder. There should be no surprises because the systems test should have identified any lingering problems, which should be resolved before the acceptance test.

Guidelines for the acceptance test must be developed in coordination with stakeholders to assure that the acceptance test is conducted accurately. These guidelines are typically the same as those used for the systems test.

Let stakeholders prepare the guidelines with your help. Stakeholders will develop a feeling of ownership in establishing the criteria. Your guidance ensures that the test criteria are realistic and achievable. Ideally, the guidelines for the acceptance are prepared before project development begins so that the project manager and stakeholders clearly have an objective measurement to judge the outcome of the project.

Stakeholders may be hesitant on setting firm criteria before development begins because changes made during development might alter the test criteria. In such a case, try to establish general guidelines with an agreement to follow up with details before the systems test begins.

The project manager must distribute the guidelines for the acceptance test to all stakeholders and to the project team. Guidelines help developers know whether their work is on target and reinforces the standard that must be met.

Guidelines must specify a time restriction for conducting the test. A time restriction is similar to duration of a task. Stakeholders must complete the acceptance test within a mutually agreed-upon time period; otherwise acceptance testing can drag on forever.

Subjectivity must be removed from the acceptance test. Only measurable criteria should be used to determine whether the project has met stakeholder expectations. For example, it isn't sufficient for the homeowner to casually stroll around the new house to determine the acceptability of the house. Instead, there should be a checklist (guidelines) that requires the homeowner to open and close windows and doors, test the air conditioner and heater, run water through every faucet and drain, flush all toilets, and to park his or her car in the garage. Each component either works or doesn't work. If they work, then the house is acceptable to the homeowner.

Keep in mind that an acceptance test may need to be conducted more than once if new changes are required. No changes are made once the acceptance test is completed successfully. Changes after the acceptance test become a new project.

Special guidelines must be developed if the project is a computer system used at a different location. In such a case, the acceptance test must include site testing. A *site test* involves testing the system at each location. Equipment could be different at each site and could therefore inhibit the system from operating properly.

MIGRATION

After testing is completed, the project moves into the final stages of development called migration. *Migration* is the process of replacing the current system with the new system. Although the term "system" is closely associated with computer application, it also refers to a way of doing something such as selling a house, buying stocks, or building an airplane.

Careful preparations must be made before migration can take place, for this is the moment when the organization depends on the new system. The project manager is responsible for developing a migration plan.

A migration plan must identify all areas of the organization that will be affected by the new system. Let's assume a new computer payroll system is being migrated. All users of the payroll system need to be trained, the application must be installed on their computers, and data from the existing payroll system must be converted to the format of the new payroll system.

The payroll system might exchange data with other computer systems; for example, it might receive information from a time-clock system and send information to the bookkeeping system. A migration plan must also assure that the data exchange functions properly.

Once all the factors that are affected by the migration are identified, the project manager must select the time to execute the migration plan. Timing is crucial because migration must take place at a time that will have the least impact on the organization.

Typically, migration is scheduled for Friday after business hours. This period gives the project team and support staff until Monday to install and test the new system. If testing does not go well, there is sufficient time to back out the new system and reinstall the old system before start of business Monday.

The migration plan must also contain a migration script. A *migration script* is a procedure that specifies what must be done, by whom, and when, for each minute during the migration period. You can consider the migration script as similar to the steps executed before the launch of the space shuttle. Every step must be executed in order.

■ DECISION MAKING AND CONTINGENCIES

There are a number of critical decisions that must be made during the migration process, and it is the responsibility of the project manager to identify them. Here are the decisions that must be made:

- Setting the cut over date. *Cut over* is the moment when the organization depends on the new system.

- Setting rehearsal dates. Migration is a critical event in the development of a project. Therefore, the project team and support staff must be certain everyone knows his or her role in the migration script. Furthermore, rehearsals will highlight areas overlooked by the migration script.

- Management of the cut over. Who is the person directing the migration?

- How do you determine if the data have been converted properly?

- How will the data be converted? Will it be gradually, i.e., will critical data be converted first? Must all the data be converted during migration?

- Is there any latitude in the cut over date? Is it possible to postpone the cut over date without affecting business operations?

- How much disruption in business operations is acceptable during the cut over? Is it possible to perform some migration activities during the business day?

- Who will decide whether or not the cut over is successful?

- Who will decide if the cut over fails and the recovery plan must be initiated? A recovery plan includes the contingency steps to be taken when the cut over fails.

SUMMARY

The project manager cannot eliminate all risk factors, but can use techniques to minimize their impact by carefully controlling the project. A project manager must institute ways to control every aspect of the project to provide checks and balances that compare planned activities against what has actually occurred. Discrepancies between the plan and execution of the plan are noted and used to determine whether corrective action is necessary.

A control takes many different forms depending on the aspect of the project that is being controlled. The project plan, monthly resource schedule and monthly budget status report are typical controls used on most projects.

A control is like a newspaper in many regards. It reports facts, but it doesn't provide information to interpret those facts. Stakeholders can inadvertently be misinformed about the project by a control, which can have far-reaching ramifications. The project manager must be proactive and carefully review and validate controls, investigate discrepancies, and forward the results to stakeholders.

A progress report communicates the current status of the project, as compared with the project plan, and can take on a variety of formats depending on the needs and expectations of the report's audience. It is the responsibility of the project manager to determine the kinds of progress reports generated and the level of detail required for each.

Each report distributed by the project manager is likely to generate a variety of inquiries ranging from serious concerns to ridiculous questions. It is important that each request be taken seriously since the manner in which you respond to the inquiry reflects on the perceived quality of the project.

It is critical that the project manager carefully review each report before the report is distributed, in order to make sure information in the report reflects the status of the project reasonably accurately.

Every change that occurs once the project plan is accepted will have a critical impact on development. The project manager must carefully control changes to the original project specifications; otherwise the project may never be completed. It is the responsibility of the project manager to educate stakeholders on the impact changes have on the development of the project.

Changes to a project tend to extend the length of the project schedule. Project managers employ various compressing techniques to deal with such situations.

An alternative to developing a project with an in-house staff is to use the services of an outside contractor, sometimes called subcontracting. The role of a subcontractor is to provide resources and fulfill tasks of a project in exchange for a fee. A contract is a legal document that specifies the terms of the agreement between the organization and outside contractor. The terms of the agreement should clearly identify the expectations of both the contractor and the subcontractor. Any item excluded from the contract is not binding.

In addition to assigning specific tasks to an outside contractor, an organization can also transfer complete functionality of one area of the organization, such as its payroll, to an outside firm. This is called outsourcing.

Before development of a project begins, the project manager must establish standards for the project team. Standards ensure that a high quality of workmanship is used in the development of the project. Standards specify that the project undergoes specific tests before the organization becomes dependent on the system.

Once the project team and stakeholders agree that the project meets the specifications of the initial request, then the migration process begins. This process replaces the current system with the new system.

MANAGEMENT CONSIDERATIONS AND CRITICAL SUCCESS FACTORS (CSFs)

Analysis, planning, and control are three cornerstones of project management. The project management process begins when the project manager analyzes the project sponsor's idea that needs to be transformed into reality. Next, a project plan must be created to provide a road map showing how to reach the destination; then controls must be imposed to assure that the project stays the course.

The fourth cornerstone of project management is management of the project team and stakeholders through the development process. Throughout the project the project manager is presented with numerous problems that could impede the success of the project, and it is his or her responsibility to address each problem in a way that will keep progress on the project moving along smoothly.

Problems will vary and can involve every aspect of management, including personnel, finances, political situations, and technical issues. Throughout the project, the project manager is required to identify critical issues, weigh risks, and decide the best alternatives to assure the project's success.

The previous sections explored analysis, planning, and controls. This section discusses management techniques, risk analysis, and how to terminate a project, which are the critical success factors for every project.

THE MANAGEMENT PROCESS

The project manager must recognize early in the project that he or she cannot fulfill the roles of every resource that is required to develop the project, even if he or she has those skills. Projects are developed by a team led by the project manager. The project manager sets the goals, hires the project team, and lets the team do its job, and then coaches team members into reaching the goal.

Being a project manager is similar to being a ship's captain when the ship is docking. The captain stands on the bridge barking out orders to steer and control the speed, but doesn't do those jobs. The helmsman does the steering and the engine room staff controls the speed based on the captain's direction.

It is the responsibility of the captain to gather information about the ship and determine which information is critical to docking, and to ignore the other information. The captain focuses on the objective, then tells the crew the tasks to perform to reach the objective.

The captain must:

- Receive all information.
- Make a correct interpretation of the information.

- Decide which orders to give.
- Properly give those orders to the crew.
- Have trained the crew to properly respond to orders.

The project manager, like the ship's captain, must hone leadership skills that encompass information-gathering skills, analytical skills, communications skills, and people skills. The way in which he or she approaches the management of the project is called a *management style*. A project manager can adopt one of six management styles:

- Boss-centered
- Decision-seller
- Idea-generator
- Straw man
- Suggestion-taker
- Group decision-maker

The *boss-centered* style requires the project manager to study the problem, decide the proper action, and give orders to the project team. Members of the project team have no input into the decision. They simply follow orders and present the project manager with any problems they encounter.

The *decision-seller* style is similar to the boss-centered style in that the project manager is solely responsible for determining how to solve the problem. However, the project manager presents the rationale for his or her solution to the project team in an effort to have the team buy into the solution. The assumption is that team members would have arrived at the project manager's solution had they studied the problem.

Project managers who use the *idea-generator* style of management devise one or more solutions to the problem, then present these solutions to the project team and invite questions. Input from the team becomes a basis for the project manager to reach a decision on which solution to initiate.

The *straw man* style is a twist on the idea-generator style. Instead of presenting alternative solutions to the project team, the project manager adopts a tentative solution and encourages the project team to recommend changes to the solution. The project manager makes the ultimate decision.

The *suggestion-taker* style presents the problem to the project team, then asks the team to propose solutions. The decision on which solution to implement rests with the project manager and not the project team.

The *group decision-maker* style is a modification of the suggestion-taker style. The project team is responsible for making the final decision.

Project managers tend to use all these styles during the life of a project, depending on the nature of the problem. For example, the decision to grant time off to a member of the project team is left solely to the discretion of the project manager. However, hiring a person typically involves input from a variety of people who provide the project manager with opinions. The project manager makes the final decision.

A complex technical problem lends itself better to a group decision—in this case, the project manager presents the problem and leads the group first to explore all possibilities, and then to a consensus. The group, rather than the project manager, makes the final decision. However, a problem that involves how the project team functions is best addressed by the project manager discussing the problem and attempting to sell his or her solution to the team.

Before the project manager decides on a management style to use, he or she must consider the ramifications of that choice. Using a style in which he or she makes the ultimate decision requires the project manager to analyze the problem and identify viable solutions to the problem. These styles enable a quick decision but increase the likelihood of errors in judgment, especially if special expertise, such as technical knowledge, is required to properly analyze the problem.

In contrast, styles requiring group input and decisions tend to reduce the risks of overlooking viable solutions and increase the likelihood that the team will readily accept the solution. However, there are two major drawbacks with these styles. First, discussions extend the time necessary to reach a decision—problems that must be addressed quickly should not be made into a group activity. Group decisions also tend to result in compromises based on group dynamics (see Section 1) and politics rather than the best way to address the problem.

Any management style that involves groups can be used as a shield to avoid accountability. When a project manager decides on a solution, he or she alone is responsible for his or her actions. However, by transferring this responsibility to a group, he or she also transfers accountability to the group.

Some project managers depend on group decisions to lower the risks of making a poor decision. Simply said, the project sponsor blames the project manager if a solution doesn't work properly. The project manager responds by passing blame to the project team, leaving the project sponsor with no one to blame.

Politicians frequently use this technique to remain in office. The art of politics is to avoid accountability by shifting blame to the legislative body—but not to any one legislator. For example, constituents are left blaming Congress, but not their Congressional representatives.

MANAGING PEOPLE

Besides the knowledge required to make a concept into reality by identifying tasks, resources, and finances to support a project, the project manager also needs to be a people-person to manage the project.

A *people-person* is someone who can relate to other people such as stakeholders and the project team. The project manager must have or develop characteristics that make others feel welcome and willing to work with him or her on developing the project.

The project manager must be able to build rapport and earn the confidence of others. The relationship must be open and one that encourages a dialogue. This helps the project manager to convince others to follow his or her plan for developing the project.

Little things, such as the mannerisms below, go a long way toward making any project manager into a people-person:

- Be a good listener.
- Have a warm smile.
- Make others feel important by encouraging them to talk about themselves.
- Become sincerely interested in what someone is saying.
- Remember a person's name.
- Talk about topics of interest to others.
- Use everyday language.
- Build a relationship from common ground, such as family, former employers, or outside interests.
- Deliver on your promises and don't promise anything you cannot deliver.
- Use a comfortable manner during conversations.
- See things from the other person's perspective.
- Be culturally sensitive to global cultures.

■ BUILD CONFIDENCE

Just as you judge stakeholders and the project team, they too are judging you. You are the leader of the project and their careers are in your hands. Every day, stakeholders and project team members have a choice. Stakeholders can refrain from participating in the development of the project or they can lend assistance to you. The project team can give their all to the project or to seek other employment. The choice they make depends on the confidence they have in the project manager. Therefore, it is critical that the project manager does everything possible to assure the success of the project.

Confidence is earned, and building confidence cannot be learned from a book or in school. There are, however, ways in which a project manager can build confidence and avoid behavior that leaves doubts about his or her ability to complete the project.

Here are a few things to do and not do when dealing with stakeholders and the project team:

- Keep good, but not excessive, eye contact with anyone who is speaking to you and to whom you are speaking. Breaking eye contact implies that what is being said isn't important to you. Eye contact conveys honesty. In contrast, too much eye contact gives the impression that you are trying to intimidate.
- Always seem relaxed, regardless of the situation. A calm person is perceived as someone who is in control and confident about how to solve a problem.
- Avoid making exaggerated gestures, since this creates the perception that you are not sincere.
- Avoid showing displeasure. Instead, discuss a negative situation rationally without exchanging harsh words, and then move on to a different topic.
- Always part as friends.
- Avoid arguments.
- Quickly admit when you are wrong.
- Respect the opinion of others.
- Never lose control.

■ KEEP COMMUNICATIONS OPEN

Everyone involved in a project must deal with an array of problems, ranging from those related to the project and the job to personal ones, such as problems arising in the family. Problems can fester and become distorted over time. Sometimes, the more someone thinks about a problem, the harder the problem seems to solve. This is much like a nervous student with an exam—the more times the student reads a question, the harder it becomes to decide on a correct answer.

Many problems can be brought back down to size by sharing them with someone else. However, sharing a problem during project development only occurs if the project manager maintains an open line of communication with stakeholders and the project team.

For example, the project sponsor may be under business pressures to implement a system three months ahead of schedule. This can seem an insurmountable task, especially if the project sponsor is devising solutions based on his or her knowledge of the project. Unfortunately, a project sponsor rarely has the detailed information necessary to determine whether the new deadline can be met. If he or she shares the problem with the project manager, the project manager might be able to adjust the project plan to accommodate the new deadline. What at first seems a critical problem to one person might be a common and easily solved problem for someone else.

Here are factors that help to maintain an open dialogue among the project manager, stakeholders, and the project team:

- Avoid criticizing, since this places the other person on the defensive—instead of discussing an issue, the other person takes a defensive position.
- Don't blow off steam in the presence of anyone. Your anger places others in the room in a difficult position, and some may think your anger is directed at them.
- Always speak in a pleasant tone.
- Give sincere appreciation when someone brings you a problem.
- Don't limit conversations to negative issues. We tend to associate the messenger with the message. If the message constantly contains bad news, we avoid the messenger.

- Be proactive and ask others to help you solve problems. This helps to foster a good team spirit.

- Never tell a person he or she is wrong. Instead, discuss the situation and let the person discover his or her error.

- Let the other person do most of the talking and feel that his or her idea has merit.

- Discuss the problem as a peer rather than as a supervisor. Conduct discussions in a neutral place such as a conference room rather than in your office.

- Always take the high road and avoid finger-pointing, threats, or making personal attacks.

- Take a break if you feel that you or the other person is becoming emotional, but always return to the discussion. Never leave any discussion on a negative point.

Ten Topics to Avoid

Appearances
Personal Hygiene
Clothes
Race
Gender
Ethnic Background
Religion
Age
Politics
Gossip

■ BE TACTFUL AND ETHICAL

The art of being tactful is a skill that every project manager needs to master. Project development frequently causes stressful situations to arise for everyone involved in the project. Simply said, things infrequently go along as planned. Mistakes are made and stakeholders and the project team fall under pressure to get the project back on track. The focal point of their anger is typically the project manager.

Throughout the development process the project manager must remain calm and respond in a tactful and ethical manner. Even in a negative situation there are ways to get your point across without injuring your relationship with stakeholders and members of the project team.

Being tactful and ethical is an art that is honed over time. You learn what to say and what not to say through trial and error. Here are a few tactics that some successful project managers use that you too can adopt as a basis for managing your project.

- Point out mistakes indirectly and let others save face. Let's say you are teaching an adult course and you pepper the class with questions. You have two choices when someone responds with a wrong answer. You can embarrass the person by telling everyone he or she is wrong. You can also say something like, "Let me see if I understand you. Correct me if I'm wrong. You're saying . . ." You use some of the same words the person said, then give the correct answer. The person knows he or she is wrong, but saves face even while you are correcting him or her.

- Point out a person's mistake and relate to how you have made similar mistakes; then show how you corrected yourself. This corrects the error and says, "It's OK to make mistakes as long as you correct them."

- Instead of giving orders, ask leading questions. A *leading question* imbeds the answer in the question. You can ask, for example, "Isn't it true that the computer network won't be able to handle the load of the new system?"

- Encourage attempts to solve a problem. If the attempt fails, then make it seem easy to correct the error. No attempt that fails should be treated as life-threatening.
- Avoid becoming emotionally involved with a situation. You'll tend to substitute your emotional judgment for a judgment based on merit. You won't look objectively at the situation.
- Be quick to recognize achievements of others.
- Avoid words that threaten the security of others.
- Avoid becoming angry. Anger reflects your inability to deal with a situation logically. When you're angry you are less likely to influence lasting change in others than if you tactfully convince others to correct their errors.
- Avoid becoming bogged down in petty disputes.
- Create an environment where others are willing to have an open dialogue and are willing to adopt your suggestions.

While being tactful you still must uphold your personal standards. At times a tactful strategy can appear to be patronizing, which isn't in anyone's best interest. Before taking any action, ask yourself, would I want someone to say this to me? If the answer is no, then change your strategy.

■ MANAGING MEETINGS

Most of a project manager's time is involved in attending meetings, many of which are his or her own meetings. Meetings are the backbone of project development. They are the place where aspects of the project are discussed, facts are reviewed, and decisions are made.

However, meetings are also time-consuming and can be looked upon as inefficient, to a point where key attendees avoid meetings. This leads to discussions being postponed because the right people are not in attendance to make decisions.

Few stakeholders and members of the project team mind attending a meeting as long as it is productive. It is the responsibility of the project manager to design a successful meeting. Here are factors to consider when holding a meeting.

- Set a time limit for the meeting, which should be no longer than an hour.
- Avoid scheduling meetings at the end of the business day.
- Take a break if refreshments are served and if the meeting lasts longer than an hour. Likewise, take a break if the meeting is scheduled immediately following lunch.
- Invite only people who can contribute to the meeting and reschedule the meeting if a key attendee is not present, e.g., if he or she sends a representative instead of attending him- or herself. The substitute is likely not authorized to make decisions. Instead, he or she is there to take notes and report back to the key attendee—and could inadvertently misrepresent information presented at the meeting.
- Create a short agenda and distribute it with the meeting announcement so attendees can prepare to address the topic.
- Make decisions in a meeting as a group. This enables any misunderstandings to be clarified immediately and lets the decision-making process continue.
- Keep the discussion on the topic. Don't let anyone babble without making a point related to the topic.
- Never end a meeting by saying that "We'll reconvene." It is the project manager's responsibility to moderate the meeting so a decision is made there.
- Realize when the meeting is not going well. You'll notice the room becomes quiet, people squirm, the subject is changed, and everyone looks away.
- Ask questions to encourage participation (see Section 1).

- Take notes, write down decisions and send the information to all attendees after the meeting.

- Start the meeting by introducing everyone, make small talk, and explain why you called the meeting. State the objective of the meeting, then place the first issue on the floor for discussion.

- Stop the meeting immediately if everyone isn't in the right mind to address the issue.

- Avoid using catchall phrases. These can lead to misunderstandings and may not convey your intent.

- Clarify terms that have multiple meanings by describing your intent in simple words. If necessary, be prepared to use examples to make your point.

- Repeat your understanding of what is being said. This enables others to correct your interpretation.

- Think of what you want to say before saying it. Pause to give yourself time to formulate your thoughts. If you are unsure of what to say, then remain silent. Your words are similar to a bullet. Once the bullet is fired, you can't take it back even if you make a mistake.

- Present your facts in a way that leads a reasonable person to reach your conclusion.

- Give everyone time to absorb what is being said at the meeting before you call for a decision.

DEALING WITH POLITICS

Political games occur not only in the public arena, but in every organization. Stakeholders who are involved in the project potentially have two political objectives: to advance within the organization and to assist the organization in achieving its objective. In theory both objectives are tied together; in reality, they can work against each other.

The project manager is likely to find him- or herself at the center of organizational politics if the project is used as a tool by some stakeholders to move up the organization's ladder or can be seen as an obstacle to other stakeholders' advancement.

In the public arena, politicians make their political preferences known; it is clear who has thrown his or her hat in the political ring and who has formed political alliances. This is not the case with organizational politics. No one solicits petitions to run for office, nor do they wear campaign buttons. This can make it difficult for the project manager to manage a project.

The degree to which politics is played within the organization is dependent upon the organization's culture. An organization that has a scarcity of powerful positions can expect managers to use political techniques to gain power.

Power is usually defined in two ways: resources and money. A manager who has a large number of resources, both human and non-human, under him or her is perceived as having power within the organization. Likewise, a manager who is responsible for a large portion of the organization's budget is also seen as a powerful person.

Politics also plays an important role in an organization that consistently hires ambitious people who compete with each other to achieve a powerful position. Politics is seen as a way to circumvent published promotion policies and to give candidates a subjective edge for a position. A manager is likely to select a candidate whom he or she perceives as doing a good job. The use of organizational political techniques creates that perception.

Regardless of the reason for organizational politics, the project manager must be able to deal with the political culture. The initial task is to identify politicians within the organization. Current power holders are easily identified because they have the largest number of resources reporting to them and manage the largest portion of the organization's budget.

Up-and-coming politicians are a little less obvious, although they leave clues. They typically imitate the behaviors of those with power, such as dressing in a similar manner. Their objective is to demonstrate that they have the same philosophy as the power holder.

Politicians tend to be manipulators who seek to get people to do things that are to the advantage of the politician, and to achieve results they may make misleading statements and try to embarrass rivals. Therefore, each time a politician gives advice to the project manager, the project manager must determine if the politician is trying to help or hinder the project.

The project manager must be sufficiently secure to be in control of his or her own destiny, while responsible for the project. Politics cannot be used as an excuse for failure of the project. The fate of the project is in the hands of politicians only if the project manager allows this to occur.

Although the project manager wants to take actions that gain him or her acceptance within the organization, he or she must also not lose sight that the project manager alone must make the project sponsor's idea a reality. Regardless of who seems to be championing the project, supporters may swiftly abandon both the project and the project manager if the project seems to be headed for disaster.

■ TYPES OF POLITICIANS

Few if any politicians set their sights on developing a political style. Instead, they tend to learn techniques from those whom they admire (and avoid techniques used by those they disdain), and then create their own style. Organizational politicians tend to fall into one of five categories. These are:

- Machiavellian
- Organizational
- Survivalist
- Straight arrow
- Power brokers

The project manager can better deal with a stakeholder by first categorizing him or her into one of these classifications.

A *Machiavellian politician* is a person who is ruthless and devious in an attempt to grab power, and whose successes are always at the cost of others. He or she is likely to seek revenge towards anyone by whom he or she feels politically injured. The downfall of such a person comes when politics interferes with achieving the organization's objectives. Few in the firm are there to sincerely offer support and instead look to increase his or her likelihood of failure.

An *organizational politician* too has a desire for power, but gains the power without defaming others in the organization. He or she is careful to plot strategy for advancement, but has the ethical and moral sense not to injure anyone in executing the strategy. This type of person tends to remain within the organization even when errors in judgment cause him or her to lose power.

A *survivalist politician* is a person who balances life and a career in the organization. Power within the organization isn't his or her objective. He or she always manages to be in the right place at the right time to take advantage of advancement opportunities, while avoiding making obvious political blunders. For example, he or she may give credit to the boss for a hot new idea that was actually created by the survivalist.

A *straight arrow politician* is someone who feels competency on the job is the best strategy for advancement. He or she has great trust in colleagues to do the right thing by him or her, although he or she avoids making obvious political blunders.

A *power broker politician* projects a powerful image and uses this perceived power to direct activities within the organization. For example, he or she is always willing to help others in the organization and thereby seems to influence their future. If this type of person doesn't have the power to do something, he or she knows how to have the person who does have power do what he or she requests. The power broker has the power to influence decision makers and withhold scarce resources, having gained this power over the years through friendship and knowledge.

◼ PLAYING THE POLITICAL GAME

Any project is a pawn in organizational politics, because a successful project is likely to bring the project sponsor and those associated with the project new power. Likewise, a project's failure is a tool for opponents to defeat the project sponsor and others associated with the project.

The project manager is in the middle of this political maneuvering and is forced to participate in the political game simply to survive in the job. The skill at playing the political game usually determines whether the project manager is successful in delivering the project on time, within budget, and in perfect working condition.

The rules of organizational politics are simple to understand. Everything is a competition in which prizes are given only to winners. The prize in an organization is power and money. Your job is to win the trust and respect of the winners and to band together to support each other against those politicians who want the project to fail.

Because politics often get in the way of developing a successful project, it is the project manager's responsibility to neutralize their effects on the project. *Neutralizing* means to remove ammunition with which the opposition can attack the project. Here are common techniques used to neutralize an opponent:

- Identify persons who are opposed to the project.

- Determine the reasons why they feel the project isn't to their advantage.

- Establish objective measurements to gauge the project's progress, such as established dates for deliverables. No one can complain if you deliver as promised.

- Make sure all stakeholders, including the opposition, agree to the measurement.

- Place all agreements and progress reports in writing. This provides an audit trail that shows that opponents agreed with your plan.

- Never hedge your comments. Speak directly and truthfully so that the opposition is unable to catch you in a lie that would discredit you.

- Distribute a memo to all stakeholders to clarify all rumors that you hear about the project. Opponents commonly use the organizational rumor mill to distribute misinformation about the project. Usually the rumor is based on half-truths that are sufficient to convince a reasonable person to believe the rumor is truthful.

- Make sure everyone on your project team supports the project rather than individual people who may oppose its success. Opponents typically attempt to recruit support from within a project team so they can receive inside information.

- Be prepared to defend any action you take. Make sure that you have a solid rationale for your decisions.

- Verify the sources of information on which you base your decisions. Ask yourself, why is this person telling me this? Make sure the information isn't being used to cause you to make an error that will be exploited by the opposition.

- Meet with anyone who directly attacks you or the project and ask that person what is troubling him or her. Be forthright and describe your concerns. Bring supporting documents too if you believe that he or she is trying to sabotage the project. Show the person how his or her action will affect the project and the organization, and then ask for suggestions to get him or her to support the project.

◼ MAKING POLITICAL MOVES

Political risks must be evaluated before any action is taken. For example, don't assume that your conversation with anyone is confidential. Chances are good that everything said in the conversation will be relayed to the project sponsor and other stakeholders.

Information is key to surviving in organizational politics. It is your job to find out as much information as possible about the organization and personalities within the organization before beginning the project. For example, you need to identify the different political factions, the political history of the organization, and the heir apparent to any power position.

This information isn't published in the organizational newsletter. Instead, it is found by tapping into the organizational underground rumor mill. The best sources of political information are those people who assist power holders. They are close to the source of power and are privy to information not available to others.

The challenge facing the project manager is how to influence these people so that they share the information. A method that many successful project managers use is to ask them for input on solving a problem. Instead of asking probing questions that imply politics, project managers ask the questions indirectly; e.g., "Who do you think would be interested in this project?"

Most of us like to be helpful and to be asked for advice as long as we're not asked to violate confidentiality. We also like to be treated as colleagues rather than subordinates, and once we trust someone, we tend to share gossip.

In turn, be willing to share your own information without violating confidentially. This helps to cultivate sources of information throughout the organization. However, you need to verify all information you receive before taking action, since the source of information may not be accurate. You can use a news reporter's rule to keep you out of trouble: Before information is treated as fact, it must be verified by two independent sources. The political situation is always in flux. Alliances change, making it critical that you keep your information about the political climate updated.

A project manager must be proactive in organizational politics to assure his or her survival, and yet be tactful enough not to make it obvious that he or she is a politician. Success is the best way to gain inroads in organizational politics; that is, the project manager must make his or her successes known to powerful stakeholders. Even errors can be turned into successes when the project manager clearly demonstrates the ability to resolve a crisis.

Show that you are serious about doing what is in the best interest of the organization by trying to fit in with the culture of the organization. Show respect for others even if they don't do the same to you. Make sure your name is in front of powerful stakeholders, and make sure you appear more interested in the project than your own career advancement. Handle situations that place you and the project in an unfair light with diplomacy. Remember that an intolerable condition is usually not long lasting.

The success of a project is dependent upon the project sponsor and the project team performing their responsibilities well. Since the project manager hires the team, he or she has control over the quality of that team. However, the project manager can still find him- or herself working with a project sponsor who is not comfortable with the project manager's role.

It is the responsibility of the project manager to compensate for any weaknesses of the project sponsor. For example, he or she should be able to take over part of the project sponsor's job if necessary, diplomatically allowing the project sponsor to save face. In a case like this, the project manager must tactfully raise doubts about the project sponsor's decisions by asking the project sponsor to explain the merits of his or her ideas. Flaws in an idea can be pointed out by following the project manager's trend of thought aloud, and then asking questions when the flaw becomes apparent.

Successful project managers stay in political control by focusing on the project and its problems rather than on political personalities. Regardless of the politics, it remains the project manager's responsibility to solve all problems that impede development of the project.

■ GETTING POWER

A project must be developed from a position of strength, and this strength must come from the power gained by the project manager. At the inception of a project, the project manager has bonded with the project sponsor, and power for the project manager to do his or her job comes directly from that person. That power must be enhanced to a point where the project manager gathers his or her own power.

Alliance with a powerful project sponsor is sufficient to work with those stakeholders who support the project. However, the project manager must also gain the support of stakeholders who see the project sponsor as the opposition within the organizational politics.

Successful project managers gain their own power to deal with all stakeholders by developing expertise in the organization through information gathering and analysis related to the project. This expertise is a valuable asset to stakeholders, regardless of their political position.

In addition, the project delineates an area of the organization that is clearly under the authority of the project manager. He or she has staff, assets, and budget under his or her control. As the project grows in scope, so does the project manager's power.

It is common for project managers to purposely plan expansion of the project into multiple phases, with each phase redeveloping a major function within the organization. Let's say the initial project is to automate the sale of merchandise in a store. The project begins by redeveloping the organization's existing system to order, receive, stock and record the sale of goods. However, the recording of sales touches the boundaries of the organization's accounting system. A project manager might propose to redevelop the accounting system in another phase of the project. In doing so, he or she increases in authority and power within the organization. However, gaining power by expanding the initial project must be performed tactfully, since otherwise the project manager will be viewed as a competitor and invite attacks.

An approach used by many successful project managers is to gain the confidence of all stakeholders immediately by sharing information and resolving their concerns. Next, the project manager discusses problems the organization faces and comes up with ideas that show how money can be saved or profits increased. The ideas become reality by expanding the original project.

Stakeholders who support the idea are encouraged by the project manager to do what is necessary to expand the project. While those stakeholders negotiate to change the scope of the project, the project manager stays out of any conflict.

■ LOSING POWER

Gaining power within an organization is a requirement if a project manager is to work in a political environment to develop the project. The project manager needs sufficient power to transform the project sponsor's idea into reality.

Although a project manager might have established a power base, he or she must take steps in order not to make blunders that cause him or her to lose power already gained. Political missteps can cause the downfall of any project. Even a subtle error in judgment can be perceived as a major lack of character and cause supporters to withdraw their support.

Successful project managers avoid committing common mistakes by avoiding situations that expose them to such risks. Here are a few situations to avoid:

- Don't fight other people's battles. Unless you are directly involved in the issue and have something to gain or lose, stay away and concentrate on issues related to the project.

- Don't be the messenger of bad news. Regardless of what is said, stakeholders tend to associate the bad news with the person who reports the news.

- Don't become personally involved with any stakeholder or their family. Always keep the relationship professional.

- Don't criticize anything unless you have all the facts, because you might be criticizing something that is important to a stakeholder.

- Don't surprise or bypass the project sponsor. Be sure to brief the project sponsor with good or bad news before the news is given to stakeholders.

- Don't challenge any of the organization's beliefs. If you do, you risk being viewed as being disloyal. Instead, stay within the organization's culture.

- Don't do anything to lose friends and supporters. You may need their help at a later date.

Be alert to recognize signs that you've lost power and that it might be time to move on rather than stay with the organization. The signs are obvious: no one responds to your memos, you lose key personnel from the project, and you are no longer invited to meetings.

MANAGING A DISASTER

Careful project planning and execution of the plan, coupled with honed political skills, is all a project manager needs to deliver the project. However, there are times when a project manager is called upon to handle a disastrous situation. A disaster can strike at any time during project development and is likely to come at the least advantageous moment.

For example, workers on a construction project could go on strike at a critical point in the project. Each day progress is delayed, the project falls farther behind schedule and costs increase because the builder must continue to pay interest on the building loan.

A project manager must also be prepared to take over a project that is in a disastrous condition. For example, when a project has fallen behind schedule, it is common for the original project manager to be terminated and a new project manager called in to revive the project.

Disaster can be caused by a loss of a key resource or a fire or natural disaster. The project manager must develop a disaster recovery plan that will allow development to continue during the disaster.

Successful project managers are able to meet such challenges by following disaster control techniques, some of which are developed by emergency service personnel. The project manager is similar to an emergency room physician who is presented with the victim of a motor vehicle accident. The patient is unresponsive and appears to have multiple injuries. It is the responsibility of the project manager to correctly assess the damage and determine the proper treatment to get the patient back on his feet—only in this case, the patient is the project.

The initial task is to assess the damage. Damage assessment begins by reviewing the project plan and changes made to the plan as well as other documents relating to the project. This provides an overview of the project status.

Next, the project team must be assessed. The project manager must learn the skills, personality and anything else he or she can about each member of the team, and then compare the outstanding tasks with the skill sets of the project team to determine whether they complement each other.

The most important question that must be answered by the project manager is, "What caused the project to fall into a crisis state?" Potential problems must be listed, so the same mistakes are not made again.

Project triage is performed next. *Triage* is the technique of organizing project components into three categories: can be saved without further work, can be saved with further work, and cannot be saved and must be rebuilt.

It is critical that an honest assessment is made, especially when deciding to scrap some components, for the organization pays double for any component that must be rebuilt. However, when there is any doubt, the project manager should rebuild a component rather than risk developing a system that has a weak foundation.

The project manager has one opportunity to fix the project; he or she may also be replaced if the project fails. Therefore, it is important that the project manager creates a new task list and formulates a new project plan that will deliver the project on time, within budget and in perfect working condition.

After the assessment is completed, the project manager must determine if the objective of the project is achievable within the current project charter. A *project charter* states the scope of the project and lists the terms within which it can be developed.

The project manager should not hesitate to request a new charter from the project sponsor if he or she feels the current charter cannot be implemented. If a new charter is not permitted, and the project manager isn't working within the original charter, then he or she should reconsider taking the position.

■ DAMAGE CONTROL

It is always gratifying to be the project manager coming to the rescue of someone else's project. However, there are times when it will be your project in trouble. You'll know if the project isn't going well long before the project sponsor and stakeholders know the status. This can happen even to the best project manager.

Successful project managers are quick to resort to damage control to contain the problem until there is time to repair the damage. *Damage control* is a technique for keeping the project afloat by minimizing the impact the damage has on the development of the project.

The initial steps in damage control are to reassess the problem by gathering information, and then reviewing the problem from various viewpoints. It is very easy to assume all facts are known when a decision is made. In reality, a critical piece of information could have been overlooked, which may make what is really the best decision seem less desirable.

After assessing the nature of the problem, the project manager must be honest with him- or herself and decide if he or she can handle the crisis alone or if additional resources are required. In either case, the project manager must devise a plan for repairing the damage by modifying the existing project plan and, if necessary, including new resources that can assist in solving the problem.

The project manager has one opportunity to recover from the damage, so the best plan possible must be developed and sold to the project sponsor. The plan must achieve results; otherwise, the project manager should anticipate being replaced.

Meet with the project sponsor and identify the problem. Be honest and provide him or her with a realistic status of the damage and the impact that damage has on the project. Remain calm and admit to any mistakes.

Let the project sponsor know whether the project is salvageable and, if it is, that you have a plan for getting the project back on course. Lay out your new project plan. Be sure to create a deliverable that is due shortly after the new project plan is implemented.

The deliverable is a test, which, if passed, will win support for the new project plan. Support for the project—and for the project manager—will increase with each deliverable because a successful trend develops.

Here are other things successful managers do to regain the confidence of stakeholders:

- Make changes visible to show that you are departing from the old ways.
- Never give the impression that you are starting over. The organization has invested funds in the development of the project and its members like to feel some part of the old project isn't a total loss. The only exception to this rule is when there is no possibility of reviving any portion of the project.
- Provide functionality as soon as possible. This shows that the investment in the project is starting to pay off.
- Develop a list of new expectations that you are to meet.
- Manage the stakeholders' expectations and ask them to modify their expectations if they are not realistic.
- Place all terms of the project, such as expectations, in writing, and distribute the information to stakeholders.
- Make sure all changes to the project plan are approved in writing.
- Create a sense of mission for the project team. If necessary, change the composition of the team to match the new project plan.
- Monitor the project carefully for any sign of a new crisis.

MANAGING DIFFICULT PEOPLE

Most of us can encounter a variety of personalities each day and are able to conduct business with them without much difficulty. A project manager also must work with some people who are likely to be more difficult to handle than those we meet daily.

A project manager doesn't have the luxury of walking away from a troublesome situation. Instead, he or she must meet the challenge head-on and be able to convince the difficult person to cooperate with the project plan.

The project manager must also be prepared to handle personal attacks from stakeholders who find the project not to their liking. Some stakeholders make their feelings known politely while others seek to demoralize the project manager.

Successful project managers are able to manage the attacks without doing anything to escalate the situation. At the heart of this management strategy is the understanding that the stakeholder's dissatisfaction lies with the situation and not with the integrity of the project manager. This is important for the project manager to keep in mind; otherwise he or she is likely to return the attack, which is counter-productive.

The project manager must manage the stakeholder during the episode until tensions ease and cooler heads prevail. Here are steps used to address a personal attack:

- Avoid the battle, since this tends to fuel the situation.
- Remain low-key and stay in control.
- Don't take the attack personally.
- Be fair and impartial. Before long the stakeholder will realize the attack is not accomplishing anything.
- Refocus the stakeholder on finding a solution. Don't be afraid to ask why he or she is becoming offensive. This question might jolt him or her back onto a productive track.
- Avoid being baited into a counter-attack. Some stakeholders who look for a fight and don't find an opponent try to use phrases that are likely to incite an opponent to fight back.
- Stand firm when confronted with threats. For example, a stakeholder may threaten to have the project manager dismissed. However, the stakeholder must present a solid case to others in the organization before such action can be taken. There is a good chance that he or she doesn't have a solid case and cannot fulfill the threat.
- Confront the stakeholder by asking him or her to prove claims against you. Volleys during the attack are typically made in general, subjective terms such as, "your project team is never around to help us." However, this is likely based on perception rather than fact. Asking for specific incidents, which the stakeholder cannot provide, neutralizes such an attack. You can always investigate if the stakeholder backs up his or her claims.
- Try to curtail the attack when tensions ease by apologizing if necessary and clarifying any misunderstanding. Say that you are looking for a fair and reasonable conclusion to the meeting rather than leaving the matter unsettled.

■ DEALING WITH PERSONALITIES

Not every stakeholder will target the project manager for attack. Many stakeholders are team players and are willing to cooperate with the project manager. However, each has a personality that can impact the project.

Successful project managers categorize stakeholders by personality traits, and then use an appropriate technique to deal with each person. There are five categories of personality traits that are useful to the project manager: the procrastinator, the analyst, the artist, the intuitive, and the decision-maker.

A *procrastinator personality* is someone who doesn't want to make a decision and will do anything to avoid it. The project manager shouldn't attempt to change the person's personality. However, he or she can use a technique that forces the person to make a decision in a particular situation.

The best way to handle a procrastinator is to lead the person into making the correct decision by creating a sense of urgency, and then reviewing the advantages and disadvantages of each option. Recognize that decisions are difficult to reach, but emphasize that the success of the project depends on making a decision immediately.

An *analyst personality* is a person who is interested in concrete facts that support a decision. A decision is postponed until the facts are known. The project manager can force a decision by anticipating the information the person requires to make a decision, and then presenting it in a concise manner. Your case must be based on fact and not intuition.

The *artist personality* is a person who is more interested in how things look rather than facts and figures. A project manager must present the situation in a way that is artistically pleasing and then concentrate on the aesthetics of the project. For example, an artistic person is likely to be more interested in the user interface and report layouts rather than a flow chart of the system.

An *intuitive personality* makes decisions based on his or her feelings rather than on facts. Therefore, it is critical that the project manager develop a strong bond with the person that allows mutual trust to build over time, after which the person listens to the project manager's case and agrees if his or her presentation is reasonable.

A *decision-maker personality* is a person who likes to make quick decisions. All he or she requires is sufficient information in order to come to a conclusion. The project manager must present all information clearly and explain why other options were rejected. It is critical that no question is left unanswered.

WHY PROJECTS SUCCEED AND FAIL

The reasons projects do not succeed as planned include the project is late, it is over budget, and it is not working properly. Projects are also canceled outright when the organizational need no longer exists for the project.

There are many underlying causes for the failure of a project. One of the most important reasons is that no one defines success. It is the responsibility of the project manager to have all stakeholders agree on how to determine whether the project is successful.

This definition must be objective and must use metrics to measure the project. For example, stakeholders may create a set of test transactions and agree the project is successful if those transactions are processed correctly. Without an objective definition of success, each stakeholder will create his or her own definition.

Another underlying cause of failure is the complexity of a project. There are countless points of failure in a project. A *point of failure* is a place in the project where failure could occur. A project manager's job is to minimize the number of points of failure in the design of a system. Let's consider a project to build front steps for a house. Points of failure are weather, delivery of supplies, workmen arriving at the job site, the truck carrying tools arriving on the job site, and proper mixing of cement. Any of these events could fail, placing the project behind schedule.

Points of failure increase proportionally with the increase in the complexity of the project. Even attempts to simplify a project by dividing it into phases can add to the complexity of the project.

Let's say a project is divided into four phases. A change in specifications in the third phase could require changes to the first two complete phases. If these modifications are overlooked, then the third phase and possibly the project will fail.

If the complexity of a project isn't considered when setting duration for tasks in the project plan, then the project is likely to fall behind schedule. This condition in turn places pressure on the project team to rush through tasks, not giving them time to complete the tasks properly. What results is a chaotic situation.

The complexity of a project also increases proportionally to the number of people who are involved in the project, because each person must fully understand and agree to project specifications and changes made to the project plan during the course of development.

Here are some other common problems that lead to a project's failure:

- Stakeholders have unrealistic expectations and the project manager fails to manage those expectations.
- Insufficient resources are available to complete the project.
- The project manager and stakeholders are unable to accommodate changes in the original project specification.
- The organization lacks technology with the capacity to handle the project. This is common with computer systems in which there are insufficient network services to transmit data, causing an inadequate response time.
- Insufficient testing.
- Lack of commitment by stakeholders to finish the project.
- Organizational politics which hinder development of the project.
- A lack among the project team of the skill set required to perform tasks.
- Inaccurate estimates of resources, duration and funding.
- Incomplete analyses of required functionality.
- Changes in the business direction, such as new markets.
- Legislative changes requiring new systems.

Signs That a Project Will Fail

There are clues that indicate stakeholders and members of the project team feel that the project is in trouble and the likelihood of completing the project is slim. Here are the subtle clues to watch for:

- Project team members resign before the end of the project.
- Deadlines of deliverables are missed.
- Stakeholders and the project team stop acting as a team and begin to protect themselves by assuring that their portion of the project isn't blamed for the project's failure.
- The project starts floundering, and drifts as if no one is in control.
- People stop communicating.

■ A SUCCESSFUL PROJECT

Nothing will guarantee the success of a project. However, there are steps that can be taken by the project manager to avoid situations that tend to cause projects to fail. The initial step is to receive a clear mandate from the project sponsor and stakeholders. The mandate establishes the project's objectives and sets the limitations within which the project team must develop the project. Furthermore, it defines what they consider is a successful project.

Once the mandate is known, the proper resources must be acquired and the organization must fully fund the project. Failure to accomplish either of these will likely doom the project before the project is launched.

Everyone involved in the project must also agree to minimize political influence during the development of the project. A project manager cannot expect to eliminate politics, but he or she can request the project sponsor to keep politics in check.

Before the project begins, the project manager must have agreement on how changes to the original project plan are handled. A change management policy must be implemented and enforced.

The project manager must empower the project team to do its job with minimum interference from stakeholders. Team members have the expertise to complete tasks specified in the project plan and likely require little direction from anyone outside of the project team.

Every component of the project must be thoroughly tested by following a test policy. Duration for testing should never be reduced unless the number of tasks is reduced from the original plan.

Deliverables specified in the project plan must be delivered on time and must work perfectly, since otherwise stakeholders and the project team will perceive that the project is in trouble. Everyone who is involved in the project must follow the project plan. If the project plan is lacking, then changes should be made to the plan.

Above all, stakeholder satisfaction is the ultimate determination of whether a project is successful, and to assure satisfaction the project manager must adopt a project methodology that includes stakeholders in the development process. Stakeholders should agree to specifications before they are incorporated into the project plan. They should see prototypes throughout the development, and should thoroughly test the project during the acceptance test. If each step is followed, then there shouldn't be any surprises when the project is completed.

■ COMMUNICATION AND REPORTING

Consistent open lines of communications and status reporting during the development of a project are two critical factors that assure that stakeholders are satisfied with the results of a project. The project manager, project sponsor, and stakeholders must recognize early on in the project's development cycle that many people in the organization have an interest in the project and those people must be updated regularly.

Updates can be provided by reports and regular project progress meetings (perhaps every two weeks). Meetings bring interested parties together to discuss the project for an hour.

The project manager is responsible for identifying everyone in the organization who must receive progress reports throughout the life of the project, and for the format of those reports. A *progress report* is a report that indicates the status of the development of the project.

The way in which information about the project is reported to stakeholders varies in format depending on the needs of the person. Reports are categorized by the degree of detail contained in the report.

For example, a resource's work schedule contains fine details such as start and end dates of all the tasks assigned to the resource. At the other end of the detail spectrum are general reports that summarize details of the project. A budget summary report is an example where only total expenses are shown.

The amount of detail required for a report is determined by assessing how the data will be used by the stakeholder. Too much information makes the report inefficient, since the stakeholder needs to sift through and analyze data. Too little data does not provide stakeholders with sufficient information and tends to generate additional requests for information.

Let's say the stakeholder needs to determine whether the project is within budget. The information can be gleaned from a detailed budget report; however, the stakeholder is only interested in the totals and deviations between the baseline budget and actual expenses. He or she must calculate these totals from the detailed data. A more desirable report contains only the totals and deviations.

Reports can be in various forms ranging from a simple verbal update to a formal presentation. The choice of form is dependent on the critical nature of the data that are contained in the report.

Some stakeholders prefer to receive verbal updates regardless of the information that is being reported. This method is a fast way to distribute the information and reduces unnecessary paper. The drawback of verbal reporting is that there is no audit trail that indicates the data were reported. In addition, misunderstandings can develop, since the project manager and the stakeholder are relying on their memories and notes to recall the details of the report.

A formal report is made in writing and can include a verbal component. For example, the project manager can distribute the printed report at a meeting of stakeholders, and then brief them on the highlights of the report. Unlike a pure verbal report, the printed report provides an audit trail and a way for stakeholders to refresh their memories following the meeting.

The frequency of the report is also a critical factor that is determined by the project manager and stakeholders who receive the report. Reports usually follow a standardized reporting period, such as once a month. Progress reports that are distributed to the project sponsor and steering committee are likely to occur once a week. A progress report contains the tasks scheduled and completed for the previous week.

After a report is distributed, the project manager must be proactive to encourage stakeholders and anyone who receives a report to provide the project manager feedback. Feedback is a response in connection with data contained in a report. Feedback completes a communications loop that ensures that a free flow of information occurs throughout the development of the project.

SMALL AND LARGE PROJECTS

Project managers must categorize a project by size—such as a small or large project. A *small size project* is less complex than other projects and has a development cycle of three months or less. In contrast, a *large size project* is complex, requires many tasks and resources to complete, and takes more than three months to develop.

Sizing a project is a subjective exercise and is very difficult to measure. Successful project managers have a saying: "I know a project is small when I see one." It is important that a project manager make an assessment of the size of a project before he or she starts developing the project plan. The size of the project determines the effort that is required to develop the project plan. A large project requires the creation of a very detailed project plan, which is not necessary for a small project.

Let's say a project manager needs to patch a link in a roof. There are a few tasks required to complete this job and it will require one human resource and very little roofing material. This is obviously a small project and doesn't require an elaborate project plan. Typically, the project manager needs only to schedule the resource and assign him or her to the single task of patching the roof. The resource decides subtasks that are necessary to complete the job.

In contrast, a more formal project plan is necessary if the roof needs to be replaced, because there are many more tasks and resources required in addition to coordinating tasks with suppliers.

■ CRITICAL ISSUES USING SOFTWARE TOOLS

Project management software such as Microsoft Project is a powerful tool that simplifies the development of a project plan. Microsoft Project calculates start and end dates, summarizes duration of subtasks, and calculates the costs. The project manager is required only to supply tasks, dependencies, duration, and resource information.

All these calculations can be performed manually without the need for Microsoft Project. However, the project manager must re-compute the calculations each time changes are made to the project plan. This is a time-consuming task and is prone to calculation errors.

The flexibility of Microsoft Project enables the project manager to repeatedly fine-tune the plan and make adjustments to develop the most efficient way to approach the project. Microsoft Project also enables the project manager to perform "what-if" analysis. *"What-if" analysis* is the process of determining how changes to the project plan affect the outcome of the project. Changes include modifying dependencies and rescheduling tasks and resources. With each change, Microsoft Project forecasts the duration of the project.

While Microsoft Project has many advantages, it, like other project management software tools, has a serious drawback in that it can impede the development of the project. Project managers must be conscious of the fact that the project plan isn't the project. That is, an excessive amount of time should not be spent developing the project plan.

TERMINATING A SUCCESSFUL PROJECT

■ PROJECT TERMINATION

Project termination is an important, yet often mismanaged phase in a project's life cycle. At some point, management must decide to terminate the project. However, this can be a difficult and agonizing activity, since projects tend to develop a life and constituency of their own. Team members, subcontractors, and other support personnel often become effective advocates for continuing a project long after its useful life has expired. Nevertheless, all projects must end and it is up to management to see that their concluding phase is smooth, timely, and as painless as possible.

The reality is that team members frequently overlook or try to delay termination to the last possible moment. Such delays can have serious consequences because they create unnecessary stress and are costly for both the organization and the project personnel. Therefore, a successful project must include a well-planned and executed termination phase that saves time and money and avoids unnecessary conflict.

Managing project termination revolves around two central questions concerned with when and how to terminate the project. The answer to the first question seems obvious: Terminate the project when its mission is accomplished. Some projects, though, are perforce canceled before this criterion is met because of changing market conditions, organizational shakeups, cost overruns, or technical difficulties. However, if a manager is convinced that a project will produce results, he or she may be predisposed to slant cost and performance data in the most favorable direction. Sometimes when managers realize that a project is in real trouble, rather than accept failure, they may choose to invest more resources. As a general rule, though, premature termination should be considered only when the probability of success is clearly too low to justify further investment in the project.

How to terminate the project requires a clear set of procedures for reassigning materials, equipment, personnel, and other resources. A project manager with good leadership skills can decrease anxiety levels within the organization and among the outside participants by carefully planning and executing the project's termination.

■ WHEN TO TERMINATE A PROJECT

In the section above we presented a simplistic answer to the question of when to cancel a project. Judging when a project's mission is accomplished is difficult because the degree of success or failure associated with most projects is tricky to measure at any specific time. The success (or failure) level tends to increase at a decreasing rate, implying that change is less visible with the passage of time. But since detecting a partial success or failure is not easy, management is wont to delay termination until the outcome is clearer or more information is available. This "wait and see" attitude can be very expensive. Project costs may escalate, and in most failed projects, these costs cannot be recovered. In many cases the project manager is forced to act subjectively without full confidence in the decision.

On the other hand, a project's termination costs may be a stumbling block to what objectively looks like the best course of action. When the initial decision to start a project is made, managers rarely know, or even consider, what the closing costs and salvage value of the project will be if it is terminated prematurely. New projects are supposed to succeed, not fail. It would be psychologically disturbing to think or plan otherwise. So when management is faced with a huge bill for project termination, the decision might be to continue spending money with the hope that the situation will improve, despite the evidence to the contrary. At the end of the Cold War, the United States was faced with just such a situation. The reality of canceling tens of billions of dollars in defense contracts meant skyrocketing unemployment in the aerospace and shipbuilding industries and huge financial penalties to buy out extant contracts. To cite one example, in 1992 the U.S. Congress decided to go ahead with a $3 billion program to build a prototype of the next-generation nuclear attack submarine to avoid closing down General Dynamic's Electric Boat Division in Groton, Connecticut. Politics and the severe short-term economic effects that the local community would probably have experienced were the determining factors.

Economics and politics alone, though, do not always drive the termination decision. The L1011 Tri-Star program of Lockheed is a prime example. For more than a decade the aircraft accumulated enormous losses and, in fact, was never really expected to earn a profit. But the program was Lockheed's reentry into commercial aviation and became a symbol that broadened the company's image beyond simply being a defense contractor (Staw and Ross 1987).

This suggests another difficulty in reaching consensus on the exact termination point of a project: namely, defining the mission. For example, consider a construction project in a residential neighborhood. The project may accomplish its mission as soon as the houses are built, as soon as they are sold and tenants move in, or possibly, as soon as the one-year contractual warranty period expires. The situation may be even more difficult when R&D projects such as the development of a space station are concerned. In this example, the design team is likely to make engineering changes throughout the station's construction, assembly, and even operation. Members of the R&D team may be assigned to other parts of the organization (NASA) or may continue as a team involved in related projects and activities. Here, project termination is almost impossible to define. A third scenario involves an engineering team designing a new product intended for mass production, such as a notebook computer. When a prototype is successfully developed, the team may be integrated into the parent company as a division to manufacture, support, and improve the new product.

Meredith and Mantel (1989) propose three approaches to project termination: extinction, inclusion, and integration.

1. *Termination by extinction* occurs when the project stops because its mission is either a success or a failure. In either case, all substantial project activities cease at the time of assessment. The project team or special project termination team conducts the phaseout. Either team's aim is to reassign resources, close out the books, and write a final project report.

2. *Termination by inclusion* occurs when the project team becomes a new part of the parent organization. Resources are transferred to the new organizational unit, which is integrated into the parent organization. This type of project termination is typical for organizations with a project/product structure.

3. *Termination by integration* occurs when the project's resources, as well as its deliverables, are integrated into the parent organization's various units. This approach is very common in a matrix organization because most people involved in a project are also affiliated with one or more functional units. When the project terminates, team members are reintegrated into their corresponding units.

As noted earlier, most projects do not reach clear success or failure points. Therefore, management should monitor each project vigilantly to look for signs that call its continuation into question. Monitoring is facilitated by the project control system. In addition, it is a good idea to conduct regular evaluations and audits to evaluate the status of critical milestones during a project's life cycle. Unlike the project control system, which is operated by the project team, an external organizational unit not directly involved with the project should conduct the audits to assure a more objective analysis. The client may also require formal evaluations and audits as each phase ends. These results may be presented at the preliminary design review, the critical design review, or other milestone dates.

The financial audits commonly used in organizations concentrate on their financial well-being and economic status. By contrast, the project audit covers a large number of aspects, including:

- The project's *current status versus stated goals* as related to schedule, costs, technology, risk, human relations, resource use, and information availability.

- *Future trends*, that is, forecasts of total project costs, expected completion time, and the likelihood that the project will achieve its stated goals.

- *Recommendations* to change the project's plans or to terminate the project if success seems unlikely.

If performed conscientiously, the audit report will be more objective than the project control system reports. However, due to auditing costs, audit reports are not issued regularly. Termination decisions, then, frequently result from information from the control system. If the cumulative information indicates that success is remote, an audit team may be assembled to evaluate the situation more closely. We note here that a decision against initiating the termination phase (i.e., the "do nothing" decision) should be based on a project's satisfactory performances, not on a lack of alarm signals. For assistance in this matter, the project manager must rely on the control system throughout the project's life cycle. The information that it provides can trigger an audit to support the termination decision.

Assuming that the control system functions well and that current information is available, management needs a methodology for reaching a termination decision. Project management researchers have developed lists of questions designed to address this issue (Buell 1967). Although most studies have focused on R&D projects, the following list is appropriate in the majority of circumstances. The questions may be difficult to answer, requiring a special audit to obtain the necessary information.

- Did the organization's goals change sufficiently so that the original project definition is inconsistent with the current goals?

- Does management still support the project?

- Is the project's budget consistent with the organizational budget?

- Are technological, cost, and schedule risks acceptable?

- Is the project still innovative? Is it possible to achieve the same results with current technology faster and at lower cost without completing the project?

- How is the project team's morale? Can the team finish the project successfully?

- Is the project still profitable and cost-effective?

- Can the project be integrated into the organization's functional units?

- Is the project still current? Do sufficient environmental or technological changes make the project obsolete?

- Are there opportunities to use the project's resources elsewhere that would prove more cost-effective or beneficial?

Based on the answers to these questions, perhaps obtained with the help of economic analysis and project evaluation/selection techniques, management should be able to decide whether it is time to cancel the project. Once a termination decision is made, the question then becomes how to minimize the likely disruption that such action would cause.

As mentioned, management should repeatedly consider whether to continue or to terminate a project throughout its life cycle. In addition, an outside group should be asked to provide input to the decision, since the project manager and team members have a vested interest that may compromise their candor. The outside analysis should be apart of the project audit effort which should be designed to yield an objective evaluation of the project's status.

Since project success (or failure) is multidimensional, the evaluation should cover at least the following:

- *Economic evaluation.* Given the costs of all project efforts to date, is project continuation justified?

- *Project costs and schedule evaluations.* Given the current costs, schedule, and control system's trend predictions, should the project be canceled?

- *Management objectives.* Given the organization's current objectives, does the project serve these objectives?
- *Customer relations and reputation.* If premature termination is justified, how will this affect the organization's reputation and its customer relationships?
- *Contractual and ethical considerations.* Is project termination possible given current client and supplier contracts? Is project termination ethical?

In conjunction with these questions, the auditing process should consider a multitude of factors as well as their impact on the organization. Building on the work of Buell, Balachandra, and Raelin (1980), identify the following quantitative and qualitative factors:

Quantitative factors

Probability of commercial success

Anticipated annual growth rate

Capital requirements

Project use

Investment return

Annual costs

Probability of technical success

Amount of time actual project costs equaled budgeted project costs

Qualitative factors

Degree of consumer acceptance of the project's outcome

Probability of government restrictions

Ability to react successfully to competition

Degree of innovation

Degree of linkage with other ongoing projects

Degree of top management support

Degree of R&D management support

Degree of the project leader's commitment

Degree of the project personnel's commitment as perceived by top management, R&D management and project leaders

Presence of persons with sufficient influence to keep the project going

One methodology supporting a project termination decision is the early termination monitoring system (ETMS) designed to generate an overall index of a project's viability (Meredith 1988). By using input from the project's control system, ETMS reports the effects of an early termination on the organization's image, the project team's performance, the marketplace economics, and the penalty costs that will be incurred.

Finally, Table 5.1 enumerates 10 critical reasons identified by Dean (1968) in a study of 36 companies for premature R&D project termination. Taken together with the lists above, we begin to see why this life-cycle phase is so difficult to manage. The difficulty stems from the many factors involved in the decision to begin phaseout, as well as in the complexity of termination planning and execution.

TABLE 5.1
Principal Reasons for Canceling R&D Projects

Factors	Reporting frequency
Technical	
Low probability of achieving technical objectives or commercial results	34
Available R&D skills cannot solve the technical manufacturing problems	11
R&D personnel or funds required for higher-priority projects	10
Economic	
Low investment profit or return	23
Individual product development too costly	18
Market	
Low market potential	16
Change in competitive factors or market needs	10
Other	
Too much time to achieve commercial results	6
Negative effects on other projects or products	3
Patent problems	1

■ PLANNING FOR PROJECT TERMINATION

Like any other phase in the project's life cycle, termination planning tries to maximize the project's probability of success. Once management approves cancellation, the following action should be taken:

- Set project termination milestones.
- Establish termination phase target costs and budget allocations.
- Specify major milestone deliverables.
- Define desired organizational structure and workforce after termination.

Although each project may have a different set of goals, some activities are required in almost all cases. Archibald (1976) suggests the following activity termination list.

Project office (PO) and project team (PT) organization

Conduct project closeout meetings.

Establish PO and PT releases and reassignments.

Carry out necessary personnel actions.

Prepare a personal performance evaluation for each PT member.

Instructions and procedures

Terminate the PO and PT.

Close out all work orders and contracts.

Terminate the reporting procedures.

Prepare the final report(s).

Complete and dispose of the project file.

Financial

Close out the financial documents and records.

Audit the final charges and costs.

Prepare the final project financial report(s).

Collect the receivables.

Project definition

Document the final approved project scope.

Prepare the project's final breakdown structure and enter it into the project file.

Plans, budget, and schedules

Document the actual delivery dates of all contractual deliverable end items.

Document the actual completion dates of all other contractual obligations.

Prepare the project's final and task status reports.

Work authorization and control

Close out all work orders and contracts.

Project evaluation and control

Assure the completion of all action assignments.

Prepare the final evaluation report(s).

Conduct the final review meeting.

Terminate the financial, personnel, and progress reporting procedures.

Management and customer reporting

Submit the project's final report to the customer.

Submit the project's final report to management.

Marketing and contract administration

Compile the final contract documents, including revisions, waivers, and related correspondences.

Verify and document compliance with all contractual terms.

Compile the required proofs of the shipment and customer acceptance documents.

Officially notify the customer of the contract's completion. Initiate and pursue any claims against the customer.

Prepare and conduct the defense against the customer's claims.

Initiate public relations announcements regarding the contract's completion.

Prepare the final contract status report.

Extensions—new business

Document the possibilities for project or contract extensions or other related new business.

Obtain an extension commitment.

Project records control

> Complete the project file and transmit it to the designated manager.
>
> Dispose of other project records as required by established procedures.

Purchasing and subcontracting (for each purchase order and subcontract)

> Document compliance and completion.
>
> Verify the project's final payment and proper accounting.
>
> Notify the vendor/contractor of the project's completion.

Engineering documentation

> Compile and store all engineering documents.
>
> Prepare the final technical report.

Site operations

> Close down all site operations.
>
> Dispose of all equipment and materials.

Based on this list and on additional (project specific) activities, management can perform a project scheduling analysis of the termination phase. The results obtained from the analysis form the basis for budgeting and staffing during phaseout. Spirer (1983) suggests the use of diagrams, matrices, and checklists as analytical tools for the management of project termination. In addition, he suggests a work breakdown structure, as shown in Figure 5-1, to identify the problems that are likely to arise in the process.

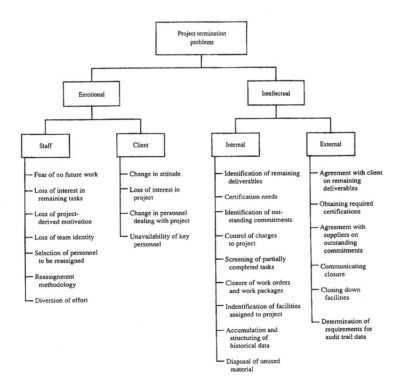

FIGURE 5-1   *Work Breakdown Structure for Problems Accompanying Termination (From Avraham Shtub, Jonathan F. Bard, and Shlomo Globerson,* Project Management: Engineering, Technology and Implementation, *© 1994 by Prentice-Hall, Inc.: reprinted by permission of the publisher.)*

The project termination phase has a significant emotional impact on the people involved. Four types of groups may be identified: end users, customers, team members and producers, and consultants and maintenance personnel. The following example clarifies the differences among the groups. A company that manufactures elevators is the producer, its customer is the builder, the end users are the tenants who are going to occupy the building. Each of the four groups is involved and affected differently by project termination. Therefore, it is extremely important to identify the nature of the impact and be able to treat any untoward consequences. Although the contractor is the immediate customer of the elevator manufacturer, the end users and the other interested parties, such as the maintenance crew and the consultants, represent future customers that should be taken into account. The immediate customer may want to terminate the project as soon as possible, even if the unit installed has not been tested sufficiently under normal operating conditions. However, if this unit does not meet the expectations of the end users, costly rework may be required and the reputation of the elevator company may be damaged.

The following list identifies typical problems that employees working on a project may face during the termination phase:

- Loss of interest in the project
- Insecurity regarding their prospect to get new jobs
- Insecurity regarding the uncertainty involved in a new project
- Problems in handing the project to the customer

From an emotional point of view, project termination has a separation effect. Each project team member faces the following troublesome questions:

- What, if any, are my plans after the project?
- What is my future role in the organization?
- What is my next assignment?

The project manager should consider specific answers as well as the best way to communicate these answers to the team members. Furthermore, the project manager may worry about his or her own future after the project. Planning ahead how to resolve these personal problems and fears will help to reduce high levels of individual anxiety among all team members.

During phaseout, due to the natural feelings of uncertainty, project team members may experience low morale, lose their interest in the project, or try to delay its termination. The frequency and intensity of conflicts tend to increase, and even successful projects may leave many members feeling angry, upset, or both. To minimize these effects, management should try to reduce the members' uncertainty levels. Suddenly canceling a project may be disastrous. Team members may find it difficult to terminate the project effectively if they face sudden unexpected changes requiring them to invest their time and energy developing adaptive strategies. Consequently, management's sensitivity, thoughtful planning, and consideration of members' emotions can reduce the negative effects of cancellation and support a project's successful closing.

■ IMPLEMENTING PROJECT TERMINATION

Once management decides to cancel a project and develops a project termination plan, a termination phase leader must be chosen. Project managers are natural candidates, but if they are emotionally unsettled and uncertain about their own futures, they might not be able to do a reliable job. A second candidate is a professional project termination manager who may be unfamiliar with the project's substance but experienced and well trained in closing down projects efficiently and effectively. The choice depends on the answers to the following questions:

- Did the project achieve its mission?
- Is the project manager assigned to a new project? If yes, when will the new assignment begin?

- Is the client satisfied?
- Is an experienced project termination manager available?

If the project is completed successfully, the client is satisfied, and the project manager knows his next assignment, the project manager is the best candidate to head up the termination effort. Otherwise, appointing an experienced alternative is a wiser choice because the current project manager may not be motivated to do the job conscientiously.

The termination leader should implement the termination plan by notifying all project team members of the decision to cancel the project. Communicating with team members and laying out a road map for their futures reduce their uncertainty levels. Once this is accomplished, the next step is to reduce and eventually eliminate the use of all resources, while implementing procedures that will facilitate a smooth transition of all personnel to their next assignments.

Throughout project termination planning, implementation, and execution, management should be extremely sensitive to the various aspects of human relations. The need for cooperation in future projects should guide all interactions with current team members, the client, suppliers, and subcontractors. The termination phase is a bridge to future projects. One cornerstone of this bridge is the project's final report.

■ FINAL REPORT

The basis of total quality management is continuous improvement. Since each project has a limited lifetime, TQM requires improvement from one project to the next. To facilitate this notion, one important outcome of the termination phase is the project's final report, documenting activities at each stage of the project's life cycle. Such a report emphasizes weak points in the planning and implementation phases in order to improve organizational procedures and practices. The report also explains working procedures developed during the project's life cycle that contributed to its success, and proposes adopting these procedures in future projects. The report helps management to plan future projects and to train future managers and team members. Thus the report forms the basis for improving organizational-project-management practices and developing new and improved working procedures.

To accomplish these goals, the final report begins by stating the project's mission. Next, it discusses in detail the plans developed to achieve that mission, the trade-off analyses conducted, and the planning tools used. Finally, the report compares the project's original mission and plans with the actual results and deviations, and explains why such deviations occurred.

Based on this analysis, the report evaluates the project's specific procedures and tools for planning, monitoring, and control. Details should be furnished on any new procedures and analytical methods developed during the project, and recommendations should be made regarding their adoption if it is believed that they can be implemented successfully by the entire organization. Recommendations on the future uses of, or modifications to, existing procedures should also be cited. Next, the report evaluates resource use and the performance of vendors and subcontractors, judging specifically whether or not they should be included in future projects. Finally, the report evaluates and documents the performance of project team members, auxiliary personnel, and functional unit managers.

Developing a standard format for final reports allows an organization to store the information collected in a database, making it accessible for future projects. Many standard formats are designed around one of the following:

- *Standard WBS*, such as the one suggested by MIL-STD-88 IA. Using a standard WBS allows management to retrieve information on relevant WBS elements in past projects.
- *Standard CBS*. Storing cost information in a standard cost breakdown structure allows cost estimators and life-cycle cost analysts easy access to this type of data for future project use.

- *Standard SOW*. Storing work statements in a standard format makes responding to future requests for proposals easier, since similar SOWs from past projects can serve as a basis for new proposals.

A well-structured final project report can help an organization improve and learn from its experience. Submitting the report to management is the last step in any well-managed project.

SUMMARY

A cornerstone of project management is for the project manager to manage the project team and stakeholders through the development process, analyze risk, and terminate a project properly. A project manager can adopt one of six management styles that will help him or her manage the project. These are boss-centered, decision-seller, idea-generator, straw man, suggestion-taker, and group decision-maker.

The *boss-centered* style requires the project manager to study the problem, decide the proper action, and give orders to the project team. The *decision-seller* style is where the project manager presents the rationale for his or her solution to the project team in an effort to have the team buy into the solution.

The *idea-generator* style of management has the project manager devising one or more solutions to the problem, then presenting these solutions to the project team and inviting questions. The *straw man* style is where the project manager adopts a tentative solution and encourages the project team to recommend changes to the solution.

The *suggestion-taker* style presents the problem to the project team, then asks the team to propose solutions. The *group decision-maker* style is where the project team is responsible for making the final decision. Project managers tend to use all these styles during the life of a project depending on the nature of the problem.

The project manager needs to be a people-person to manage the project. A *people-person* is someone who can relate to other people, such as stakeholders and the project team. These skills help build the confidence of stakeholders and the project team in the project manager.

Problems can fester and become distorted over time. In some cases, the more someone thinks about a problem, the harder the problem seems to solve. Any problem can be brought back down to size by sharing the problem with someone else. However, sharing a problem only occurs if the project manager maintains an open line of communication with stakeholders and the project team. A project manager must handle all stressful situations tactfully so that problems are not exaggerated and energy is focused on problem solving rather than voicing anger.

Meetings are the backbone of project development. There should be regular project progress meetings that focus everyone's attention on recent developments in the project. Meetings are the place where aspects of the project are discussed, facts reviewed, and decisions are made. It is the responsibility of the project manager to manage meetings so they are efficient and productive.

A project manager is likely to find him- or herself at the center of organizational politics, since the project is likely to be used as a tool by some stakeholders to move up the organization's ladder and can be seen as an obstacle to other stakeholders' advancement.

There are five categories of organizational politicians that a project manager will encounter. These are: a *Machiavellian politician*, which is a person who is ruthless and devious in an attempt to grab power. An *organizational politician* also has a desire for power, but gains the power without defaming others in the organization.

A *survivalist politician* is a person who balances life and a career in the organization. Power within the organization isn't his or her objective. A *straight arrow politician* is someone who feels competency on the job is the best strategy for advancement. A *power broker politician* projects a powerful image and uses this perceived power to direct activities within the organization.

Politics get in the way of developing a successful project. It is the project manager's responsibility to neutralize the effects on the project. Neutralizing means to remove ammunition with which the opposition can attack the project.

Political risks must be evaluated before any action is taken. A project manager must be proactive in organizational politics to assure his or her survival, yet be tactful enough not to make it obvious that he or she is a politician. Success is the best way to gain inroads in organizational politics.

A project must be developed from a position of strength. The strength must come from the power gained by the project manager. Steps must be taken not to make blunders that cause the loss of power he or she has gained. Political missteps can cause the downfall of any project. Even a subtle error in judgment can be perceived as a major lack of character and cause supporters to withdraw their support.

There are times when a project manager is called upon to handle a disastrous situation. A disaster can strike at any time during project development and is likely to come at the least advantageous moment. A project manager must also be prepared to take over a project that is in a disastrous condition. It is common that when a project has fallen beyond schedule that the project manager is terminated and a new project manager is called in to revive the project.

Successful project managers handle disasters by following disaster control techniques, some of which are developed by emergency service personnel. The project manager must assess the damage and the project team. Next, project triage is performed. Project triage organizes project components into three categories: can be saved without further work, can be saved with further work, and cannot be saved and must be rebuilt. Once triage is completed, the project manager must ask for a new project charter, and then create a new project plan.

Successful project managers are quick to resort to damage control if their project runs into difficulties. Damage control contains the problem until there is time to repair the damage. The project manager must reassess the situation and choose the best course of action to fix the problem. The project sponsor must also be kept informed of the problem and of the corrective action.

The project manager must be able to handle a variety of personalities if he or she is to successfully manage the project. There are five categories of personality traits that are useful for the project manager to know. These are the *procrastinator personality,* who is someone who doesn't want to make a decision and will do anything to avoid a decision. The *analyst personality* is a person who is interested in concrete facts that support a decision. The *artist personality* is a person who is more interested in how things look than in facts and figures. An *intuitive personality* makes decisions on feelings rather than on facts. A *decision-maker personality* is a person who likes to make quick decisions.

There are many underlying causes for the failure of a project. One of the most important reasons is no one defines success. Another underlying cause of failure is the complexity of a project. There are countless points of failure in a project. Points of failure increase proportionally with the increase in complexity of the project.

A project manager can increase the chance of a successful project by receiving a clear mandate from the project sponsor and stakeholders and acquiring proper resources to develop the project. Further, the project must be fully funded by the organization. Organizational politics must be held to a minimum and a change management policy must be imposed on all changes to the original project plan.

The project team must be empowered to do its job without interruptions, components must be thoroughly tested, and stakeholders must be involved in the development of the project once the project is launched.

Archibald, R. D., *Managing High Technology Programs and Projects,* Wiley, New York, 1976.

Balachandra, R., and J. A. Raelin, "How to Decide When to Abandon a Project," *Research Management*, Vol. 23, No. 4 (1980), pp. 24–29.

Buell, C. K., "When to Terminate a Research and Development Project," *Research Management*, Vol. 10, No. 4 (1967), pp. 275–284.

Dean, B. V., *Evaluating, Selecting, and Controlling R&D Projects*, American Management Association, New York, 1968.

Meredith, J. R., "Project Monitoring and Early Termination," *Project Management Journal*, Vol. XIX, No. 5 (1988).

Meredith, J. R., and S. J. Mantel, Jr., *Project Management: A Managerial Approach*, Second Edition, Wiley, New York, 1989.

Spirer, H. F., "Phasing Out the Project," in D. I. Cleland and W. R. King (editors), *Project Management Handbook*, Van Nostrand Reinhold, New York, 1983, pp. 245–262.

Staw, B. M., and J. Ross, "Knowing When to Pull the Plug," *Harvard Business Review*, Vol. 65, No. 2 (1987), pp. 68–74.

INDEX

CD-ROM INSTRUCTIONS

SYSTEM REQUIREMENTS

Windows PC

— 386, 486, or Pentium processor-based personal computer

— Microsoft Windows 95, Windows 98, or Windows NT 3.51 or later

— Minimum RAM: 8 MB for Windows 95 and NT

— Available space on hard disk: 8 MB for Windows 95 and NT

— 2X speed CD-ROM drive or faster

— Browser: Netscape Navigator 3.0 or higher or Internet Explorer 3.0 or higher*

— Reader: Adobe Acrobat Reader 3.0 or higher (on the enclosed CD-ROM)*

Macintosh

— Macintosh with a 68020 processor or higher, or Power Macintosh

— Apple OS version 7.0 or later

— Minimum RAM: 12 MB for Macintosh

— Available space on hard disk: 6 MB for Macintosh

— 2X speed CD-ROM drive or faster

— Browser: Netscape Navigator 3.0 or higher or Internet Explorer 3.0 or higher*

— Reader: Adobe Acrobat Reader 3.0 or higher*

* You can download any of these products using the URL below:

— **NetscapeNavigator: http://www.netscape.com/download/index.html**

— **Internet Explorer: http://www.microsoft.com/ie/download**

— **Adobe Acrobat Reader: http://www.adobe.com/proindex/acrobat/readstep.html**

GETTING STARTED

Insert the CD-ROM into your drive.

— Windows PC users should double click on My Computer, then on the CD-ROM drive. Find and double-click on the Index.html file.

— Macintosh users should double click on the CD-ROM icon on the screen, then find and double-click on the Index.html folder. (Index.html may come up automatically on the Macintosh.)

You will see an opening screen with the Welcome page and other navigation buttons. From this screen, you can click on any button to begin navigating the CD-ROM contents.

MOVING AROUND

If you have installed one of the required browsers, you will see three frames on your screen. The frame on the left-hand side contains a navigational toolbar with buttons. From this toolbar you can click on the buttons to navigate through the CD-ROM, which will then appear in the frame on the right-hand side. Note: At any time, you can use the Back button on your browser to return to the previous screen.